SUPERHEROES ORPHANS
AND ORIGINS

►

Eighteenth-century rebus token: 'I want relief'. Placed with their child by mothers, tokens were a simple way to reclaim their child if circumstances improved. Every one of the 18,000 tokens in the Foundling Museum's collection is a life and a story; each infused with a sense of loss, connection and hope.

Overleaf:
Superman, Vol. 1, #53
Cover art by Wayne Boring, Aug. 1948

Cover features imagery from:
Street Angel: Deadliest Girl Alive, *Paracuellos*, *Nubia: Real One*, *Superman* Vol. 1, #53, *Zenobia*, *Gasoline Alley* and *Street Angel*.

Published in 2022 by Unicorn,
an imprint of Unicorn Publishing Group LLP
Charleston Studio,
Meadow Business Centre
Lewes BN8 5RW
www.unicornpublishing.org

ISBN 978-1-914414-24-4
10 9 8 7 6 5 4 3 2 1

Editor: Laura Chase
Designer: Felicity Price-Smith
Printed by Fine Tone Ltd

Supported using public funding by
ARTS COUNCIL ENGLAND
LOTTERY FUNDED

DAIWA ANGLO-JAPANESE **FOUNDATION**

The Great Britain **SASAKAWA FOUNDATION**
グレイトブリテン・ササカワ財団

SUPERHEROES
ORPHANS
AND ORIGINS

125 YEARS IN COMICS

UNICORN

Foundling
Museum

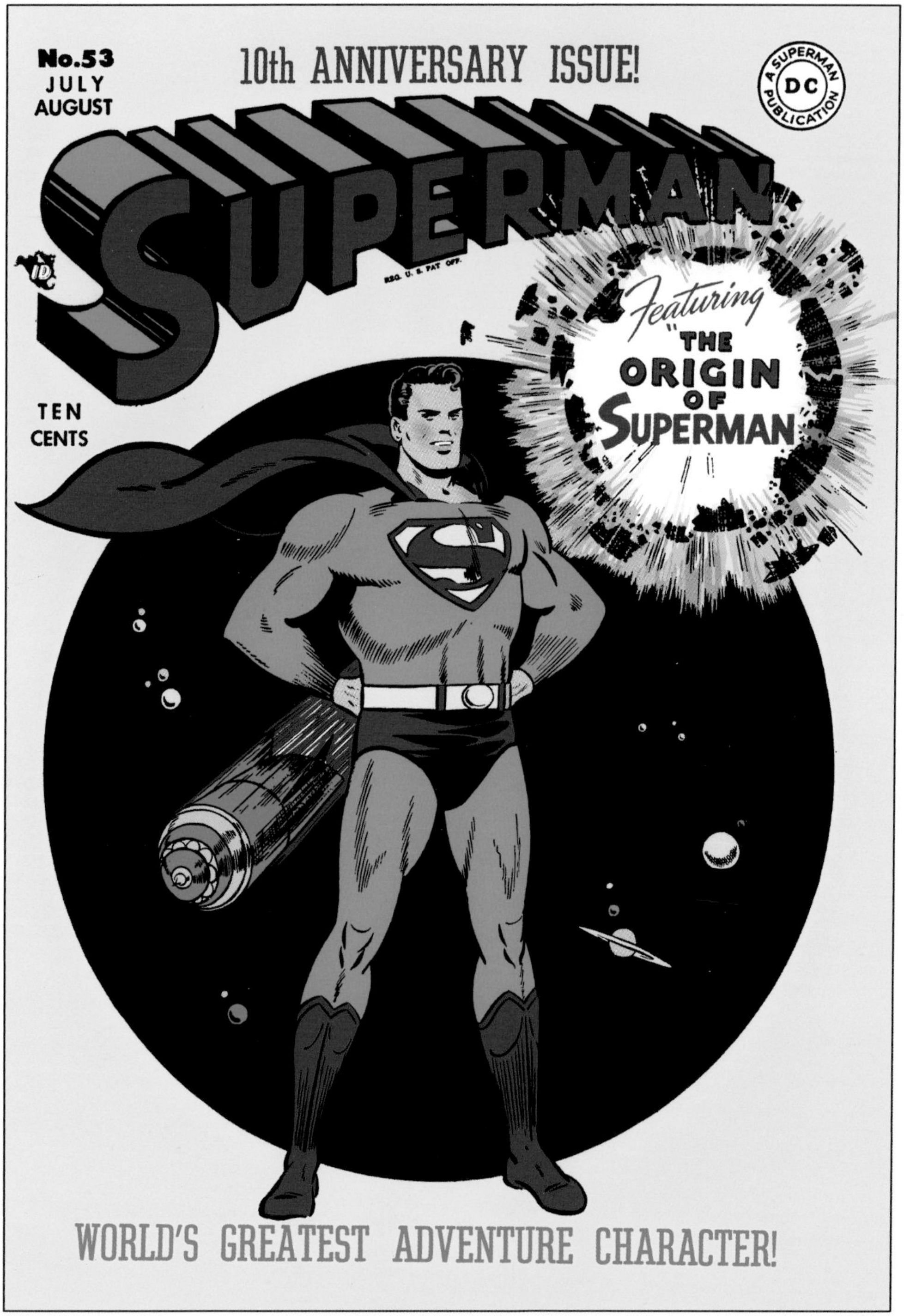
No.53
JULY
AUGUST
10th ANNIVERSARY ISSUE!
A SUPERMAN PUBLICATION
DC
SUPERMAN
REG. U. S. PAT. OFF.
TEN
CENTS
Featuring
"THE
ORIGIN
OF
SUPERMAN"
WORLD'S GREATEST ADVENTURE CHARACTER!

CONTENTS

Heathcliff was a foundling. Harry Potter was fostered. Estella Havisham was adopted. Her

Becky Sharp was orphaned. Alem
Kelo was fostered. Dick Whittington
was orphaned. Asajj Ventress was
orphaned. Cinderella was fostered.
Dorothy Gale was adopted. Gideon
Smeed was a foundling. Han Solo
was orphaned. Harriet Beadle was
a foundling. Rapunzel was fostered.
Hotaru Tomoe was adopted. James
Bond was fostered. Romulus and
Remus were found. Jane Eyre
was fostered. Hashio Miya was
a foundling. Lyra Belacqua was
fostered. Frodo Baggins was adopted.
Jack Worthing was a foundling.
Tom Riddle was orphaned.

Scarlett O'Hara w
Twist was orphar
a foundling. Chri
fostered. Princes
Jean Valjean wa
Feather was a
Mohammed was
Salander was
was a foundling
fostered. Spider
Madeline was
Xiao was adop
was adopted.
adopted. Viole
fostered. Wolve
Yuri Zhivago

FOREWORD

CARO HOWELL, FOUNDLING MUSEUM DIRECTOR

SINCE ITS INSTALLATION in 2014, Lemn Sissay's mural, *Superman was a Foundling*, has captivated visitors and resonated with audiences far beyond our walls. Framed by the Foundling Museum's story, Sissay's poem which lists over 100 orphaned, adopted, fostered and found characters from fiction, presents an implicit challenge to the viewer: Why, when looked-after children have such a powerful presence in culture, are they so marginalised in real life?

The mural's provocation has been a source of inspiration for us ever since. In 2016, it prompted the exhibition *Drawing on Childhood*, which explored illustrators from the eighteenth century onwards, who have created powerful images of these fictional characters. Now, with *Superheroes, Orphans and Origins: 125 years in comics*, our focus turns to comics and graphic novels across nine countries, three continents and 125 years.

In addition to examining the social context behind many well-known comic origin stories, the exhibition moves beyond fictional characters to embrace autobiography. This shift has enabled the voice of lived experience to move from the margins to the centre. Excitingly, it has also enabled us to commission new work from Asia Alfasi, Bex Glendining and Woodrow Phoenix. Their creative responses to Sissay's work return the exhibition to its conceptual origin and further animate the emotional reality behind the superhero narrative.

For people who grew up without birth parents, the Foundling Museum is a place of visibility and even validation. Like superheroes, care-experienced people hide in plain sight, intersecting the museum's life as visitors, artists, supporters and participants. Within our space, they share experiences of childhoods in care and its impact on their adult lives. While some are heartening, many are not and most are rarely revealed. In exploring this overlooked aspect of the superhero origin story, we hope to raise awareness of the immense resilience needed to overcome separation, loss,

◀
Superman was a Foundling
Lemn Sissay
2014, the Foundling Museum
Photo by Louis Mealing, 2022

NEW YORK
WORLD'S FAIR
COMICS
1940 ISSUE
96
THRILLING
PAGES IN
FULL
COLOR!
SUPERMAN • BATMAN AND ROBIN
THE SANDMAN • SLAM BRADLEY

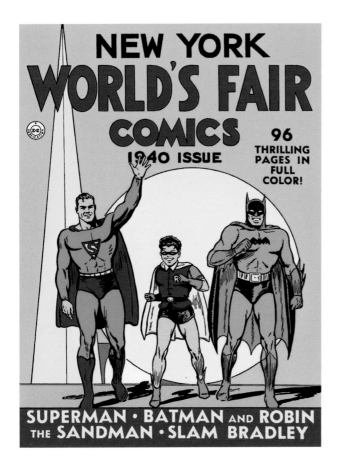

stigma and society's indifference, and to build a sense of self and self-worth.

I would like to thank our Artisa Curatorial Fellow, Laura Chase, and the Artisa Foundation, who enabled us to translate an idea into an exhibition. I would like to thank Will Tuckett for having the idea and our generous lenders, without whom this exhibition would have remained on the page: the Billy Ireland Cartoon Library and Museum, the V&A National Art Library, the British Library, Shogakukan, the Sanmao Group, the Cartoon Museum and artists Carlos Giménez, Lisa Wool-Rim Sjöblom, Taiyō Matsumoto, Robyn Smith, Morten Dürr, Lars Horneman and Jim Rugg. Thanks, too, to Asia Alfasi, Bex Glendining and Woodrow Phoenix, for enriching the exhibition's narrative with their work. We are immensely grateful to Arts Council England, Daiwa Anglo-Japanese Foundation and the Great Britain Sasakawa Foundation for their financial support, which enabled the exhibition's creative potential to be realised fully, and to DC for their generous assistance. Finally, I would like to thank Lemn Sissay for being a constant source of inspiration, encouragement and creativity – a superhero in fact.

Caro Howell
Director, the Foundling Museum

◀
New York World's Fair Comics
Vol. 1, #2
Jack Burnley
Jul. 1940

▶
Gasoline Alley
Frank King
28 Jun. 1925
Chicago Sunday Tribune

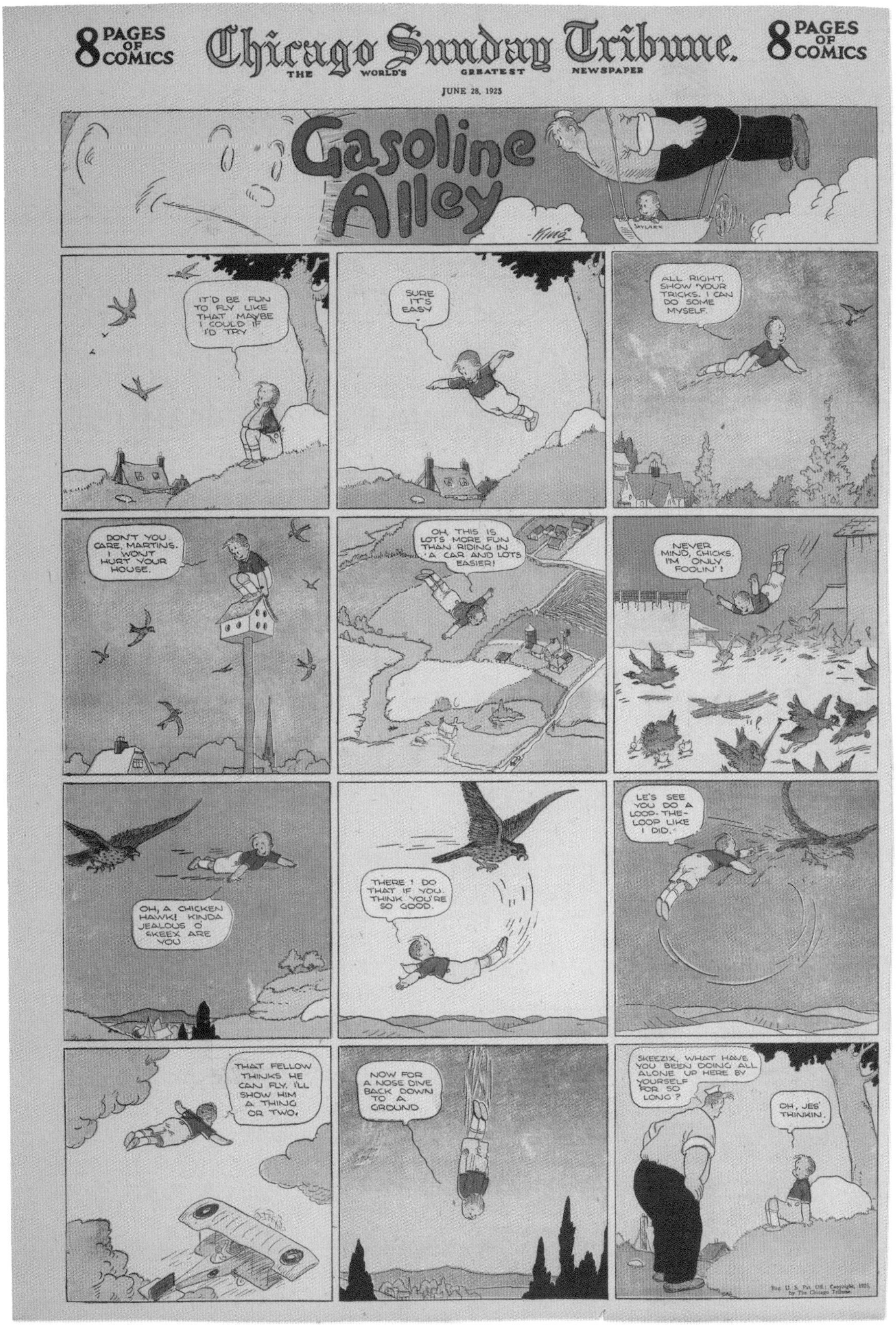
8 PAGES OF COMICS
Chicago Sunday Tribune.
THE WORLD'S GREATEST NEWSPAPER
8 PAGES OF COMICS
JUNE 28, 1925
Gasoline Alley
SKYLARK
KING
IT'D BE FUN TO FLY LIKE THAT. MAYBE I COULD IF I'D TRY
SURE IT'S EASY
ALL RIGHT, SHOW YOUR TRICKS. I CAN DO SOME MYSELF.
DON'T YOU CARE, MARTINS. I WONT HURT YOUR HOUSE.
OH, THIS IS LOTS MORE FUN THAN RIDING IN A CAR AND LOTS EASIER!
NEVER MIND, CHICKS. I'M ONLY FOOLIN'!
OH, A CHICKEN HAWK! KINDA JEALOUS O' SKEEX ARE YOU
THERE! DO THAT IF YOU THINK YOU'RE SO GOOD.
LE'S SEE YOU DO A LOOP-THE-LOOP LIKE I DID.
THAT FELLOW THINKS HE CAN FLY. I'LL SHOW HIM A THING OR TWO.
NOW FOR A NOSE DIVE BACK DOWN TO A GROUND
SKEEZIX, WHAT HAVE YOU BEEN DOING ALL ALONE UP HERE BY YOURSELF FOR SO LONG?
OH, JES' THINKIN.
Reg. U. S. Pat. Off.; Copyright, 1925, by The Chicago Tribune.

SUPERMAN WAS A FOUNDLING

LEMN SISSAY, FOUNDLING MUSEUM TRUSTEE

COMICS, COMICS, GLORIOUS comics. They line the shelves of Mr and Mrs Jolly's shop, bursting with pride, joy and primary colours. Pride because they knew they were good. Joy because they knew they were exciting. And primary colours because they also knew a child like me could not miss them. Could anything connect to a child like a comic? I was besotted. Friends swapped them at school, beneath our desks like comics were contraband smuggled by spies across the communist checkpoint. They were made for us and for all we knew they were made *by* people like us in a secret factory, then shipped at night to newsagents across England. Ha!

I used to sit with *Roy of the Rovers* – a football comic about Roy Race – and devour every single action-packed panel. I immersed myself in his pitch adventures. The outside world melted away. I am on the soccer field. England must win. It's the last minute. A thought balloon appears above Roy's head. He is flanked by Yugoslavian defenders. It reads: 'Need

to get in the centre box position.' Close up on Roy as he flies through the air. He is heading the ball. It's the last minute of the game. The crowd rises to their feet: 'Will he do it? Roy the Rocket!! GOAL.' Roy is held on the shoulders of his teammate with his fist in the air. I am there. Speech bubble: 'Yes!'

I made that last paragraph up, but it goes to show the drama. Comics, comics, comics. The kinetic energy between literature and art awoke my imagination without fail. There is something very adult about comics. The thought bubble was the first time I saw in words what someone was thinking. *Roy of the Rovers* was about football adventures. *Commando* was about war adventures. *New Hotspur* was about the wild west. Then there was DC's *Superman* and Marvel's *The Amazing Spider-Man*.

Superheroes saving the world saved me! But *Beano* and *Dandy* were also filled with the adventures of characters we all loved. We loved them because of who they were and the ridiculous things they did.

SUPERHEROES, ORPHANS AND ORIGINS – 125 YEARS IN COMICS

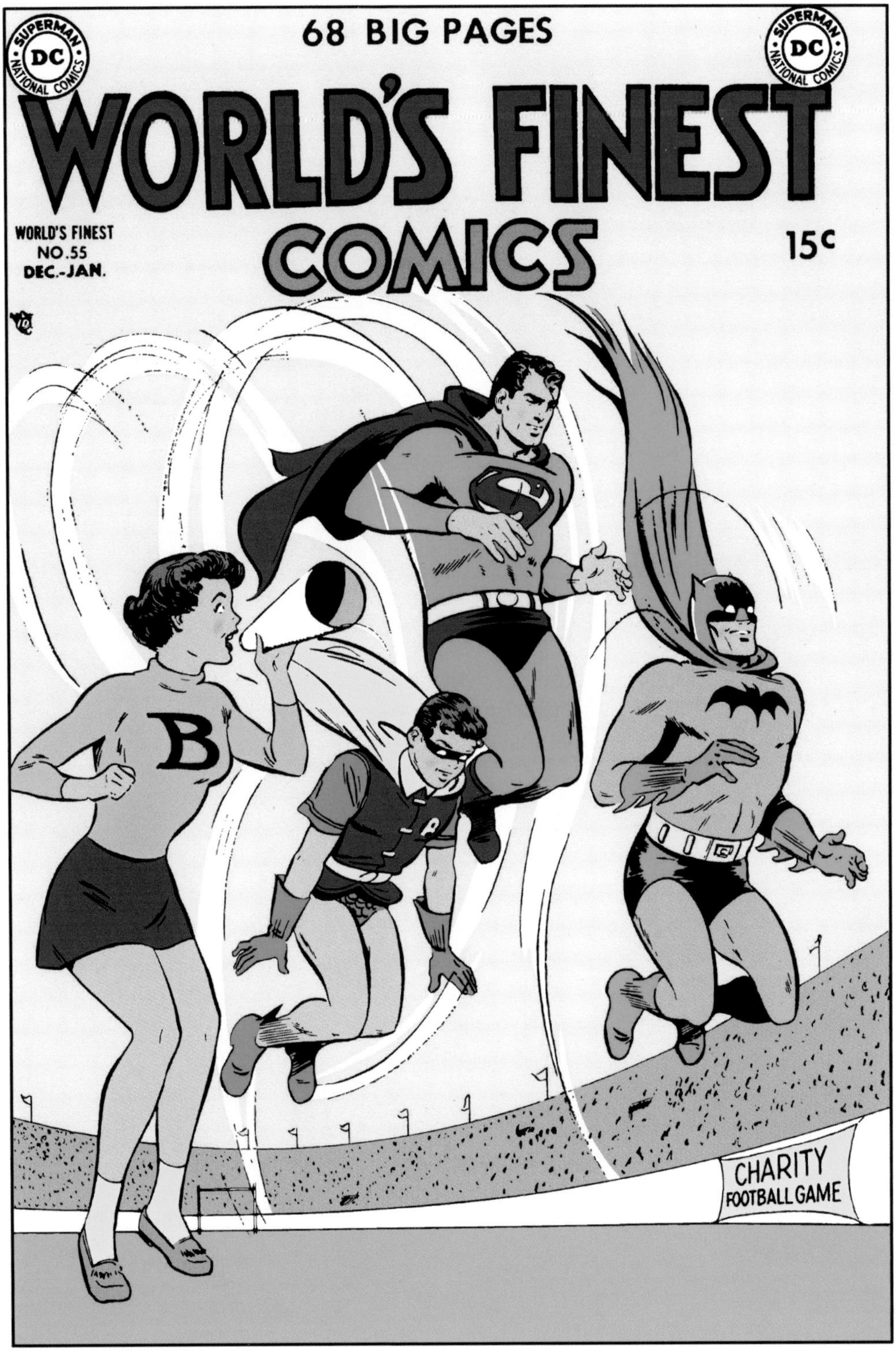

68 BIG PAGES
SUPERMAN DC NATIONAL COMICS
WORLD'S FINEST COMICS
WORLD'S FINEST NO.55 DEC.-JAN.
15¢
B
CHARITY FOOTBALL GAME

World's Finest Comics #55
Win Mortimer
Dec. 1951

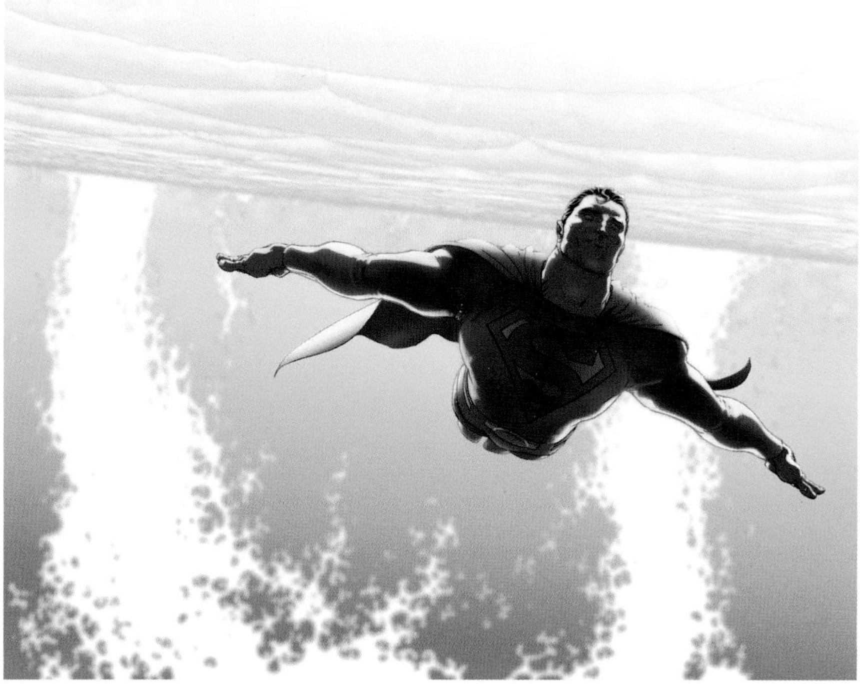

▲
All Star Superman #1
Grant Morrison,
Frank Quitely
Jan. 2006
pp. 2-3

The opposite to saving the world, they created mayhem in it.

Every year Santa brought me *The Beano Annual* which was a bumper hardback yearbook jam-packed with cartoon strips of my favourite characters: Dennis the Menace, Billy the Whiz, Gnasher, the Bash Street Kids. They were as daring as I wished I could be. They were as irreverent and funny as any child wishes to be. They got into all sorts of hilarious tangles. Adults seem to flock together with similar adults. Children don't care and neither did the characters in *Beano*. Was there any form other than a comic which could light up a young boy like me? The answer to that question is 'No.'

At twelve, the comic reading abruptly stopped. I was sent to a children's home. IRL. In real life. If it were a comic everything would be black, white and grey. The block of text on the first page reads: 'A young boy finds himself in a place he has never known, with strangers he has never met.' Next to it the first panel depicts a dormitory at night. In the foreground you see the shape of my body under the sheets. In the background you see the other beds and the text above them: 'Zzzzz, Zzzzz, Zzzzz.' A thought bubble appears above my bed: 'Where am I? What am I doing here?' Behind me is an open window and through it a moon above trees. In the next panel, you see through the fully open window on to the ground where there's a long shadow of a boy disappearing beneath the trees. The adventure begins.

I actually did that! Comics were a place to escape to, but when I really needed to escape, they were not there. So, my comic reading stopped. There were none in the children's home. No books either. No safe place for the imagination. And yet the children's home was filled with characters worthy of any comic. Characters with incredible back stories. But, somehow, we were deemed unworthy. Not even the people in the town liked us. Not really. But what none of them knew was that we were the closest examples to the people they all read in their own comics.

Many comic heroes of my past are now stars of a billion-dollar industry. The first to break the mould from comic to cartoon to billion-dollar film star is Superman. Look at his origin story. Superman was found by Jonathan and Martha Kent. Then they took him to children's home. Then they adopted him. Wait a minute. How did I not notice that before?! Superman was a foundling!

I looked at other origin stories and there they were in plain sight. Spider-Man was fostered, as was Wolverine of *The X-Men*. Then I started to look at books. Heathcliff of *Wuthering Heights* was orphaned. Oliver Twist was fostered. Roald Dahl's Matilda was in children's homes. Then there is film. James Bond was a foster child, and Leila of *Star Wars* was adopted. Harry Potter was fostered. Setsuko was adopted in *Graveyard of the Fireflies*. Fostered, adopted, orphaned or found characters are everywhere in popular and classic culture. And for me it all started with Superman and that original comic!

A revealingly adult reaction to my hypothesis is to assume that this broad-brush approach is untenable due to the fictional 'hero' narrative, which assumes a glow of purity. But this is not true… Superman caused mayhem at the children's home because of his incredible strength and because only his birth parents knew of it. Notice how, as an adult, he does everything to hide his past. Notice how he secretly feels like two people. Notice how he avoids telling people the truth about his past. And notice how difficult he finds relationships.

No, the closest examples in real life, to *Superman* or *Superboy*, are the children who were sleeping in those beds in the dormitory on my first night in the children's home. Now who is going to tell them? Comics, comics, comics.

ABOUT LEMN SISSAY:

Lemn Sissay OBE is a BAFTA-nominated award-winning writer, poet, performer playwright, artist and broadcaster. He has read on stage throughout the world: from the Library of Congress in the United States to Addis Ababa University, from Singapore to Sri Lanka, Bangalore to Dubai, from Bali to Greenland and Wigan Library. He was awarded an OBE for services to literature and charity by Queen Elizabeth II. Along with Chimamanda Ngozi Adichie and Margaret Atwood, he won a PEN Pinter Prize in 2019. He is Chancellor of the University of Manchester and an Honorary Doctor from the Universities of Huddersfield, Manchester, Kent and Brunei. He is Dr Dr Dr Dr Lemn Sissay. He was the first poet commissioned to write for the London Olympics and poet of the FA Cup. He has been a trustee of the Foundling Museum since 2017.

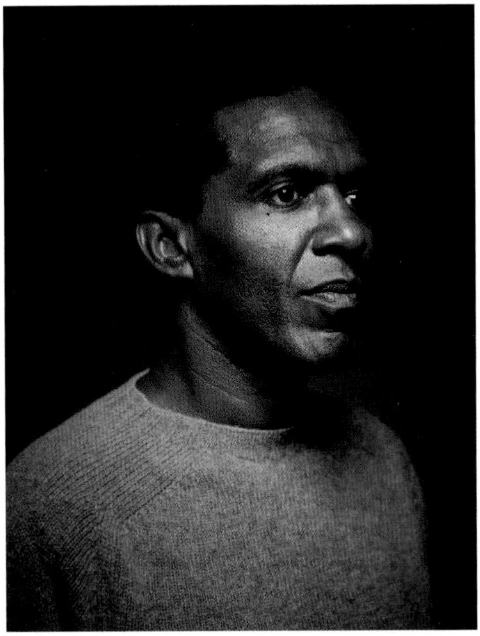

▸ Lemn Sissay 2021, photo by Hamish Brown

FINDING CATHARSIS IN COMICS

AN INTERVIEW WITH CARLOS GIMÉNEZ

INTERVIEWED BY LAURA CHASE
TRANSLATION BY ESTEFANIA ROBINSON-VEIRA

HOW DID YOU develop the idea to create *Paracuellos*, especially at a time when there weren't any other autobiographical comics in existence in Spain? How did it feel to share such personal experiences with readers?

I would frequently tell my friends some of the experiences I had lived in the so-called 'Homes' of Social Assistance, an institution in which I had spent eight years of my childhood ... practically all my childhood. And they would always tell me: *What a shame that you cannot tell these stories in your comics*.

Indeed, these stories (most stories, actually) couldn't be told through my comics. It was still the time of the Franco dictatorship and the world of publishing was controlled by strict censorship. But as soon as I could do it – in the seventies, after the death of the dictators – I began telling those stories in my comics. I did this, not so much with the aim of denouncing what those children's institutions had been (even though there

was an element of this), but with the intention of telling more real-life stories, stories that were not only of intrepid and brave adventurers or romances, which were the themes that appeared in most comics in those years. But after the death of the dictator and once the censorship laws were relaxed, magazine editors were seeking something else. They wanted to cheer the readers up and make them laugh, and it quickly became evident that my stories of poor and sad children were depressing, rather than cheering.

It was not until France published these stories in the magazine *Fluide Glacial* (a humour magazine!) with some success that the Spanish editors became interested in *Paracuellos*.

You have previously described the process of drawing *Paracuellos* as one in which you 'exorcised your demons'. What is it about the act of **drawing** – rather than writing – these experiences that you think provoked such a strong reaction?

▶
Paracuellos 1
Carlos Giménez
1976, p. 14

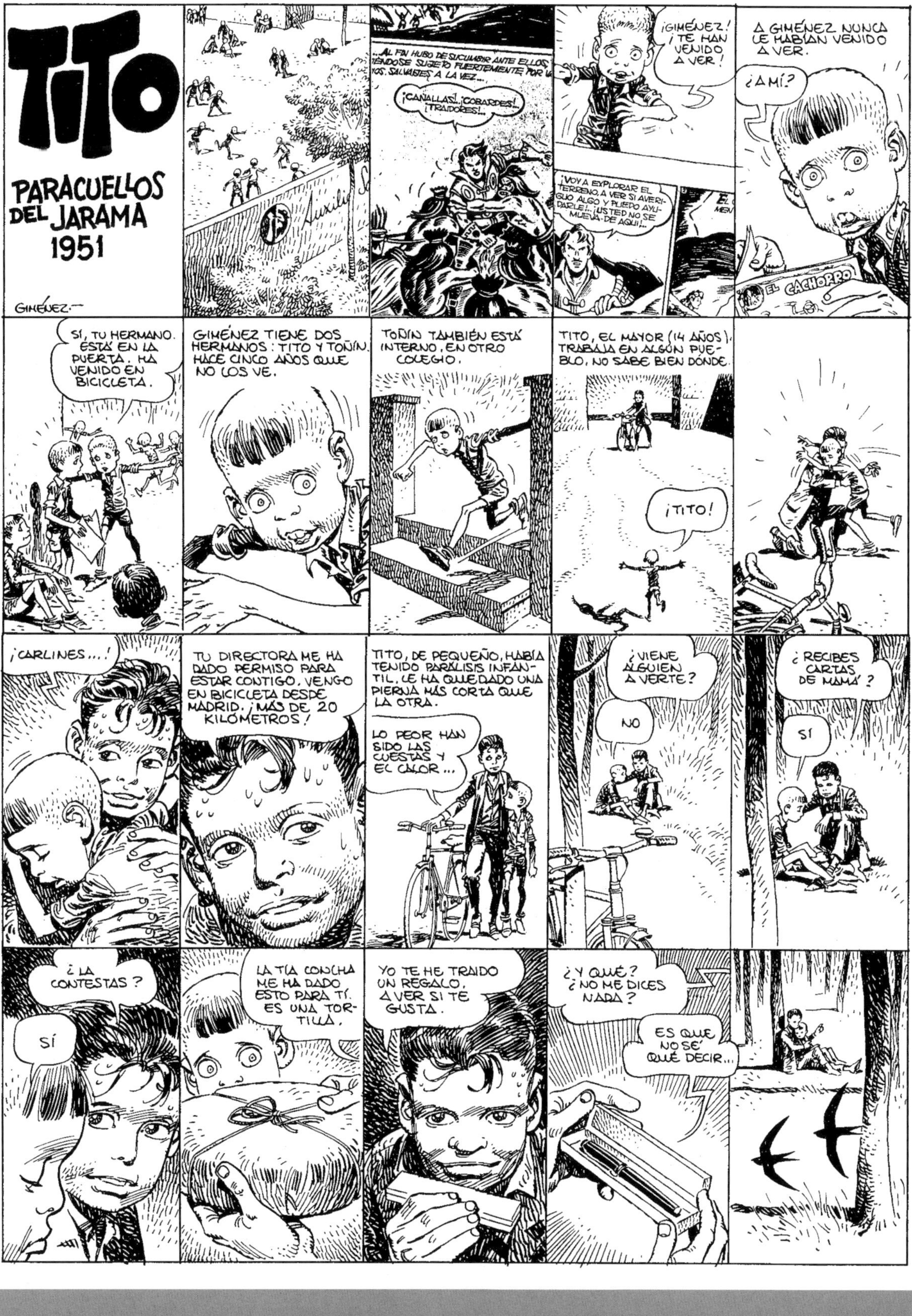

TITO
PARACUELLOS DEL JARAMA 1951
GIMÉNEZ
...AL FIN HUBO DE SUCUMBIR ANTE ELLOS, TÉNDOSE SUJETO FUERTEMENTE POR LA YOS. SALVAJES A LA VEZ...
¡CAÑALLAS!..¡COBARDES!.. ¡TRAIDORES!..
¡GIMÉNEZ! ¡TE HAN VENIDO A VER!
¡VOY A EXPLORAR EL TERRENO, A VER SI AVERIGUO ALGO Y PUEDO AYUDARLE!.. ¡USTED NO SE MUEVA DE AQUI!..
A GIMÉNEZ NUNCA LE HABÍAN VENIDO A VER.
¿A MÍ?
EL CACHORRO
SÍ, TU HERMANO. ESTÁ EN LA PUERTA. HA VENIDO EN BICICLETA.
GIMÉNEZ TIENE DOS HERMANOS: TITO Y TOÑÍN. HACE CINCO AÑOS QUE NO LOS VE.
TOÑÍN TAMBIÉN ESTÁ INTERNO, EN OTRO COLEGIO.
TITO, EL MAYOR (14 AÑOS), TRABAJA EN ALGÚN PUEBLO, NO SABE BIEN DÓNDE.
¡TITO!
¡CARLINES...!
TU DIRECTORA ME HA DADO PERMISO PARA ESTAR CONTIGO. VENGO EN BICICLETA DESDE MADRID. ¡MÁS DE 20 KILÓMETROS!
TITO, DE PEQUEÑO, HABÍA TENIDO PARÁLISIS INFANTIL. LE HA QUEDADO UNA PIERNA MÁS CORTA QUE LA OTRA.
LO PEOR HAN SIDO LAS CUESTAS Y EL CALOR...
¿VIENE ALGUIEN A VERTE?
NO
¿RECIBES CARTAS DE MAMÁ?
SÍ
¿LA CONTESTAS?
SÍ
LA TÍA CONCHA ME HA DADO ESTO PARA TÍ. ES UNA TORTILLA.
YO TE HE TRAÍDO UN REGALO. A VER SI TE GUSTA.
¿Y QUÉ? ¿NO ME DICES NADA?
ES QUE NO SÉ QUÉ DECIR...

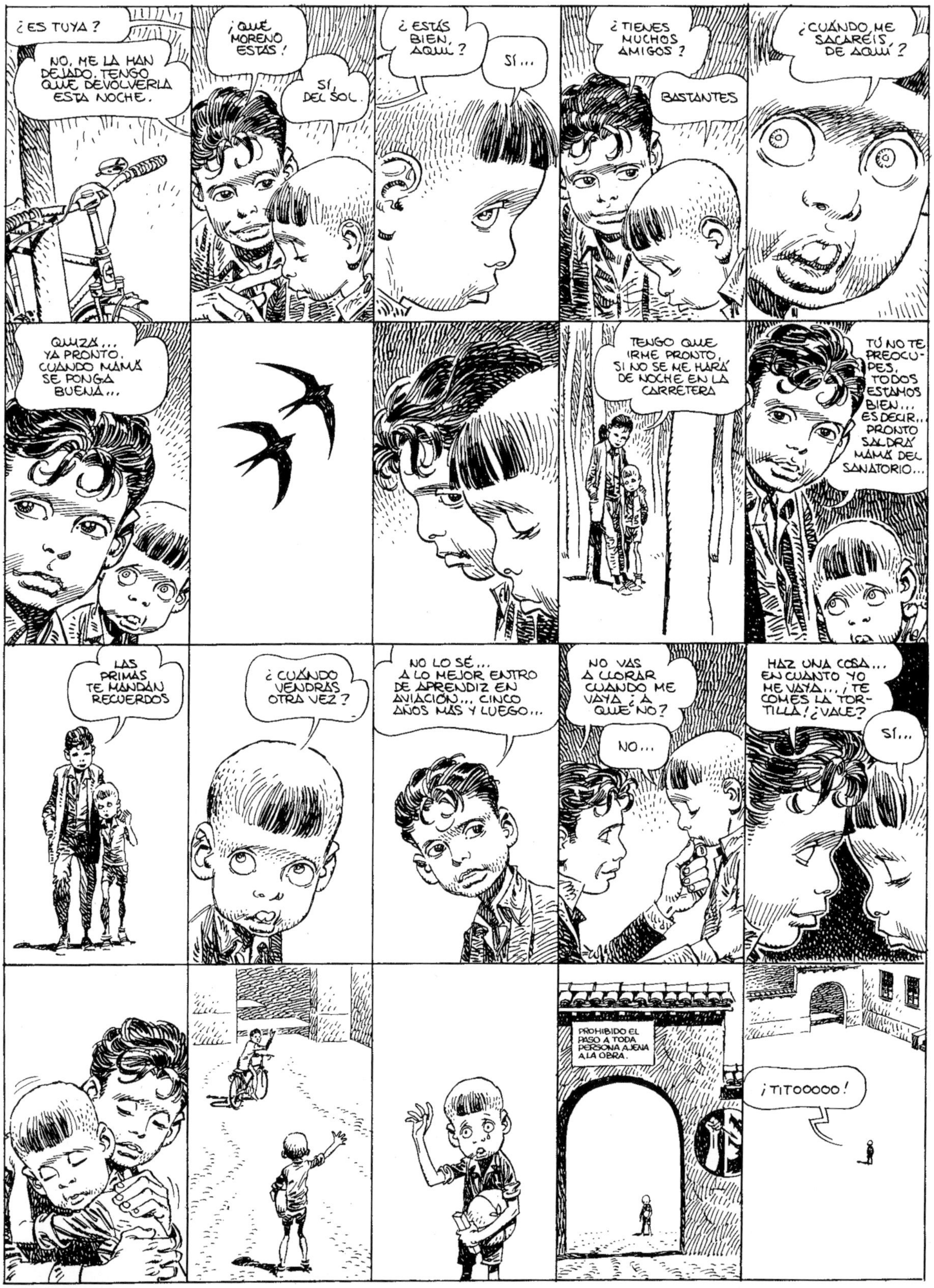
¿ES TUYA?
NO, ME LA HAN DEJADO. TENGO QUE DEVOLVERLA ESTA NOCHE.
¡QUÉ MORENO ESTÁS!
SÍ, DEL SOL.
¿ESTÁS BIEN, AQUÍ?
SÍ...
¿TIENES MUCHOS AMIGOS?
BASTANTES
¿CUÁNDO ME SACARÉIS DE AQUÍ?
QUIZÁ... YA PRONTO. CUANDO MAMÁ SE PONGA BUENA...
TENGO QUE IRME PRONTO, SI NO SE ME HARÁ DE NOCHE EN LA CARRETERA
TÚ NO TE PREOCUPES, TODOS ESTAMOS BIEN... ES DECIR... PRONTO SALDRÁ MAMÁ DEL SANATORIO...
LAS PRIMAS TE MANDAN RECUERDOS
¿CUÁNDO VENDRAS OTRA VEZ?
NO LO SÉ... A LO MEJOR ENTRO DE APRENDIZ EN AVIACIÓN... CINCO AÑOS MÁS Y LUEGO...
NO VAS A LLORAR CUANDO ME VAYA ¿A QUE NO?
NO...
HAZ UNA COSA... EN CUANTO YO ME VAYA... ¡TE COMES LA TORTILLA! ¿VALE?
SÍ...
PROHIBIDO EL PASO A TODA PERSONA AJENA A LA OBRA.
¡TITOOOOO!

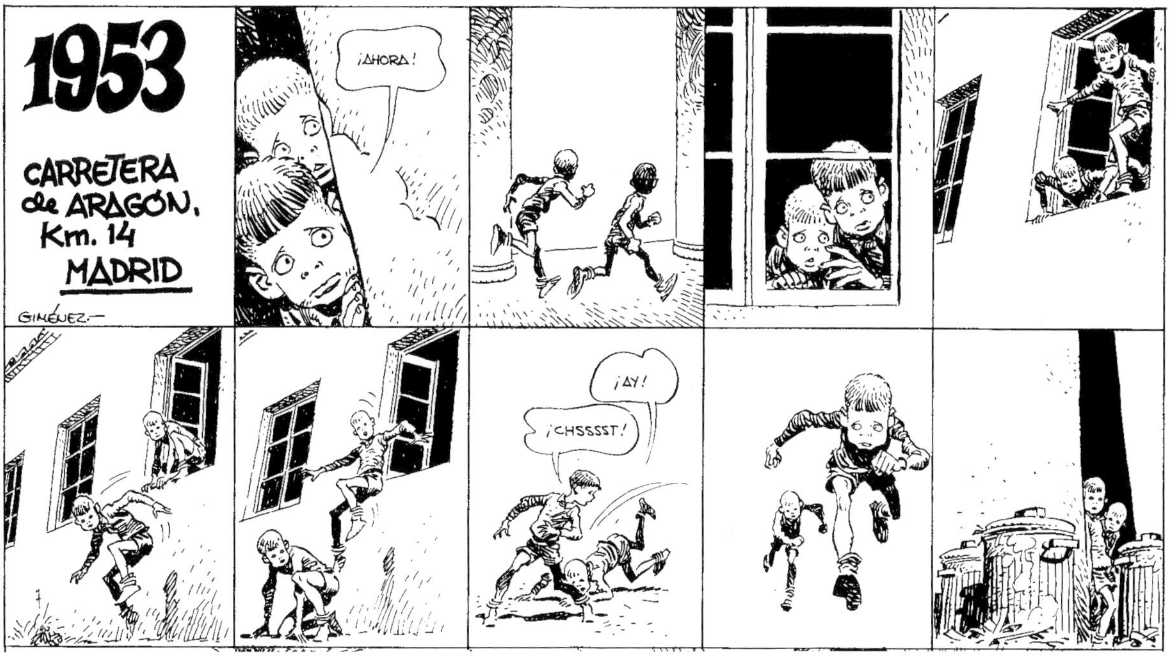
1953
CARRETERA de ARAGÓN, Km. 14 MADRID
GIMÉNEZ.—
¡AHORA!
¡AY!
¡CHSSSST!

▲ *Paracuellos 1* p. 6 (detail)

In this case, drawing or writing is the same. It is the fact of telling it – and above all publishing it – which exorcises. Once I started to tell and publish the anecdotes and events of my childhood, I stopped telling them to my friends. There even came a time when talking about all this again was monotonous to me. But it is a subject that has transcended so much that I feel obliged to continue talking about it.

My humble comics have served as a starting point for other people (sociologists, writers, historians, scholars) to investigate and write about those institutions. Now there is a vast bibliography on the subject and people can study it further, which fills me with satisfaction. If I hadn't spoken about these 'homes' when I did, maybe no one else would have. This is why I'm very happy to have done it.

◀ *Paracuellos 1* p. 15

Comic books feature repeatedly in *Paracuellos 1* and *Paracuellos 2*. What do you remember about your early experiences of reading comics?

Throughout the nine books that make up the *Paracuellos* series, comic books (called *tebeos* in Spain) are another character in the story. Comics are present in *Paracuellos* in the same way that they were in my life during those years of my childhood. In those boarding schools, all we – the children – did was pray and do semi-military training. It was about making us – the children of fascist Spain – 'half monks, half soldiers'. That was the slogan.

In such a closed and mannered world, comics were like a breath of fresh air. The modest post-war comics were, for us boarders, the only window open to the world of imagination. They were our role models when it came to games, our drawing boards, our currency, the textbooks we would use to learn about science and geography. In comics, there is talk of friendship. The heroes are generous.

In the absence of better books, I learned a lot from those comics: I learned what a shark and a reptile was, what a vessel was, what a bow and stern were in a ship… I fell in love with the pirate comics, from which I learned about the existence of Maracaibo, the Caribbean Sea, Turtle Island and the Sargasso Sea. Those simple comics inspired me as a child to become what I am today.

How do you feel now when you look at the character 'Giménez' in *Paracuellos*?

I don't know quite how to answer this question. My childhood is so far away, and I have already spoken, written and drawn so much about it. Sometimes I find it difficult to differentiate the memories of experiences I actually lived from the memories of things I was told as a child.

Your work introduced readers to an entirely unique genre and style of comic. What would you say to someone

Paracuellos 1 p. 7 (detail)
▼

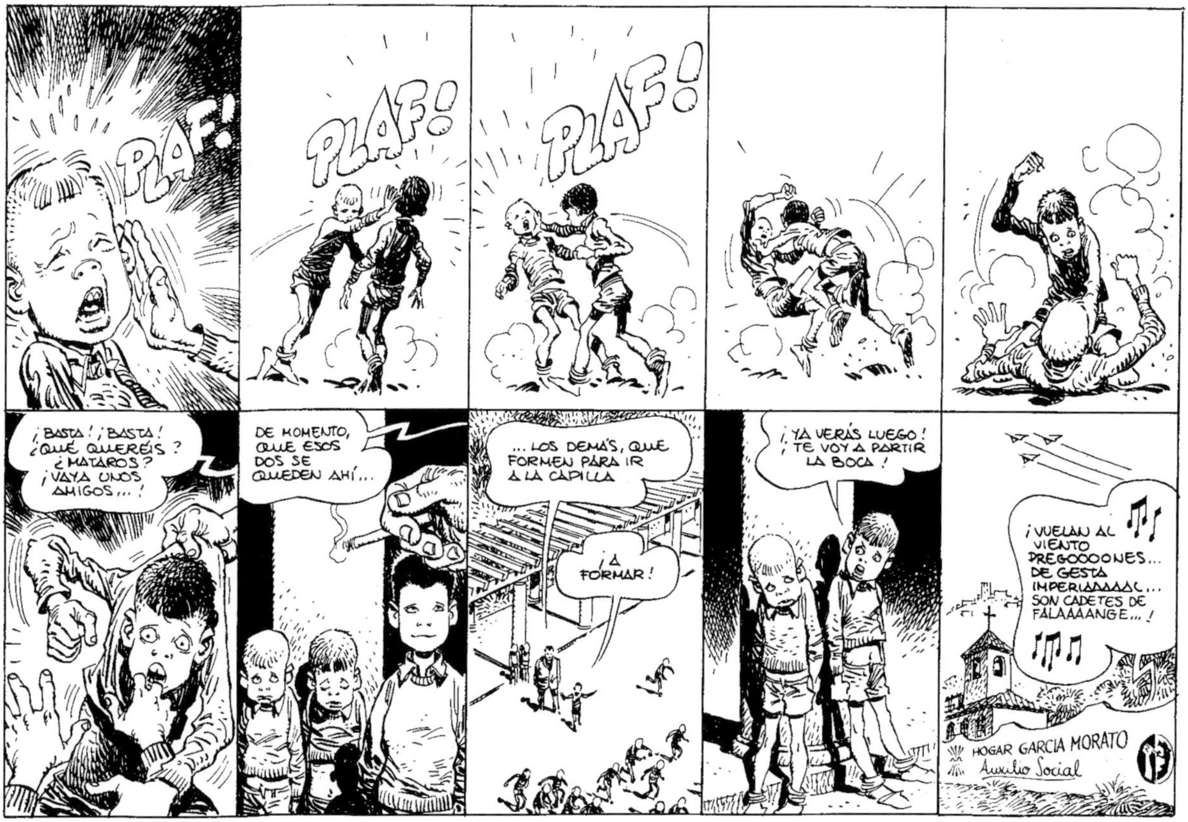
PLAF!
PLAF!
PLAF!
¡BASTA! ¡BASTA! ¿QUÉ QUERÉIS? ¿MATAROS? ¡VAYA UNOS AMIGOS...!
DE MOMENTO, QUE ESOS DOS SE QUEDEN AHÍ...
... LOS DEMÁS, QUE FORMEN PARA IR A LA CAPILLA
¡A FORMAR!
¡YA VERÁS LUEGO! TE VOY A PARTIR LA BOCA!
¡VUELAN AL VIENTO PREGOOOONES... DE GESTA IMPERIAAAAAL... SON CADETES DE FALAAAANGE...!
HOGAR GARCIA MORATO
Auxilio Social

who wants to document their personal experience through comics?

When I began to write and draw these kinds of stories – not only the *Paracuellos* comics, but also some other ones – it was not usual to speak about these themes of real life. I still remember the shocked face of some editors when they came across my comics, which they didn't quite understand.

It is true that if I hadn't done it myself, another author would have done it. The time to do it had come. I do not intend to put on medals that do not belong to me, but it is true that I was the first one, or one of the first ones, who started to speak, and denounce through comics real issues that until then have never been addressed. And when I started to speak about the things that I had known, the experiences that I had lived, diving into my own biography, it was in the same way that before me, many other authors had done in film, theatre and novels. I have always believed that comics shouldn't be only for children, or for comic fans who enjoy stories of good and evil with a happy ending.

I think that in order to tell something that is worthwhile and that has overtones of authenticity, first you should have lived or fully known the experiences you want to narrate. Otherwise, the stories that are told are anodyne or lack the necessary stamp of authenticity. I am sometimes asked, 'Were the Social Aid Homes that you say you went to really as you describe them?' If I say: 'No, that place has never existed, I invented it,' then people say, 'You can't have invented it; what you describe is too real.'

Overleaf:
Paracuellos 1
◀ p. 10
▶ p. 11

ABOUT CARLOS GIMÉNEZ:

Carlos Giménez is an award-winning and internationally acclaimed cartoonist. One of the first Spanish cartoonists to make autobiographical comics, Giménez first began serialising Paracuellos *in 1975. The comic tells stories from Giménez's own childhood, most of which was spent growing up in the Social Aid Homes that were established by Francisco Franco following the Spanish Civil War. Managed by Catholic nuns, the Social Aid system was created to provide care for war orphans and children whose parents were unable to look after them as a result of being hospitalised or, in many cases, imprisoned for opposing the Franco regime.*

Giménez entered the Social Aid system when he was six years old and remained in care until he was fourteen. He lived in five different homes during this period. His drawings reveal an environment in which children are regularly terrorised by violence and cruelty. The series was not published in Spain until 1981, and its searing honesty and criticism of the regime sent shockwaves through the country.

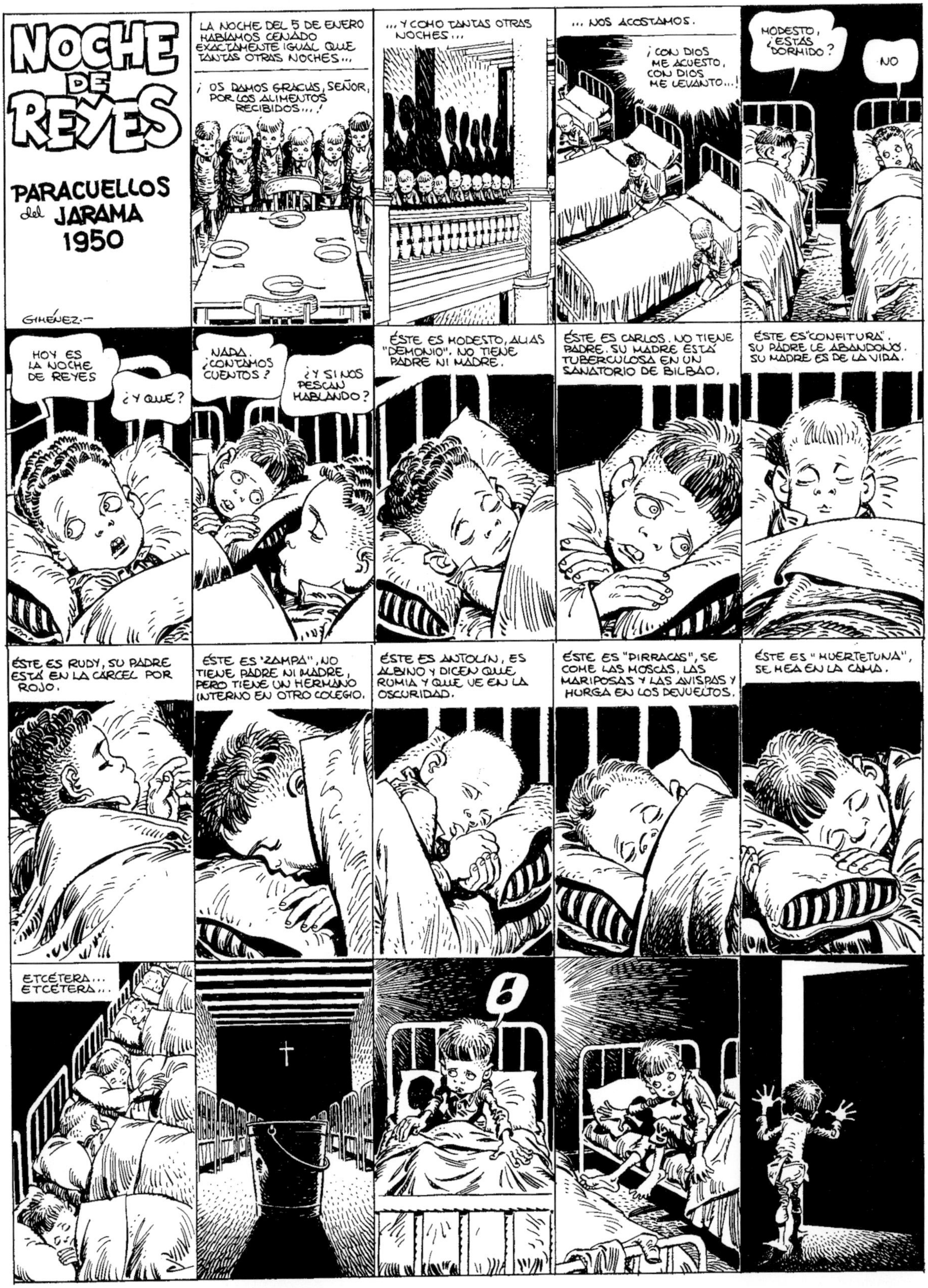
NOCHE DE REYES
PARACUELLOS del JARAMA 1950
GIMÉNEZ.-
LA NOCHE DEL 5 DE ENERO HABÍAMOS CENADO EXACTAMENTE IGUAL QUE TANTAS OTRAS NOCHES...
¡OS DAMOS GRACIAS, SEÑOR, POR LOS ALIMENTOS RECIBIDOS...!
...Y COMO TANTAS OTRAS NOCHES...
...NOS ACOSTAMOS.
¡CON DIOS ME ACUESTO, CON DIOS ME LEVANTO...!
MODESTO, ¿ESTÁS DORMIDO?
NO
HOY ES LA NOCHE DE REYES
¿Y QUÉ?
NADA. ¿CONTAMOS CUENTOS?
¿Y SI NOS PESCAN HABLANDO?
ÉSTE ES MODESTO, ALIAS "DEMONIO". NO TIENE PADRE NI MADRE.
ÉSTE ES CARLOS. NO TIENE PADRE. SU MADRE ESTÁ TUBERCULOSA EN UN SANATORIO DE BILBAO.
ÉSTE ES "CONFITURA". SU PADRE LE ABANDONÓ. SU MADRE ES DE LA VIDA.
ÉSTE ES RUDY, SU PADRE ESTÁ EN LA CÁRCEL POR ROJO.
ÉSTE ES "ZAMPA", NO TIENE PADRE NI MADRE, PERO TIENE UN HERMANO INTERNO EN OTRO COLEGIO.
ÉSTE ES ANTOLÍN, ES ALBINO Y DICEN QUE RUMIA Y QUE VE EN LA OSCURIDAD.
ÉSTE ES "PIRRACAS", SE COME LAS MOSCAS, LAS MARIPOSAS Y LAS AVISPAS Y HURGA EN LOS DEVUELTOS.
ÉSTE ES "HUERTETUNA", SE MEA EN LA CAMA.
ETCÉTERA... ETCÉTERA...
¿

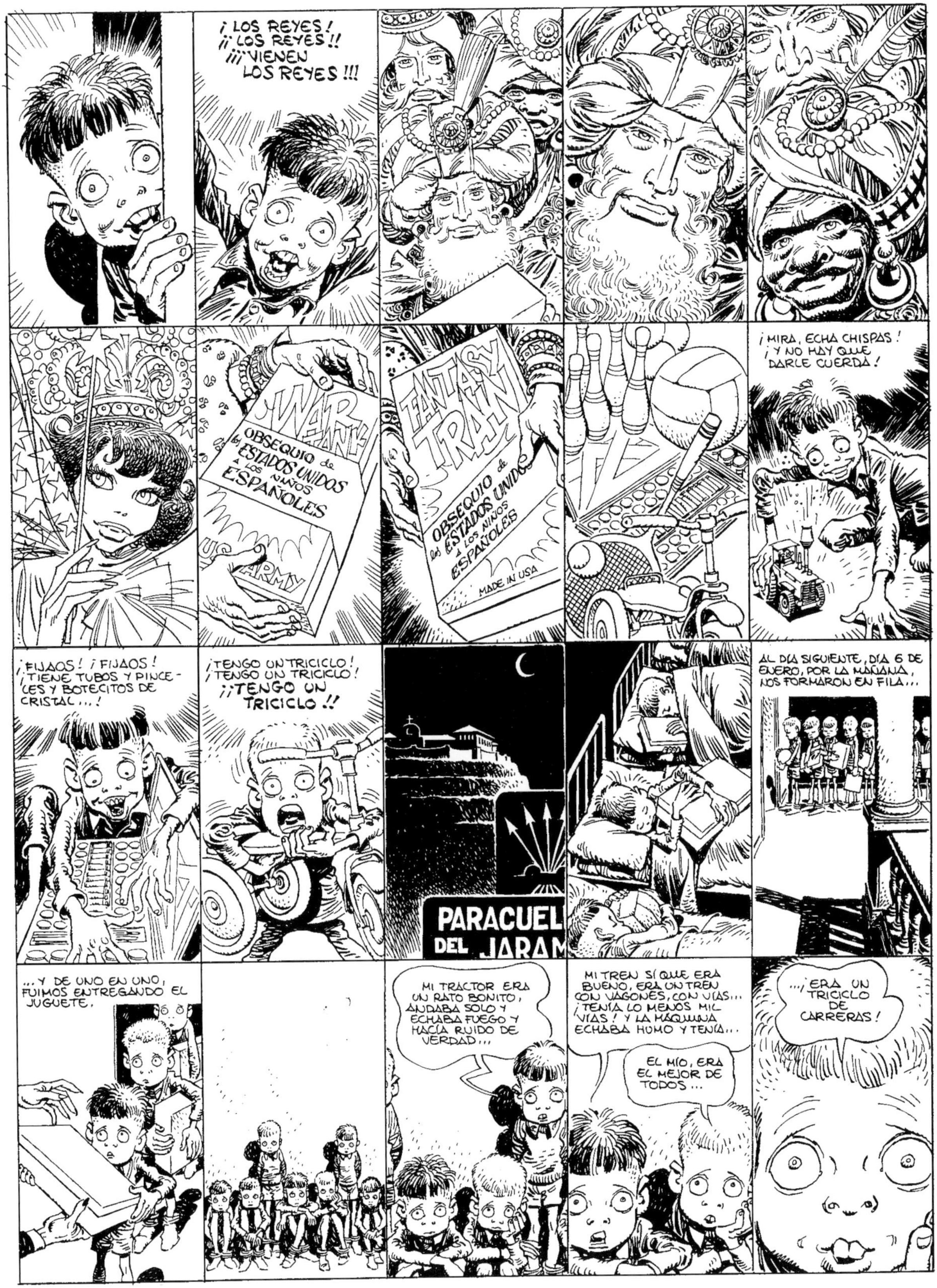
¡ LOS REYES !
¡¡ LOS REYES !!
¡¡¡ VIENEN LOS REYES !!!
WAR TANK
OBSEQUIO de los ESTADOS UNIDOS a LOS NIÑOS ESPAÑOLES
US ARMY
FANTASY TRAIN
OBSEQUIO de los ESTADOS UNIDOS a LOS NIÑOS ESPAÑOLES
MADE IN USA
¡ MIRA, ECHA CHISPAS ! ¡ Y NO HAY QUE DARLE CUERDA !
¡ FIJAOS ! ¡ FIJAOS ! ¡ TIENE TUBOS Y PINCE-CES Y BOTECITOS DE CRISTAL ... !
¡ TENGO UN TRICICLO ! ¡ TENGO UN TRICICLO ! ¡¡ TENGO UN TRICICLO !!
PARACUEL DEL JARAM
AL DÍA SIGUIENTE, DÍA 6 DE ENERO, POR LA MAÑANA, NOS FORMARON EN FILA ...
... Y DE UNO EN UNO, FUIMOS ENTREGANDO EL JUGUETE.
MI TRACTOR ERA UN RATO BONITO, ANDABA SOLO Y ECHABA FUEGO Y HACÍA RUIDO DE VERDAD ...
MI TREN SÍ QUE ERA BUENO, ERA UN TREN CON VAGONES, CON VÍAS ... ¡ TENÍA LO MENOS MIL VÍAS ! Y LA MÁQUINA ECHABA HUMO Y TENÍA ...
EL MÍO, ERA EL MEJOR DE TODOS ...
... ¡ ERA UN TRICICLO DE CARRERAS !

ORIGIN STORIES

FRAMING CARE IDENTITIES IN COMICS

LAURA CHASE, CURATORIAL FELLOW

PEOPLE TEND TO associate comics with funny stories for children. Although many of the most popular comics are *about* children, the issues raised in these stories can be surprisingly serious. Little Orphan Annie, one of the most famous children in comics, battles enormous obstacles – homelessness, social stigma and violence, to name a few – in her playful day-to-day adventures. Orphans, foundlings, adoptees, foster children and many other 'care identities' have featured prominently in newspaper strips and on comic book covers for over a century. Throughout this time, the portrayal of so-called looked-after children has evolved from superficial stereotypes to complex characters steeped in emotion and lived experience. What is it about the comic strip that makes it such an effective place to tell these stories?

The emergence of care identities in comics can be traced back to the late nineteenth century, when Victorian literature was utterly saturated with orphan narratives. Characters like Huck Finn, Oliver Twist and Heidi entertained readers with their adventures and exploits. However, the freedom these characters enjoyed also made them outsiders, highlighting the social anxieties that parentless children provoked at this time. On 5 May 1895, readers of the *New York World* were introduced to a bald, buck-toothed child wearing only an oversized yellow nightshirt in *Hogan's Alley*, a new addition to the newspaper's colourful Sunday comics page.[1] The 'Yellow Kid' – later

YA-A-A!
ANNIE DIDN'T GET ANY ICE CREAM- ANNIE DIDN'T GET ANY-
AW- LEAVE ME ALONE-
CHASE YOURSELVES OR YOU'LL GET THIS RIGHT IN YOUR MUSH!

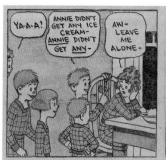

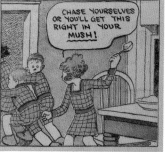

▶ 'McFadden's Row of Flats' in *Hogan's Alley* R.F. Outcault 18 Oct. 1896 *New York Journal*

◀ *Little Orphan Annie* (detail) Harold Gray 2 Nov. 1924 *Chicago Tribune*

McFADDEN'S ROW OF FLATS.

By E. W. TOWNSEND, Author of "CHIMMIE FADDEN."

Illustrated by R. F. OUTCAULT, - - - - - - - Originator of "HOGAN'S ALLEY."

"MARY ELLEN MURPHY! Mary Ellen Murphy, hasten quickly dear, and tell the Fresh Cop from Oak street to turn in a hurry ambulance call. And"—continued Mrs. Murphy, glancing up the street from her window—"and a fire alarm. Hasten quickly, darlint, or I'll break your face, dear!"

"What for?" demanded Mary Ellen; but just then her eye caught the amazing sight her mother, from her elevated lookout, had first discovered; and Mary Ellen uttered a whoop of joy and started up the street, yelling to the Dunnigan Twins, who were both trying to sit on Congo's head, "Come on, youse. It's a cirkis, and a chowder party, and a mad dog, and a fight!"

Mary Ellen's delighted announcement brought all the inhabitants of Tim McFadden's Flats to their doors and windows. Truly it was a sight as wonderful as it was enlivening. There came down the street from up Cherry Hill way a procession, which warranted Mary Ellen in her description. The leader was a shaved youth, arrayed simply in a sack of such yellow hue as would have excited the envy of Li Hung Chang. By his side pranced a knowing looking goat, sandwiched between two dogs, the three drawing a cart, luggage-laden, and surmounted by a wonderful maid with a much more wonderful hat. In one arm the yellow-clad boy carried a black cat, whose distressed yowlings competed in the general racket with a bass drum and a bass horn. There was a girl near the yellow kid with hair of such redness that Congo, who was, until he saw her, only slowly reviving from his encounter with the Twins, jumping high in the air when he first caught sight of its radiant brightness. There were banners and flags and shouting and cheering; there were fights and laughter, and everything, indeed, calculated to arouse the curiosity and enthusiasm of McFadden's Row of Flats.

"Dot's no showder barty," said Kramer, the grocer, in high excitement. "It's a masquerade ball, already. Don't it, Kelly?"

Kelly, the barkeeper, for once had no opinion to offer. He was dumb with amazement, as was Riccadonna, the pushcart man. They could only look in amazement at the oncomers, and naturally join with Mrs. Murphy and the Riccadonna girls in a chorus of demands for Tim McFadden.

He would know; nothing could happen in or near the Flats which Tim could not explain. There was comfort in that.

"Tim McFadden," cried Mrs. Murphy, "tell us what is this coming. Hasten quickly, Tim, for the love of hivin, and tell me what is this coming befoor I fall out of this windy wid wonder!"

They gathered about Tim, who was standing on the stoop of his Flats, looking proud and happy, but not excited. Ti mis never that.

"My friends," said McFadden, "what you observe and hear coming down the street is a migration."

There was a moment's hush, until Mrs. Murphy called down to Kelly, the barkeeper :

"Kell, what's a migration?"

"A migration," replied Kelly, bound not to be again caught in ignorance —"a migration is a Raines Law Hotel—when it's pulled."

"Not so bad for you, my boy," assented McFadden. "The celebration coming toward us now, which, by the same token, is now headed by the Dunnigan Twins and Mrs. Murphy's Mary Ellen, is the pick and flower of Hogan's Alley."

"I know 'bout deese ting," interrupted Riccadonna. "Hogan's Alley is corna down by da law."

"Right you are, Ricco," Tim explained. "The tinements of Hogan's Alley, by the power of the Health Board in or dinance assembled thereunto, being condemned as befit human habitation, I induced the flower thereof to migrate here by my hand and seal thereunto affixed. The weeds of Tim McFadden's Row of Flats is dispossessed, as you are all knowing thereof. The same is now moving out, and if you, Casey, hasn't a care with the stove you are putting out of the window, you'll be having ribs to mend. The vacancies thereof, accruing by due process of law, will be filled, habituated and occupied by the aforetime flower and pride of Hogan's Alley."

"I tell you bout dese ting," cried Riccadonna. "Tim McFadden is greata oratory dan deese Garibaldi. I second da motion to elect heem"——

"Murder alive!" broke in Mrs. Murphy. "What's this the Dunnigan Twins has betune thim? Is it a little Li Hoong Choong, or a kid wid the cholera, having the quarteeeen flag on him? Hasten quickly, Kramer, and inform me befoor I die wid worrymint."

"Dose kid mit de yellow nightie?" asked Kramer.

"The same," Mrs. Murphy said—"the little one wid de shaved pate on him."

It was a proud day for McFadden's Row of Flats. All four of the Riccadonna girls came down to the sidewalk to join the Reception Committee, headed by Tim himself, and including Mrs. Dunnigan, Kelly's wife and three children, not forgetting Congo, with eyes looking like two hard-boiled eggs, spotted with ink.

The procession swept into the block with a shriek and a cheer and a song and a hurrah. The Fresh Cop from Oak street looked as if he thought of calling out the reserve, and Riccadonna hastily threw a tarpaulin over his fruit. The discarded ones who were moving from the flats hastened the details of their departure with the zeal they would have displayed had there been a fire. Mrs. Murphy swirled her beer can in nervousness, and only Tim remained calm. The Flatters all waited for him to speak.

"I bid you welcome," he said to the newcomers, when the Fresh Cop had untangled a bounding ball composed of the Dunnigan Twins, the Yellow Kid, Mary Ellen and Congo, who were fighting for possession of the parrot. "I bid you welcome to McFadden's Flats by proclamation, all laws to the contrary being repealed thereof."

Then there were introductions, which did not, however, disclose the identity of the Yellow Kid.

"Whose little one are you, dear?" asked Mrs. Murphy of the Kid, observing the omission.

"Say, I aint nobody's child. I belongs t' de gang. See?" answered the Kid.

"Our gang can lick yourn," Congo suggested; and in the scrap that followed Mary Ellen, who is a good child and has a great eye for the main chance, captured the parrot, cage and all, and tied the cage to the string Mrs. Murphy uses when she makes a short cut with her growler.

The disturbance between Congo and the Yellow Kid was called off temporarily to allow the Kid to present a number of the members of his party to the Flatters. He made them acquainted with Liza, the red-headed girl, Terence McSwatt and others of his companions, who were distributed according to their family connections in the recently vacated portions of the Flat. There was no room or portion of a room assigned to the Yellow Kid, but he discovered a little closet in the hall adjoining the door to Tim's room.

Such was the migration of Hogan's Alley to Tim McFadden's Row of Flats, where the joined communities will be observed from time to time, for the benefit of the readers of this page, by the present historian and artist.

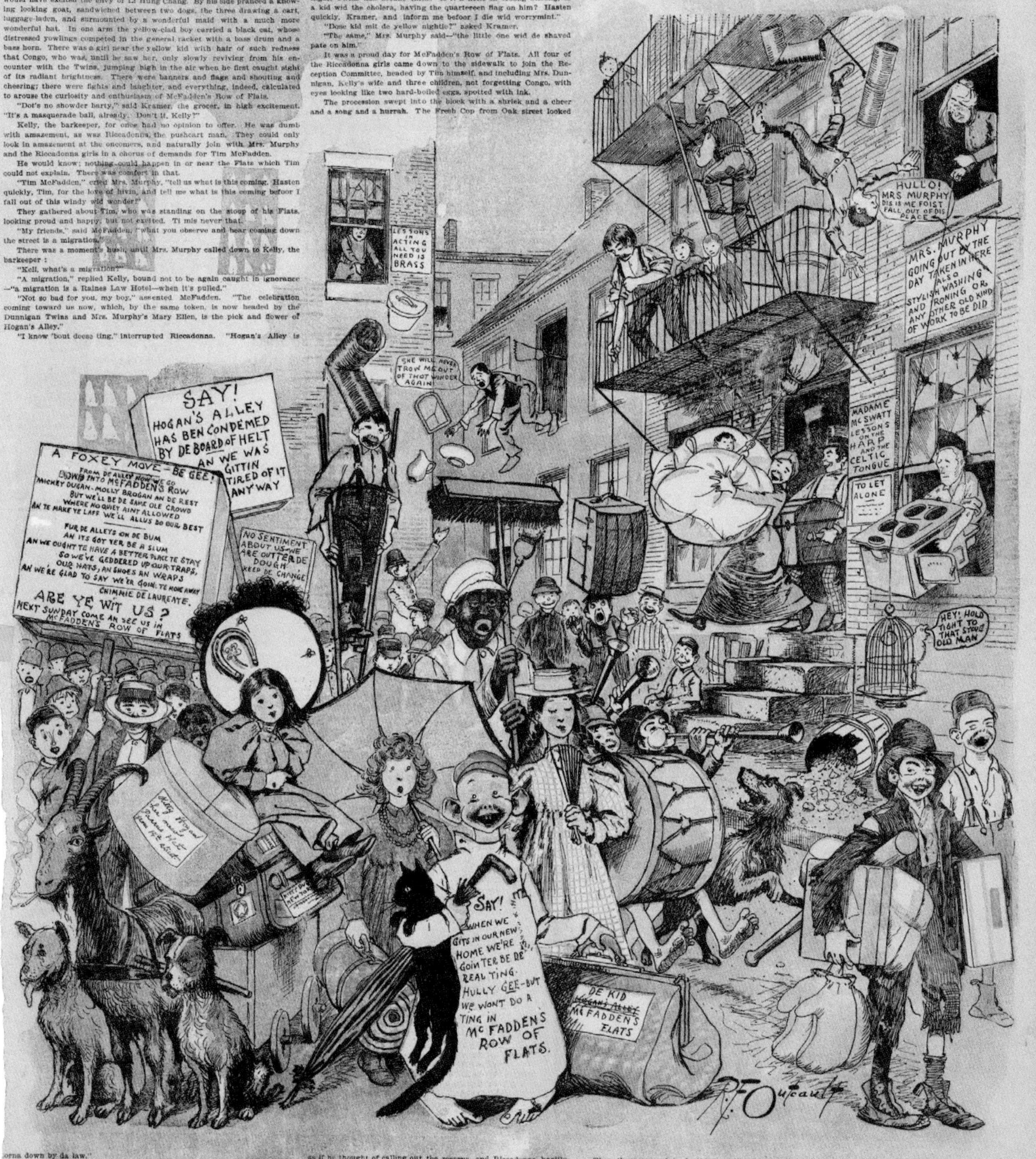
LESSONS IN ACTING ALL YOU NEED IS BRASS
HULLO! MRS MURPHY DIS IS ME FOIST FALL OUT OF DIS PLACE
MRS. MURPHY GOING OUT BY THE DAY TAKEN IN HERE ALSO STYLISH WASHING AND IRONING OR ANY OTHER OLD KIND OF WORK TO BE DID
SHE WILL NEVER TROW ME OUT OF THOT WINDER AGAIN
MADAME MC SWATT LESSONS ON THE HARP AND THE CELTIC TONGUE
TO LET ALONE
SAY! HOGAN'S ALLEY HAS BEN CONDEMED BY DE BOARD OF HELT AN WE WAS GITTIN TIRED OF IT ANY WAY
A FOXEY MOVE—BE GEE!
FROM DE ALLEY NOW WE GO
DOWN INTO McFADDEN'S ROW
MICKEY DUGAN—MOLLY BROGAN AN DE REST
BUT WE'LL BE DE SAME OLE CROWD
WHERE NO QUIET AINT ALLOWED
AN TE MAKE YE LAFF WE'LL ALLUS DO OUR BEST
FUR DE ALLEYS ON DE BUM
AN ITS GOT TER BE A SLUM
AN WE OUGHT TE HAVE A BETTER PLACE TE STAY
SO WE'VE GEDDERED UP OUR TRAPS,
OUR HATS, AN SHOES AN WRAPS
AN WE'RE GLAD TO SAY WE'R GOIN TE MOVE AWAY
CHIMMIE DE LAUREATE.
ARE YE WIT US?
NEXT SUNDAY COME AN SEE US IN McFADDEN'S ROW OF FLATS
NO SENTIMENT ABOUT US—WE ARE OUTTER DE DOUGH KEEP DE CHANGE
HEY! HOLD TIGHT TO THAT STOVE OLD MAN
SAY! WHEN WE GITS IN OUR NEW HOME WE'RE GOIN TER BE DE REAL TING. HULLY GEE—BUT WE WONT DO A TING IN Mc FADDEN'S ROW OF FLATS.
DE KID HOGAN'S ALLEY McFADDEN'S FLATS
R. F. Outcault

named Mickey Dugan – was an unlikely protagonist who swiftly became a household name.[2]

The Yellow Kid secured popularity through his ambiguous, infantile appearance, which juxtaposed the more 'adult' activities he took part in, like cockfighting. More importantly, the Yellow Kid's surroundings were relatable to American readers. The world of *Hogan's Alley* took inspiration from the tenement communities – also referred to as 'slums' – that were popping up in rapidly expanding metropolises like New York City and Philadelphia. The Yellow Kid's creator, Richard Felton Outcault, examined contemporary social issues like immigration and urbanisation through a humorous lens, following a tradition established by William Hogarth, who captured the foibles of eighteenth-century London society in sharp-witted satirical prints.[3] Outcault's visual formula consisted of highly detailed, chaotic scenes in which the Kid gazes out towards the reader. His trademark yellow shirt – a visual trope that would later evolve into the speech bubble – broadcasts a bit of witty commentary about the action swirling around him.[4] Outcault's comic soon migrated to the *New York Journal*, where it was aptly renamed *The Yellow Kid*.[5] The comic ran for only three years (1895-98), but its lead character remained a fixture in popular culture for decades.

The Yellow Kid is wholly unique among other comics from this period. With a twinkle in his eye, he guides the reader through his world: a neighbourhood rife with poverty, crime, disease and general disorder. Over the course of the comic, the reader learns very little about the Yellow Kid's personal story. The fate of his family remains a mystery, and the Kid's own future is similarly framed as a distant concern. From this perspective, Outcault's portrayal of care experience is undoubtedly limited, not to mention very clearly hindered by racial and social stereotypes.

NEW YORK JOURNAL, SUNDAY, NOVEMBER 22, 1896.
A FEW THINGS THE VERSATILE YELLOW KID MIGHT DO FOR A LIVING.

▲
'A Few Things the Versatile Yellow Kid Might Do For A Living' in *Hogan's Alley* 22 Nov. 1896

Although he regularly comes into contact with the middle and upper classes, the Kid indicates little interest in elevating his own social position. On the contrary, he seems to delight in the instability and vitality of Hogan's Alley, and defends himself against those who might try to make him feel inferior. These interactions often result in physical fights from which the Kid always emerges smiling, even on the occasions when he is the loser. This aspect of the Yellow Kid's lively personality reflects the pioneering nature of the comic strip. The Kid may be destined to inherit a grim fate, but his undercutting humour and defiant body language convey a self-awareness and resilience that – at this time – were radical for a parentless child.

The serial nature of the comic strip provides a crucial tool for exploring the

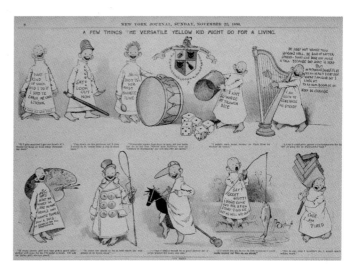

complexities of care identities. In 1922, artist Frank O. King was advised by his editor to add an infant to his comic strip *Gasoline Alley*, in an effort to expand its appeal to female and family audiences. When the character Skeezix made his debut on 14 February, it was the image of a foundling baby in a basket that drew in new readers.[6] Skeezix's gradual assimilation into a small town community in midwestern America is charted on a daily basis in *Gasoline Alley*. King made this reading experience even more emotive by having the characters age in real time, a brilliant and entirely new narrative device in comics.[7] Over the years, readers watched Skeezix attend college, serve in the Second World War, marry his childhood sweetheart, take over his adoptive father's car repair shop and have children and grandchildren of his own.

Through the chronicling of everyday events, *Gasoline Alley* celebrates a love story between adoptive father (Walt Wallet) and son. The most poignant panels are ones which show Walt and Skeezix out in nature, either sharing observations or simply sitting together in silence.

These moments convey an astonishingly progressive image of parental care. While Skeezix's 'foundling' status never fades away completely, it becomes rooted in affection and gratitude. This dynamic is most clearly conveyed in the comic strips that mark significant holidays (like New Year's Eve and Skeezix's birthdays), during which Walt invariably retells the 'origin story' of Skeezix's arrival and their enduring relationship as part of the celebration.

Gasoline Alley shows how the act of reading a comic requires an acute awareness of the passage of time. New storylines are introduced on a regular basis (daily, weekly or monthly), and past events are frequently integrated into ongoing narratives as flashbacks. The ability to move both forward and

Gasoline Alley (detail) 31 Dec 1922 ▼

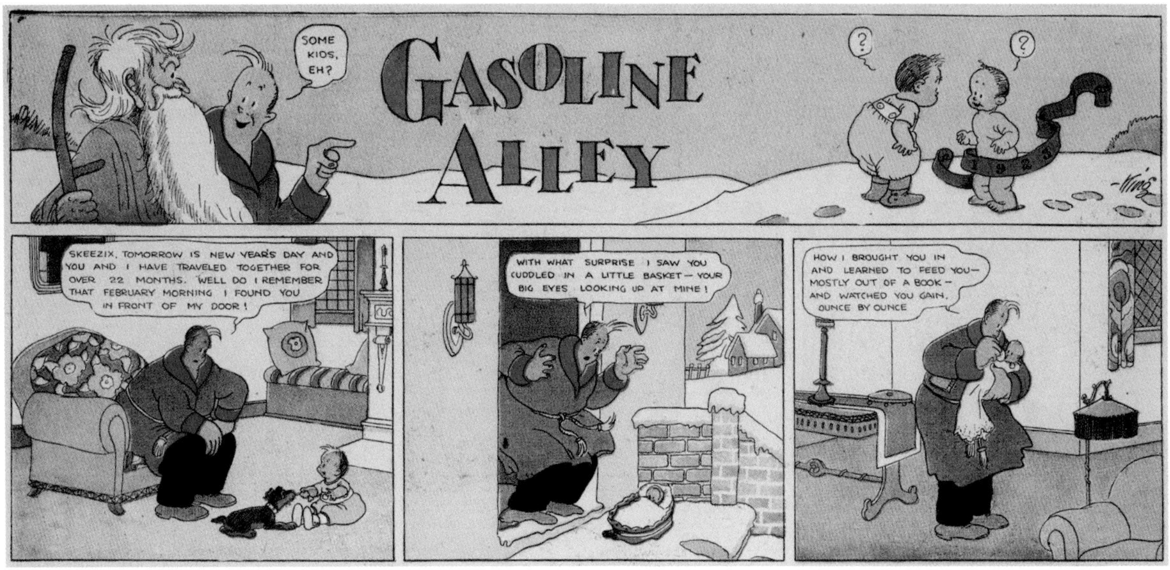
SOME KIDS, EH?
GASOLINE ALLEY
?
?
1923
KING
SKEEZIX, TOMORROW IS NEW YEAR'S DAY AND YOU AND I HAVE TRAVELED TOGETHER FOR OVER 22 MONTHS. WELL DO I REMEMBER THAT FEBRUARY MORNING I FOUND YOU IN FRONT OF MY DOOR!
WITH WHAT SURPRISE I SAW YOU CUDDLED IN A LITTLE BASKET — YOUR BIG EYES LOOKING UP AT MINE!
HOW I BROUGHT YOU IN AND LEARNED TO FEED YOU — MOSTLY OUT OF A BOOK — AND WATCHED YOU GAIN, OUNCE BY OUNCE

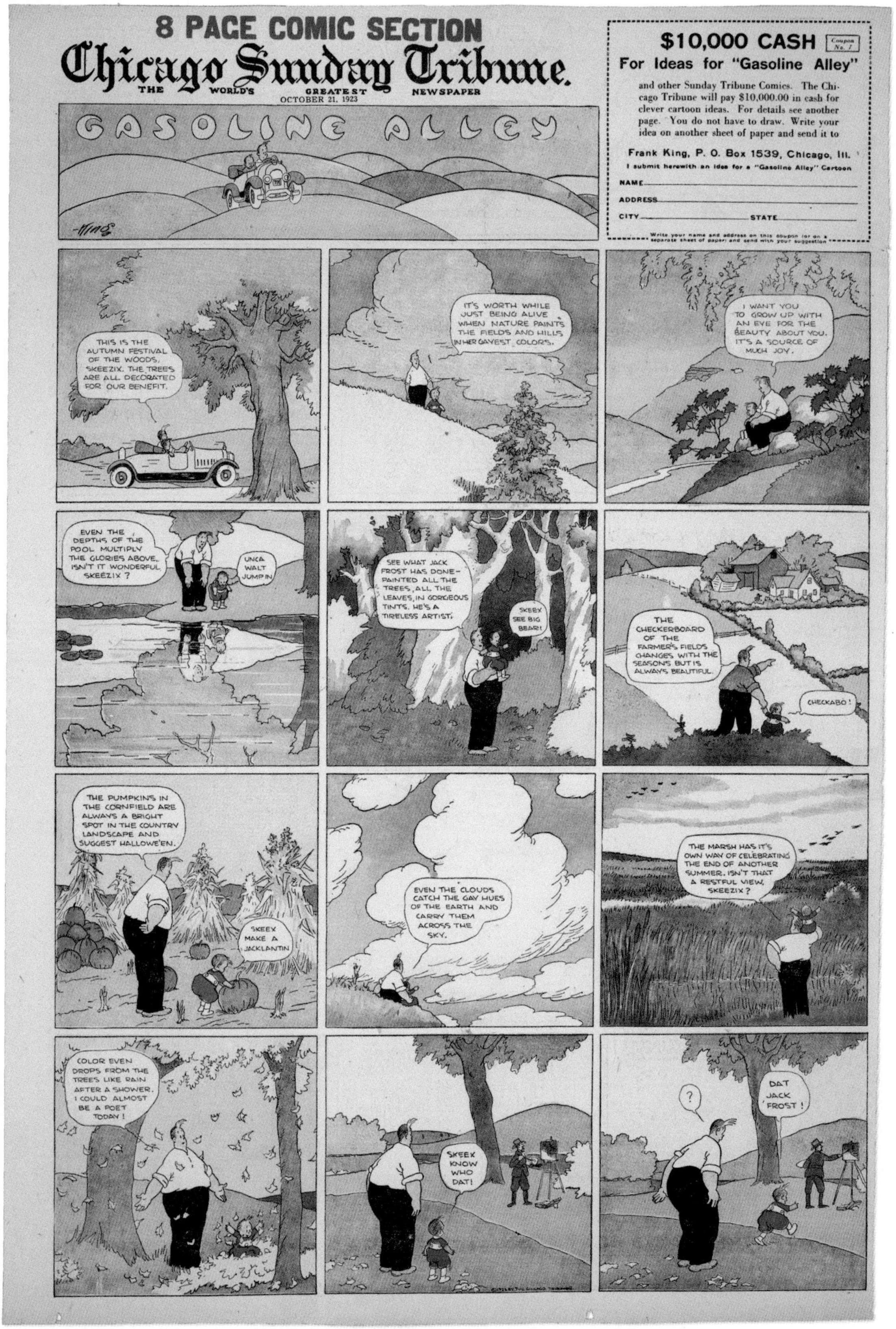
8 PAGE COMIC SECTION
Chicago Sunday Tribune.
THE WORLD'S GREATEST NEWSPAPER
OCTOBER 21, 1923
$10,000 CASH
Coupon No. 7
For Ideas for "Gasoline Alley"
and other Sunday Tribune Comics. The Chicago Tribune will pay $10,000.00 in cash for clever cartoon ideas. For details see another page. You do not have to draw. Write your idea on another sheet of paper and send it to
Frank King, P. O. Box 1539, Chicago, Ill.
I submit herewith an idea for a "Gasoline Alley" Cartoon
NAME
ADDRESS
CITY
STATE
GASOLINE ALLEY
KING
THIS IS THE AUTUMN FESTIVAL OF THE WOODS, SKEEZIX. THE TREES ARE ALL DECORATED FOR OUR BENEFIT.
IT'S WORTH WHILE JUST BEING ALIVE WHEN NATURE PAINTS THE FIELDS AND HILLS IN HER GAYEST COLORS.
I WANT YOU TO GROW UP WITH AN EYE FOR THE BEAUTY ABOUT YOU. IT'S A SOURCE OF MUCH JOY.
EVEN THE DEPTHS OF THE POOL MULTIPLY THE GLORIES ABOVE. ISN'T IT WONDERFUL, SKEEZIX?
UNCA WALT JUMP IN
SEE WHAT JACK FROST HAS DONE—PAINTED ALL THE TREES, ALL THE LEAVES, IN GORGEOUS TINTS. HE'S A TIRELESS ARTIST.
SKEEX SEE BIG BEAR!
THE CHECKERBOARD OF THE FARMER'S FIELDS CHANGES WITH THE SEASONS BUT IS ALWAYS BEAUTIFUL.
CHECKABO!
THE PUMPKINS IN THE CORNFIELD ARE ALWAYS A BRIGHT SPOT IN THE COUNTRY LANDSCAPE AND SUGGEST HALLOWE'EN.
SKEEX MAKE A JACKLANTIN
EVEN THE CLOUDS CATCH THE GAY HUES OF THE EARTH AND CARRY THEM ACROSS THE SKY.
THE MARSH HAS IT'S OWN WAY OF CELEBRATING THE END OF ANOTHER SUMMER. ISN'T THAT A RESTFUL VIEW, SKEEZIX?
COLOR EVEN DROPS FROM THE TREES LIKE RAIN AFTER A SHOWER. I COULD ALMOST BE A POET TODAY!
SKEEX KNOW WHO DAT!
?
DAT JACK FROST!

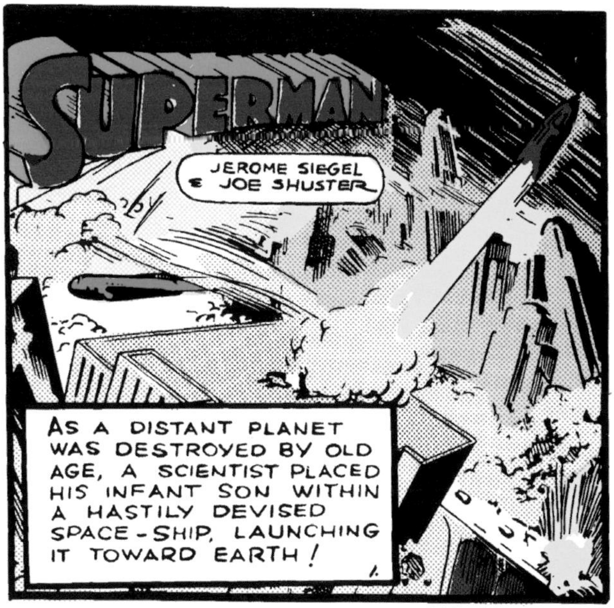
SUPERMAN
JEROME SIEGEL & JOE SHUSTER
AS A DISTANT PLANET WAS DESTROYED BY OLD AGE, A SCIENTIST PLACED HIS INFANT SON WITHIN A HASTILY DEVISED SPACE-SHIP, LAUNCHING IT TOWARD EARTH!

▶
Action Comics Vol. 1, #1
Joe Shuster, Jerry Siegel
Jun. 1938, p. 1 (detail)

backward in time lets comics embed care identities more meaningfully into their narrative structure. The flashback technique is particularly significant in the development of the classic superhero narrative as seen in major comic book series like DC's *Superman* and *Batman*. The story of Kal-El's (Superman's birth name) journey from his home planet Krypton to Earth is referenced repeatedly throughout the comic series. A particularly powerful image that resurfaces in early issues shows Kal-El's birth parents, Lara and Jor-El, placing their child in a rescue spacecraft moments before Krypton is destroyed. Similarly, the origin story of *Batman* can be compressed into a single panel that shows the child Bruce Wayne kneeling over the bodies of his parents after witnessing their murders in an alleyway.

Each of these panels clearly conveys the hero's care identity: Superman is a foundling and Batman is an orphan. The act of repeatedly inserting these images into subsequent storylines introduces an aspect of visual memory that is especially powerful. As Superman and Batman flashback to these significant memories, so too does the reader. These events are not fixed to a single point on each hero's journey, rather the past continuously shapes the character's perspective, ambition and actions. Moreover, these are deeply traumatic moments that – when they appear on the page – trigger an intensification of emotion for the character and reader alike. Throughout their respective battles for justice, Superman and Batman are also constantly reconciling a conflicted sense of self (who they are as adults), which is largely the result of the injustice they personally experienced as children.

The inclusion of traumatic subject matter doesn't diminish the mass appeal of works like *Superman* and *Batman*. Quite the opposite! Comics have the power to

◀
Gasoline Alley
21 Oct. 1923

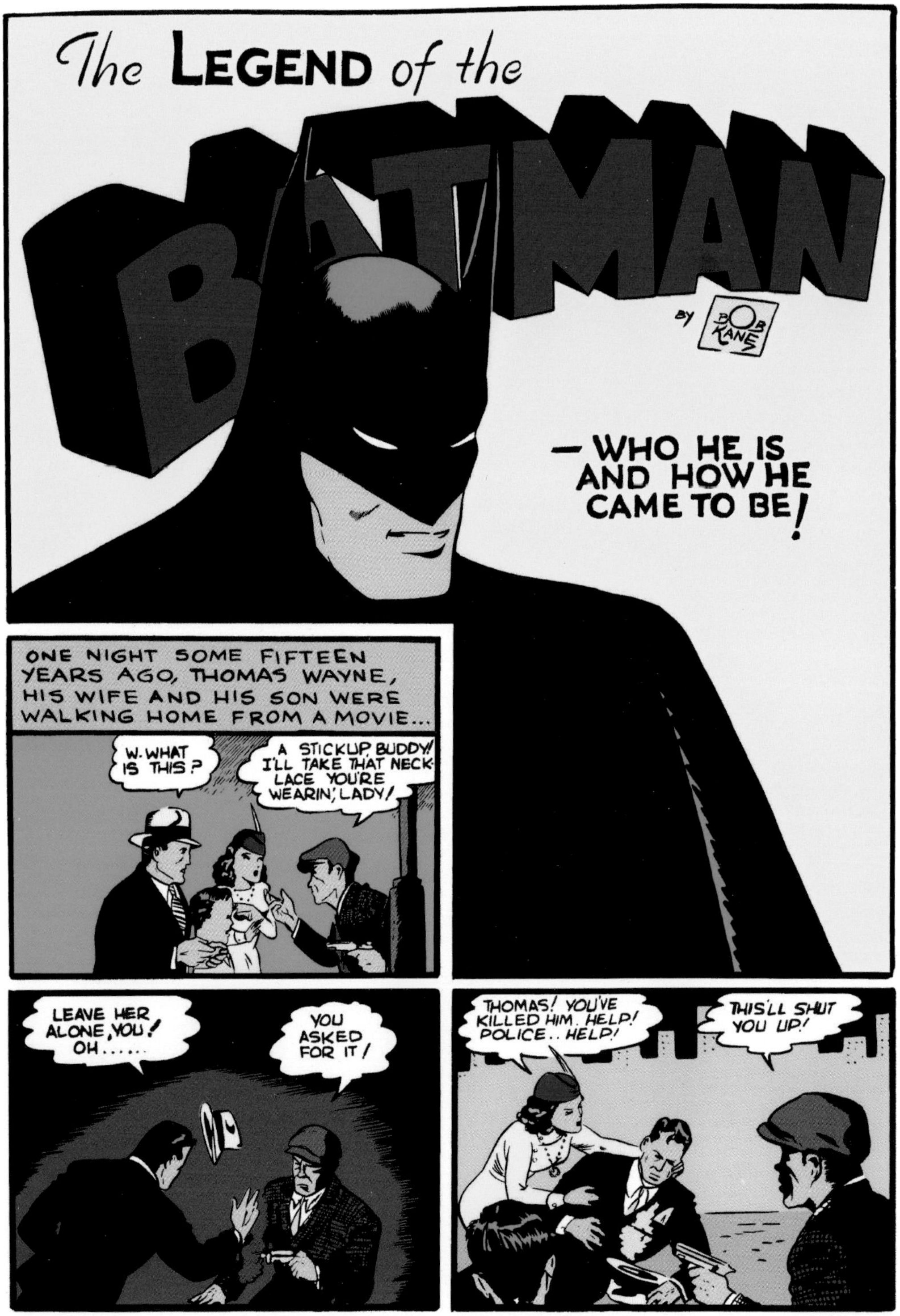
The LEGEND of the
BATMAN
BY BOB KANE
— WHO HE IS AND HOW HE CAME TO BE!
ONE NIGHT SOME FIFTEEN YEARS AGO, THOMAS WAYNE, HIS WIFE AND HIS SON WERE WALKING HOME FROM A MOVIE...
W. WHAT IS THIS?
A STICKUP, BUDDY! I'LL TAKE THAT NECKLACE YOU'RE WEARIN', LADY!
LEAVE HER ALONE, YOU! OH......
YOU ASKED FOR IT!
THOMAS! YOU'VE KILLED HIM. HELP! POLICE.. HELP!
THIS'LL SHUT YOU UP!

◀ ▶
Batman Vol. 1, #1
Bill Finger,
Bob Kane,
Sheldon Moldoff
Mar. 1940, pp. 1–2

THE BOY'S EYES ARE WIDE WITH TERROR AND SHOCK AS THE HORRIBLE SCENE IS SPREAD BEFORE HIM.

FATHER.. MOTHER!

...DEAD! THEY'RE D..DEAD

DAYS LATER, A CURIOUS AND STRANGE SCENE TAKES PLACE.

AND I SWEAR BY THE SPIRITS OF MY PARENTS TO AVENGE THEIR DEATHS BY SPENDING THE REST OF MY LIFE WARRING ON ALL CRIMINALS

AS THE YEARS PASS, BRUCE WAYNE PREPARES HIMSELF FOR HIS CAREER. HE BECOMES A MASTER SCIENTIST.

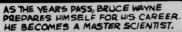

TRAINS HIS BODY TO PHYSICAL PERFECTION UNTIL HE IS ABLE TO PERFORM AMAZING ATHLETIC FEATS.

DAD'S ESTATE LEFT ME WEALTHY. I AM READY.. BUT FIRST I MUST HAVE A DISGUISE.

CRIMINALS ARE A SUPERSTITIOUS COWARDLY LOT, SO MY DISGUISE MUST BE ABLE TO STRIKE TERROR INTO THEIR HEARTS. I MUST BE A CREATURE OF THE NIGHT, BLACK, TERRIBLE .. A.. A..

AS IF IN ANSWER, A HUGE BAT FLIES IN THE OPEN WINDOW!

A BAT! THAT'S IT! IT'S AN OMEN.. I SHALL BECOME A **BAT**!

AND THUS IS BORN THIS WEIRD FIGURE OF THE DARK.. THIS AVENGER OF EVIL.. THE **BATMAN**

Forty-three seconds later, 1,800 feet over Hiroshima, the atomic bomb named Little Boy exploded with a white-hot light. It was like a million flashbulbs going off at once...
FLASH
ROARRR

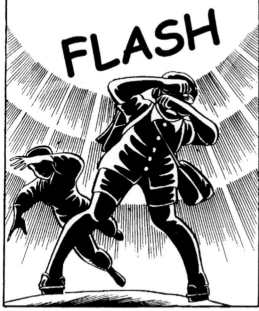

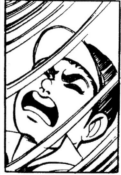

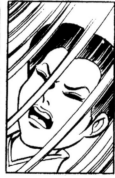

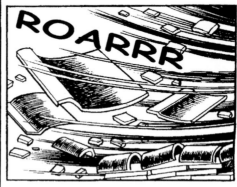

◀ *Barefoot Gen* Vol. I
Keiji Nakazawa
1978 (English translation)
p. 250 (detail)

distil complex and challenging content into a single-framed image that is accessible, compelling and entertaining for readers of all ages. Moving across the world to Japan, this power is evident in Keiji Nakazawa's ground-breaking *Barefoot Gen (Hadashi no Gen)*, a ten-volume manga series heavily inspired by the author's own experience of surviving the atomic bombing of Hiroshima by American military forces on 6 August 1945.[8] Nakazawa doesn't hold back in his depiction of the carnage that ensues: page after page shows victims staggering through piles of rubble, their bodies mutilated with burns and shards of glass endured from the nuclear blast.

It is through the wide eyes of six-year-old Gen Nakaoka that the reader experiences the hellish transformation of Hiroshima. Similarly to the Yellow Kid, Gen frames our understanding of this environment through his own reactions. But whereas the Yellow Kid's observations usually serve as a punchline, Gen's thoughts echo and amplify the turbulence of the world that has collapsed around him. His emotions swing wildly from grief – mourning the deaths of his father, brother and sister – to rage, before pivoting to courage, as he makes valiant efforts to help other survivors.

Gen's internal monologue is a testament to the tenacity of the human spirit, as he reacts to the violence that envelops him. It is Gen's voice that offers crucial

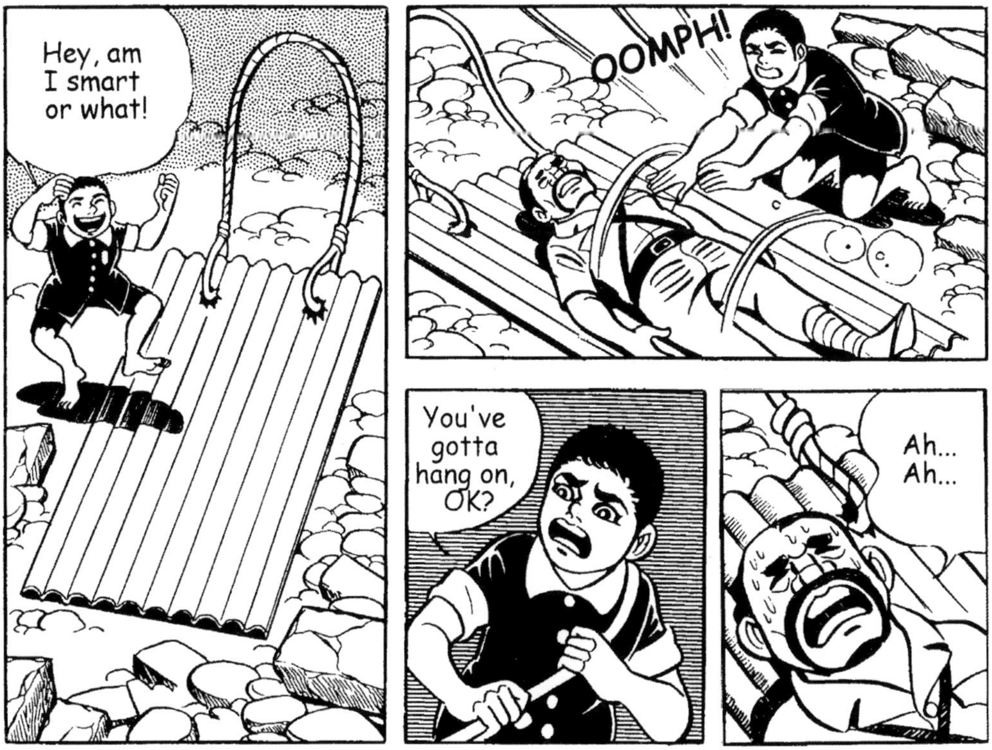
Hey, am I smart or what!
OOMPH!
You've gotta hang on, OK?
Ah... Ah...

▶ *Barefoot Gen* Vol. 2 1979 p. 39 (detail)

moments of respite – and even humour – which give the reader an opportunity to recover from the harrowing content in preceding panels. Nakazawa emphasises the complexity of Gen's identity through the character's internal voice, which evolves and matures over the course of the manga series. Gen is shaped significantly by his grief and vulnerability, but he also showcases incredible levels of resourcefulness, humour and dogged determination. Through painstaking visual detail and complex narrative voice, Nakazawa demonstrates the devastating immediacy and profound intimacy that can be achieved in comics.

Although Nakazawa incorporated fictional details at certain points in the story to increase dramatic effect, his own memories form the foundation for *Barefoot Gen*. The relationship between comics and autobiographical narratives is striking. In her memoir comic *Palimpsest*, Lisa Wool-Rim Sjöblom navigates the questions and missing details that obscure her own origin story. An international adoptee, Sjöblom was born in Korea, where she lived in an orphanage for two years before she was adopted and raised by a family in Sweden. Unlike the other comics discussed here, *Palimpsest* focuses completely on care identity. Using soft, muted colours, Sjöblom draws a world in which her questions are muffled and obstacles overwhelm her efforts to know her birth family and ancestral home. Sjöblom weaves together childhood memories and adult struggles, exposing so many layers

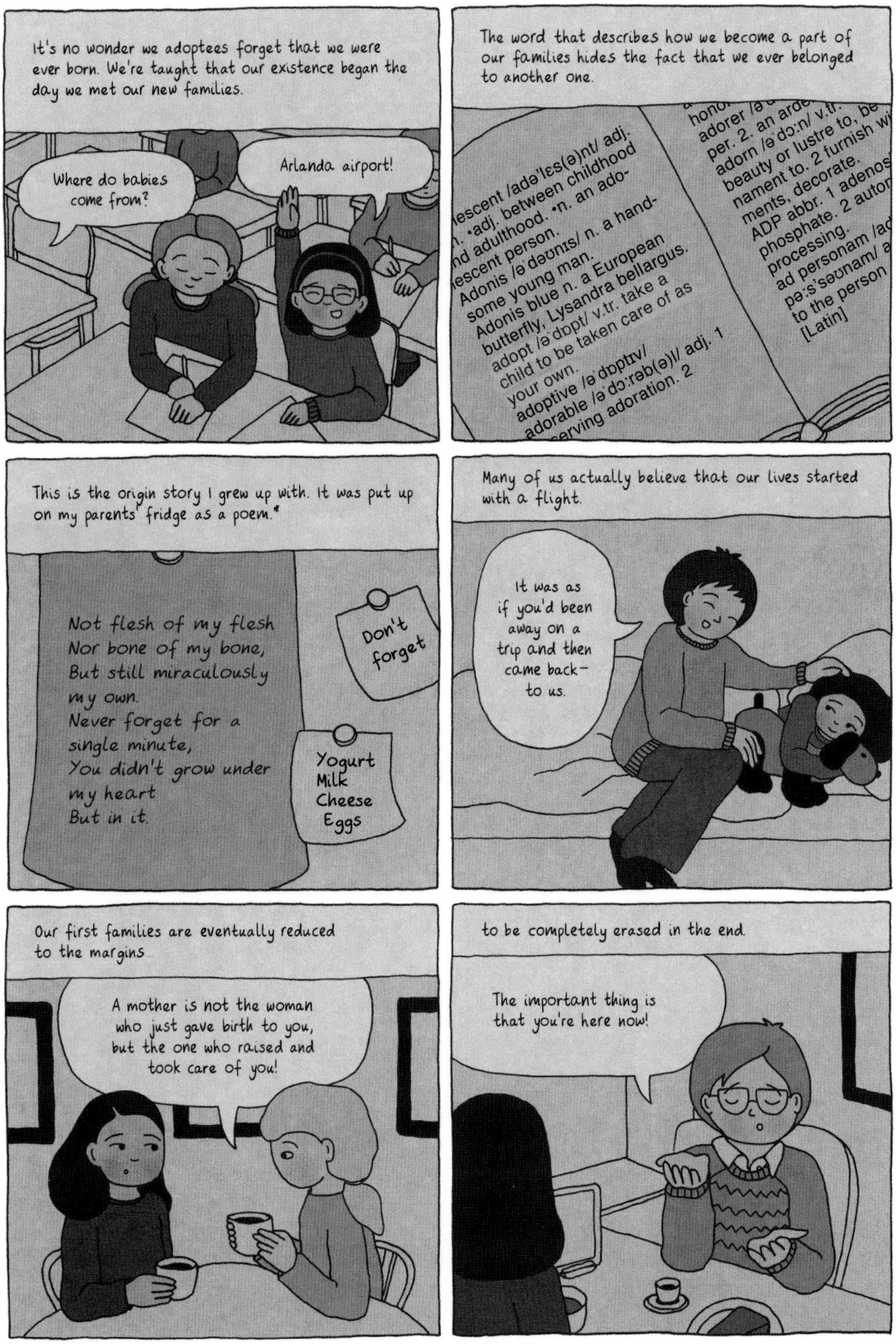
It's no wonder we adoptees forget that we were ever born. We're taught that our existence began the day we met our new families.
Where do babies come from?
Arlanda airport!
The word that describes how we become a part of our families hides the fact that we ever belonged to another one.
lescent /adə'lɛs(ə)nt/ adj. n. •adj. between childhood nd adulthood. •n. an ado- lescent person.
Adonis /ə'dəʊnɪs/ n. a hand- some young man.
Adonis blue n. a European butterfly, Lysandra bellargus.
adopt /ə'dɒpt/ v.tr. take a child to be taken care of as your own.
adoptive /ə'dɒptɪv/
adorable /ə'dɔːrəb(ə)l/ adj. 1 serving adoration. 2
adorer /ə'd per. 2. an ard
adorn /ə'dɔːn/ v.tr. beauty or lustre to, be nament to. 2 furnish wi ments, decorate.
ADP abbr. 1 adenos phosphate. 2 autor processing.
ad personam /ad pəːs'səʊnam/ a to the person [Latin]
This is the origin story I grew up with. It was put up on my parents' fridge as a poem.*
Not flesh of my flesh
Nor bone of my bone,
But still miraculously
my own.
Never forget for a
single minute,
You didn't grow under
my heart
But in it.
Don't forget
Yogurt
Milk
Cheese
Eggs
Many of us actually believe that our lives started with a flight.
It was as if you'd been away on a trip and then came back— to us.
Our first families are eventually reduced to the margins
A mother is not the woman who just gave birth to you, but the one who raised and took care of you!
to be completely erased in the end.
The important thing is that you're here now!

◀
Palimpsest
Lisa Wool-Rim Sjöblom
2019, p. 13

Many adoptees feel an inexplicable grief on their birthdays. They somehow remind us of a loss that no one will talk about.
We mourn in silence. We don't want to risk upsetting or hurting our adoptive parents, so when our losses are talked about as a positive, we keep quiet.
I'm sure your mom loved you, but she gave you away to give you a better life.

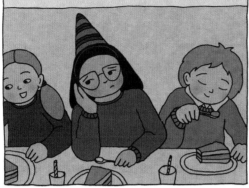

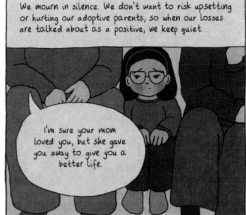

▸ *Palimpsest* p. 14 (detail)

of thought and emotion in each panel that reading the comic often feels like reading a diary. Moving beyond words, Sjöblom's illustrations convey a deep reservoir of feelings, including loss, brokenness and detachment.

Sjöblom frames her own story within the context of much larger issues, including the inequalities that corrupt the adoption system and the marginalisation of adoptee voices. Similarly to *Barefoot Gen*, Sjöblom demonstrates a comic book's vast potential to deconstruct global issues by highlighting one person's experience. *Palimpsest* isn't simply a memoir; it is a tool that Sjöblom uses as an adoptee rights activist. The ease with which comics like *Palimpsest* can be adapted as a medium for both storytelling and political engagement, indicates that the correlation between comics and care identities has immense scope for creative development.

Despite its printed format, the experience of reading a comic book has more in common with cinema than with other forms of literature. Image and sound collide as the reader deciphers the text, space, line, colour, expression and movement found on every page. Characters leap off the page as we share their memories and absorb their most private thoughts. We bear witness to vulnerability and can celebrate growth, because we know full well how the stories first began. It is not surprising that comics have produced intensely spirited and sensitive depictions of orphans, foundlings, adoptees and foster children. The nuance and sophistication with which these figures are drawn today reflects the vastly expanded language used to describe the range of identities grouped in the term 'looked-after children'. In turn, the subject of care identity has attracted a global fanbase and continues to be explored in some of today's most critically acclaimed and commercially successful graphic novels and comic book franchises.

NOTES

1. The Yellow Kid first appeared in 'At the Circus in Hogan's Alley.' (Robinson, J., 'The Yellow Kid,' p. 128).

2. Robinson p. 131. The commercial success of the Yellow Kid is difficult to overestimate. At peak popularity in the 1890s, the character was celebrated in books, plays and popular songs, and his image could be found on cigar boxes, whiskey bottles, cigarette packs, gum packets and even fancy soaps.

3. Robinson, p. 131.

4. Robinson, p. 128.

5. Robinson, p. 132.

6. The nickname 'Skeezix' (a rural slang term referring to a motherless calf) is provided by Walt Wallet, who also officially names the child Allison Wallet.

7. Chris Ware captures the impact of this artistic convention with his assessment that '[t]aken as a body of work, *Gasoline Alley* is not only a 50-year-long comic strip novel that captures and distills the inevitable, ineffable passage of time through the regular touch of an artist's pen to paper; it is also a semi-autobiographical recreation of the feeling of life itself.' (Ware, C., 'Frank King's *Gasoline Alley*,' 162).

8. Nakazawa's motivation for writing *Barefoot Gen* came after the death of his mother in the 1960s due to prolonged effects of radiation poisoning sustained from the nuclear blast. Nakazawa described the manga series as a means of 'avenging his mother' while also promoting messages of world peace and anti-nuclear policies. (Nakazawa, K., 'The Birth of Barefoot Gen.')

WORKS CITED

Robinson, J., 'The Yellow Kid,' in *Cartoon America: Comic Art in the Library of Congress*, ed. H. Katz, New York: Abrams (2006), pp. 128-132.

Nakazawa, K., 'The Birth of Barefoot Gen', in *Barefoot Gen: A Cartoon Story of Hiroshima*, San Francisco: Last Gasp (2004), pp. 7-9.

Ware, C., 'Frank King's *Gasoline Alley*', in *Cartoon America: Comic Art in the Library of Congress*, ed. H. Katz, New York: Abrams (2006), pp. 162-166.

ABOUT LAURA CHASE:

Laura Chase is a curator and arts educator who has cultivated exhibition projects in partnership with a number of museums in London and abroad. She developed Superheroes, Orphans & Origins *while serving as the Foundling Museum's Artisa Curatorial Fellow (June 2020 – March 2021).*

▶
Little Orphan Annie
7 Dec. 1924
Chicago Tribune

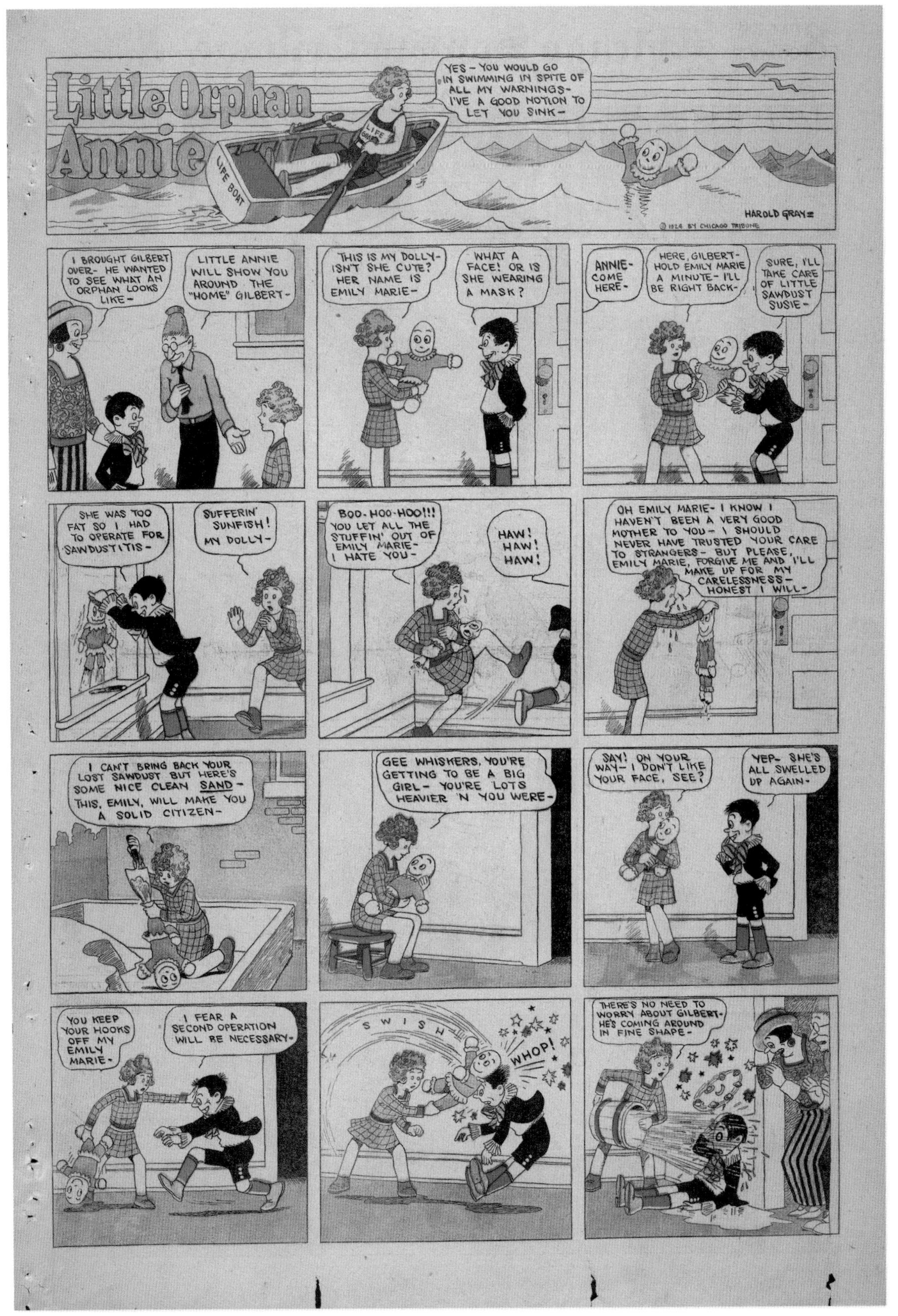
Little Orphan Annie
YES - YOU WOULD GO IN SWIMMING IN SPITE OF ALL MY WARNINGS - I'VE A GOOD NOTION TO LET YOU SINK -
LIFE BOAT
HAROLD GRAY
© 1924 BY CHICAGO TRIBUNE
I BROUGHT GILBERT OVER - HE WANTED TO SEE WHAT AN ORPHAN LOOKS LIKE -
LITTLE ANNIE WILL SHOW YOU AROUND THE "HOME" GILBERT -
THIS IS MY DOLLY - ISN'T SHE CUTE? HER NAME IS EMILY MARIE -
WHAT A FACE! OR IS SHE WEARING A MASK?
ANNIE - COME HERE -
HERE, GILBERT - HOLD EMILY MARIE A MINUTE - I'LL BE RIGHT BACK -
SURE, I'LL TAKE CARE OF LITTLE SAWDUST SUSIE -
SHE WAS TOO FAT SO I HAD TO OPERATE FOR SAWDUSTITIS -
SUFFERIN' SUNFISH! MY DOLLY -
BOO-HOO-HOO!!! YOU LET ALL THE STUFFIN' OUT OF EMILY MARIE - I HATE YOU -
HAW! HAW! HAW!
OH EMILY MARIE - I KNOW I HAVEN'T BEEN A VERY GOOD MOTHER TO YOU - I SHOULD NEVER HAVE TRUSTED YOUR CARE TO STRANGERS - BUT PLEASE, EMILY MARIE, FORGIVE ME AND I'LL MAKE UP FOR MY CARELESSNESS - HONEST I WILL -
I CAN'T BRING BACK YOUR LOST SAWDUST BUT HERE'S SOME NICE CLEAN SAND - THIS, EMILY, WILL MAKE YOU A SOLID CITIZEN -
GEE WHISKERS, YOU'RE GETTING TO BE A BIG GIRL - YOU'RE LOTS HEAVIER 'N YOU WERE -
SAY! ON YOUR WAY - I DON'T LIKE YOUR FACE, SEE?
YEP - SHE'S ALL SWELLED UP AGAIN -
YOU KEEP YOUR HOOKS OFF MY EMILY MARIE -
I FEAR A SECOND OPERATION WILL BE NECESSARY -
SWISH
WHOP!
THERE'S NO NEED TO WORRY ABOUT GILBERT - HE'S COMING AROUND IN FINE SHAPE -

DRAWING *NUBIA* FOR A NEW GENERATION

AN INTERVIEW WITH ROBYN SMITH

INTERVIEWED BY CARO HOWELL

HOW DID COMICS come into your life? What made you want to start drawing?

I actually started out as a portrait artist. It's something that I was initially interested in doing because my father is a portrait artist. At some point I realised that what I wanted to do was tell stories. While this is possible to do with portraiture, I also realised that most people only want really 'nice' – for example, smiling – pictures of themselves, which doesn't leave much room for storytelling.

I was reading mainly *Archie* comics at the time, which I still really love a lot and consider to be my main influence. I was reading *Archie* before I even really knew what comics were. While reading these comics, I was thinking about how to tell a story – specifically how to combine words and pictures – because I wasn't interested in being a novelist. It became a process of slowly figuring out that *comics* were the thing that I was looking for. There are so many different kinds of comics, and I think that's why it took me so long to 'get into'

them. I've been a comics artist for about six years now, while many of my peers have been working for much longer. It's simply because I didn't think that I could do it; I didn't think I had the ability to put words and pictures together in tiny boxes and tell a story the whole way through. After studying more about the history and theory of comics, I applied to the Center for Cartoon Studies (CCS) in Vermont, where I was told that anyone can make comics. I was like, okay!

What was the first comic you drew before applying to CCS?

It was a sort of superhero comic but mixed with Caribbean folklore. I'm from Jamaica and studied Jamaican history in depth while attending high school there. I went to America for university and kept studying independently after I couldn't find any classes that focus on this particular subject. I studied at Hampshire College (Amherst, MA), where I had a gallery show that featured twenty pages from this comic that I created as part of my final undergraduate studies project. The pages were gigantic because I didn't know what I was doing! They focused on the stories of the descendants of historical figures who have a lot of myth tied around them, and how their powers evolve over time.

> Nubia was briefly introduced as a supporting character in *Wonder Woman* before she disappeared from comics for twenty years (1979–99). What did it mean to bring Nubia back to life and into the spotlight after so many years in obscurity?

I feel like it was my destiny. I really cared about telling stories about Black superheroes while I was working on my undergraduate thesis. DC initially reached out to say that they were thinking of revamping Nubia's image and story, and asked whether I would be interested in auditioning a character design. I thought it was a prank! I was so excited to have the chance to tell a superhero story the way I would want to experience it. When I was hired, I remember thinking, *this is what I've been working toward.*

This was an opportunity to focus on a character who has been left behind. I don't think the original Nubia was

Nubia: Real One
Robyn Smith and L.L. McKinney, 2021
p. 139 (detail)
▼

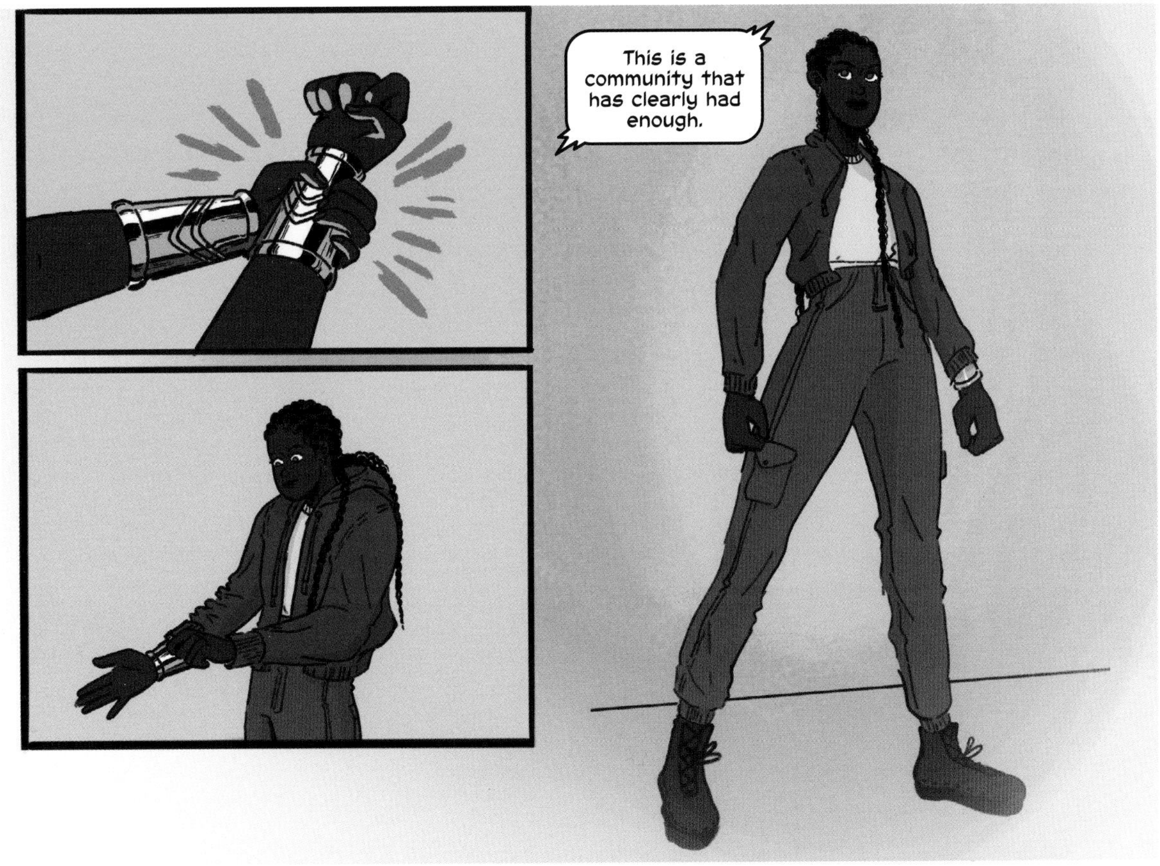
This is a community that has clearly had enough.

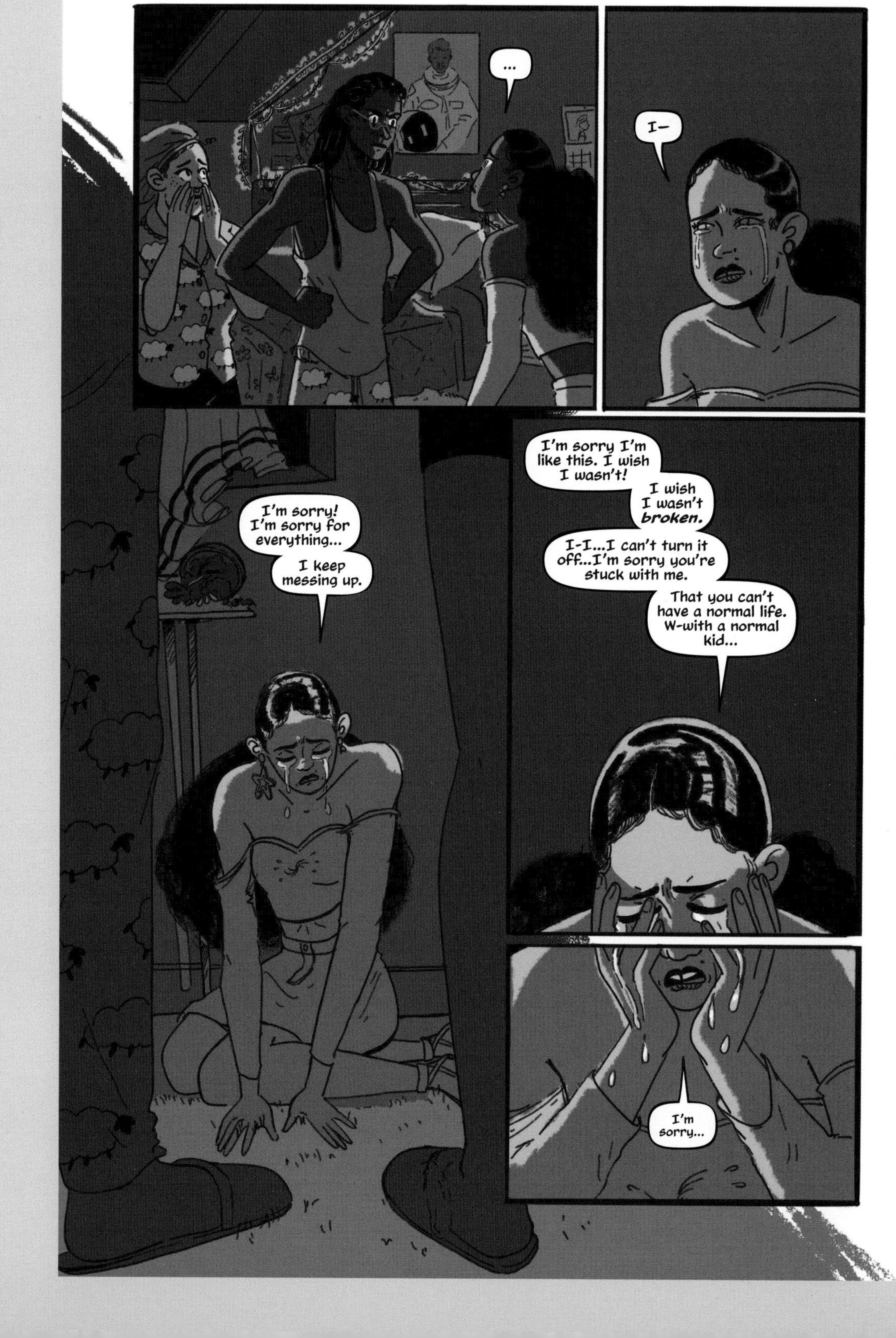
...
I–
I'm sorry! I'm sorry for everything...
I keep messing up.
I'm sorry I'm like this. I wish I wasn't!
I wish I wasn't **broken.**
I-I...I can't turn it off...I'm sorry you're stuck with me.
That you can't have a normal life. W-with a normal kid...
I'm sorry...

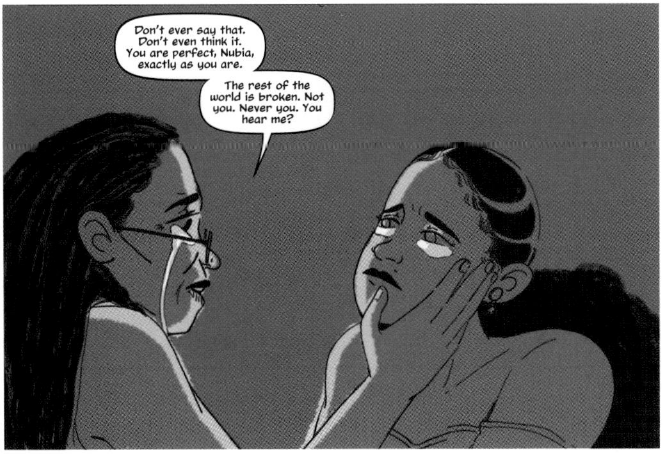
Don't ever say that. Don't even think it. You are perfect, Nubia, exactly as you are.
The rest of the world is broken. Not you. Never you. You hear me?

▲ *Nubia: Real One* p.115 (detail)

created to be a powerful Black female icon at the time, but was more the product of the Blacksploitation period in media. I did explore a lot of *Nubia* history while working on the comic, but I focused more on the negative criticism because I pretty much agreed with it. Someone gave me one of the very first comics that Nubia appears in (from the 1970s), and throughout the issue she is presented as a character that has been taken over by an evil force. She's wearing leopard print – which is in keeping with how Black superheroes were presented during that time – because it was exotic. I have never worked harder on a character study or sample design in my life! It felt good.

So in fact, she wasn't in obscurity – she was simply waiting for you?

Right!

When you first took on the challenge of drawing Nubia, what was your impression of the superhero universe?

◀ *Nubia: Real One* p. 114

It's funny because so much of my undergraduate thesis was hyper-focused on the representation of Black superheroes. I felt like this was something I had to do right, because I spent so much time studying this field, and I care so much about it. When it came down to working with it, I was a little worried about potential restrictions or preconceptions about how Nubia and her friends should be represented. I was wary of stereotypes and was concerned that feedback might focus on whether or not a scene was 'urban' enough. But none of this happened! Our editor was very open to a lot of what we made. Working with Elle (L.L. McKinney, author of *Nubia: Real One*) was great because I feel like we had a very similar vision of how to represent Black girlhood and what that doesn't look like in other media. I feel that *Nubia* is more of an indie comic because of the more mundane moments where Nubia just gets to be herself. These are also my favourite moments to draw!

How would you describe your collaboration with L.L. McKinney? What kind of creative relationship was required to bring Nubia to life through image and text?

Elle left a lot of it wide open for me to explore. She would broadly describe what was going on in the scene, but she trusted me enough to know that I've had similar experiences. There's a scene where Nubia's doing her hair, and Elle's description was *she puts her hair back*. My thinking was that Nubia wouldn't want her hair to get in the way of what's she doing, so she would cane row it back to keep it in place. When the characters go to a party, they do a line dance, which is something that happens at a lot of Black teenage parties. Nubia is really a collection of small moments that my friends and I have experienced. Nubia's best friend (Quisha) is a mash-up of all of my best friends. Jason is modelled after my brother.

So much of the process of making the panels and moving between the mundane and the superhero moments comes down to the help of my family. I need a lot of help with reference images, so there are thousands of pictures of my family pretending to punch one another, pretending to hold up a car. There are so many pictures of them, especially my brother, who was the body model for Nubia. I always tell him that he has 'Nubia shoulders' because they are perfectly square! When I look at this comic, I am really looking at a collection of family members and friends just pretending to be Nubia and her friends.

It's interesting, because in a way the comic incorporates an element of portraiture. You've circled back to find

your own way of creating portraits of your family.

That's true!

Certain details – especially the Black Lives Matter movement – make the experience of reading *Nubia* feel incredibly immediate. Why was it important to root Nubia's story in current events?

I think Elle did a great job of making the story feel current but not preachy. Elle was very intentional about what to include in the story, and it all weaved together beautifully to make a story about this girl and her family.

The real-life issues that are presented in the comic are things that younger generations have to deal with and talk about, and the process of illustrating these moments was very heart-wrenching. The protest scenes took the longest to draw. It took me over a month to draw just one of those pages, firstly because there are a lot of people in it and it's very dense. Usually when I draw crowd scenes, I default to the *'Archie* method,' which is to draw some bumps in the background and then fill it with colour. Here, I wanted to show the individual t-shirts and picket signs. When I think of the protests that I've been to, it feels so big but when you look at the people around you, they all have their reasons for being there. I wanted every person to have their reason for being

◀
Nubia: Real One
p. 139 (detail)

▶
Nubia: Real One
Draft artwork for
p. 151

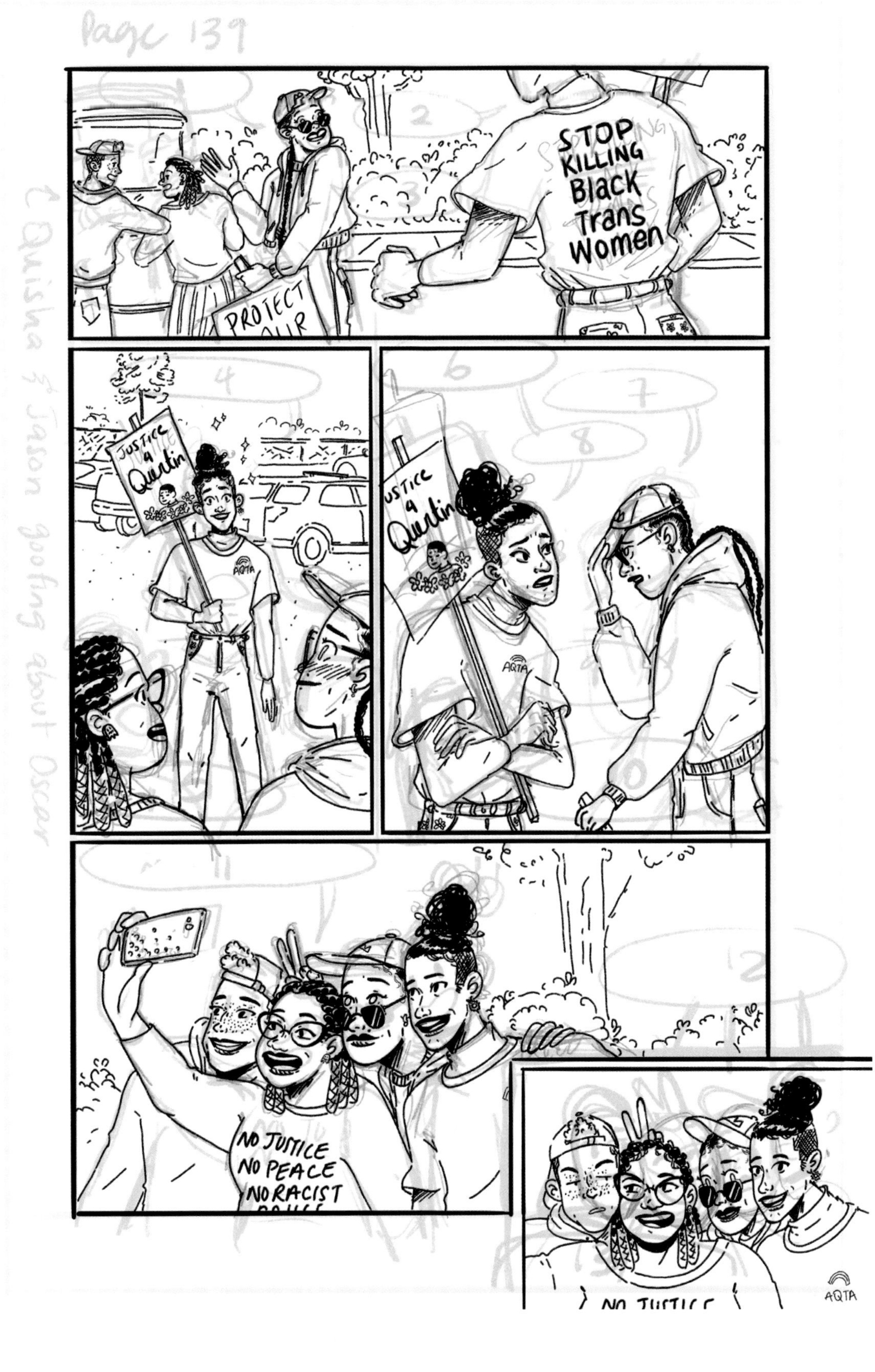
Page 139
Quisha & Jason goofing about Oscar
STOP KILLING Black Trans Women
PROTECT
JUSTICE 4 Quentin
AQTA
JUSTICE 4 Quentin
AQTA
NO JUSTICE NO PEACE NO RACIST
AQTA
NO JUSTICE

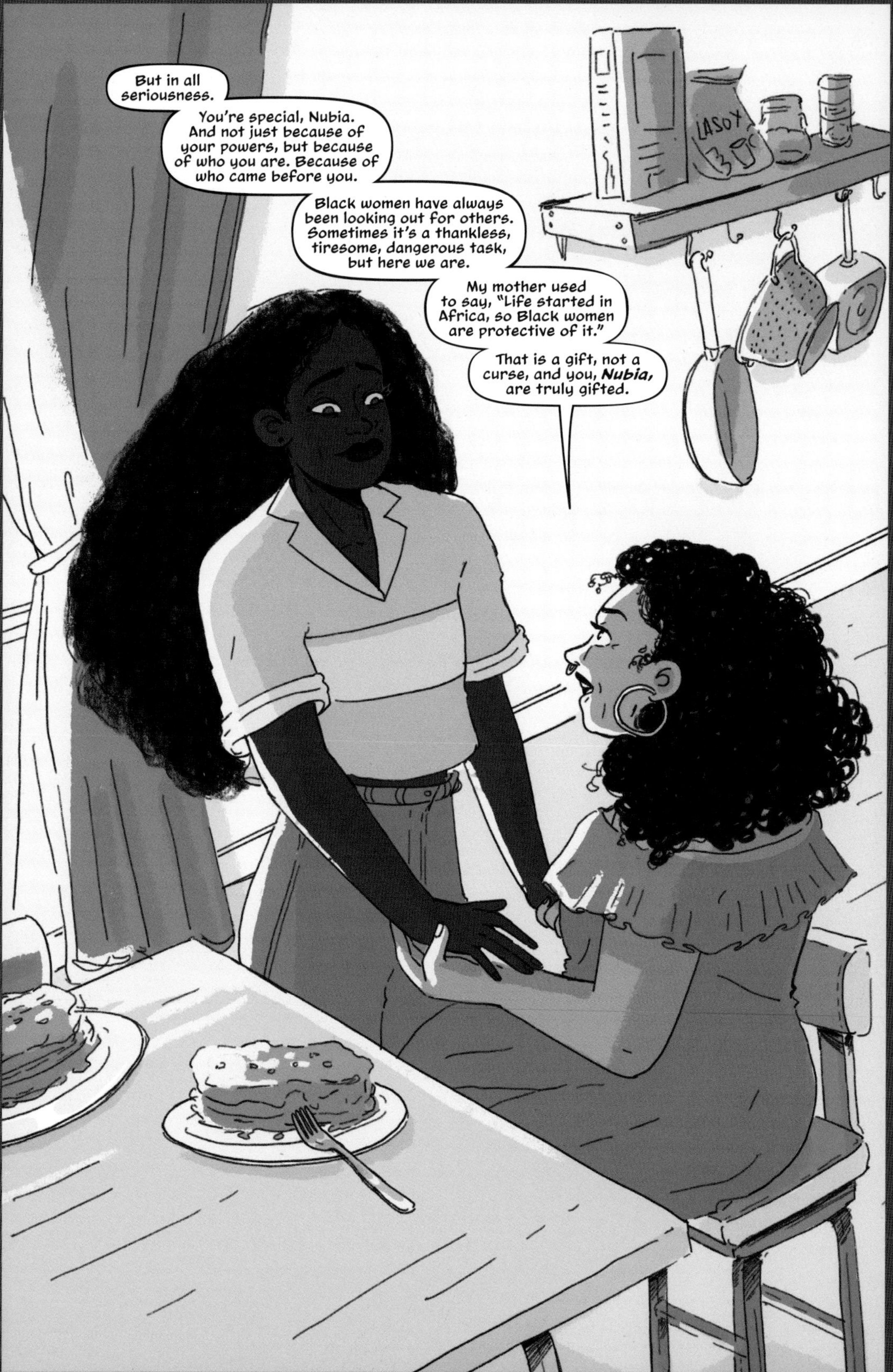

But in all seriousness.
You're special, Nubia. And not just because of your powers, but because of who you are. Because of who came before you.
Black women have always been looking out for others. Sometimes it's a thankless, tiresome, dangerous task, but here we are.
My mother used to say, "Life started in Africa, so Black women are protective of it."
That is a gift, not a curse, and you, ***Nubia,*** are truly gifted.

there in the *Nubia* protest scenes.

When I think about the violence that can take place at these protests – particularly those for Black lives – it's overwhelming to draw because I'm again looking at reference images. I have to actually see it and then process that reality before recreating those scenes on paper. DC was really understanding about this process – especially my editor, Sara Miller – and that it was a lot for me. I think another important aspect of making comics is that you have to consider the relationship the creator has with the media and subject they are creating. It takes a toll for the creator to rehash the trauma they've experienced that goes into both memoir comics and fictionalised narratives, and I don't think many people take the time to acknowledge that.

Nubia explores aspects of Blackness that you have previously touched on in *The Saddest Angriest Black Girl in Town* (2016), specifically feeling invisible and yet also hyper-visible. How did it feel to inscribe these real, shared issues within a superhero narrative?

I think there is a way to do this without intentionally teaching anyone, and I think this is the best approach with a superhero comic. I made *The Saddest Angriest Black Girl in Town* with the intention of giving it to classmates and telling them to read it instead of speaking to me directly. I'm bad at expressing myself in the moment, which is why I enjoy making memoir comics. I get to sit down and think about what it is that I want to say, and then make it.

I made *Nubia* for Black readers, and so didn't really set out to make it educational.

I wanted it to be filled with moments that Black readers could identify with and then just keep reading. I also wanted *Nubia* to offer readers of other cultures and races moments to think about, rather than respond to it with the feeling that 'I don't get this, so I'm going to put it down.' I didn't want to take up Black readers' time explaining things they already know, when the book is about them and their experiences. I feel like I've seen this happen way too often. I made a very conscious effort to avoid doing this, and yet at the same time I think this process came naturally because I am a Black creator. I don't overthink what it is that I'm trying to say in *Nubia* because it already feels very real to me.

As you've already mentioned, your comics delve into challenging and emotionally complex issues. What aspects of the comic strip do you think make it an effective space in which to tackle these kinds of issues?

One of my favourite aspects of comics is that readers can always turn back the page. You can always go back, look, process what's happening and then keep moving. This is what makes comics one of the best tools for learning about new ideas and experiences. They really allow you to exist inside someone else's experience and to immerse yourself in that world. I feel that the way a comic is paced is essential to this process. Sure, the creator can control the pace of the story, but the reader has just as much power here.

Nubia's adoptive mothers repeatedly advise her not to draw attention to

Nubia: Real One
p. 40 ◀

herself, concerned that some will see her powers as a threat, rather than a gift. What did you most want readers to observe and take away from the story regarding the dynamic between Nubia's super abilities and her Blackness?

I just don't want readers to think that she is somehow special in this regard. She is obviously very special, but she is also fundamentally like every other Black girl. This is the message we wanted to drive home regarding who Nubia is. I feel like the tension that is felt when telling a superhero story in which the superhero is Black is how not to suggest that somehow their Blackness is magical. It's just who they are, and they also happen to have these superpowers.

This is why I really enjoyed Nubia having two adoptive Black moms. I can't imagine Wonder Woman raising Nubia and having too much of a clue of what's going on with a Black person living in America! It's way more of a benefit for Nubia to have these two women taking care of her. One of her mothers is an Amazonian, so she has both the Black Amazonian and Black American experiences to draw from at home. Nubia's moms were some of my favourite characters to draw. Their love for each other and their child – making sure that she is as safe as possible because the world doesn't want to keep her safe – is just so sweet. I thought about this a lot while drawing the scenes that feature the entire family.

What's next for you?

A mini-comic that my friend Jamila Rowser

Nubia: Real One p. 132

and I made in 2017 is being developed into a graphic novel. It was originally called *Wash Day* and has been extended into the *Wash Day Diaries*. It's dedicated to Black women and their hair, and each story is a very meditative process showing a character performing an act of self-care that centres around her hair. For example, one character gets braids while another installs a wig. It focuses on 'mundane' moments, which is really what I love to draw!

If you had the opportunity to reimagine another superhero for contemporary audiences, who would you choose to draw? And why?

Yes! I really love Miss Martian (DC). She's not a very popular character, but I learned about her after watching *Young Justice*. I related so deeply with her! She is from Mars, and she lives among these kids who clearly are Earthlings. She just reminded me so much of what it's like to be an immigrant. She copies the personalities from very old sitcoms and makes them her own. Because the sitcoms are so old, the other kids don't pick up on it right away but eventually find out that everything she's told them about herself isn't real. I did this a lot when I first moved to America! I watched so many sitcoms and learned to replicate an American accent from the TV. It's what I use to relate to people around me as much as possible because I didn't grow up here. I don't have the same cultural touchstones except for sitcoms, because so many American television shows were played in Jamaica. I feel like her story just needs to be told as an immigrant story, and I would love to dive into this issue even further.

What do you think is the best piece of advice to give to a young person aspiring to create a superhero in which they can see themselves?

I'd say start super small and don't overthink it – this doesn't need to be your magnum opus! If you get into that mindset, it really trips you up and you don't go anywhere. Just make the comic. Even if it's just one panel, you will learn so much from that experience, as opposed to months of 'world-building'. You draw

the panel, then draw the character in it, and pick a simple moment to illustrate, like going to get coffee or something. Then you'll think: *Wait, why is the character getting coffee? Are they tired? From what?* All of these ideas spring from a small, specific moment, which can then grow into something big. It is so much harder to start with a big concept that you then need to rein in.

ABOUT ROBYN SMITH:

Robyn Smith is a Jamaican cartoonist known for her mini-comic The Saddest Angriest Black Girl in Town, *illustrating DC's* Nubia: Real One *(written by L.L. McKinney) and Black Josei Press'* Wash Day *(written by Jamila Rowser). She has an MFA from the Center for Cartoon Studies and has also worked on comics for CollegeHumor, Nike and The Nib. She loves cake and her cat, Benson, and holds on to dreams of returning home to the ocean.*

Overleaf:
Nubia: Real One
◀ p. 137
▶ p. 174

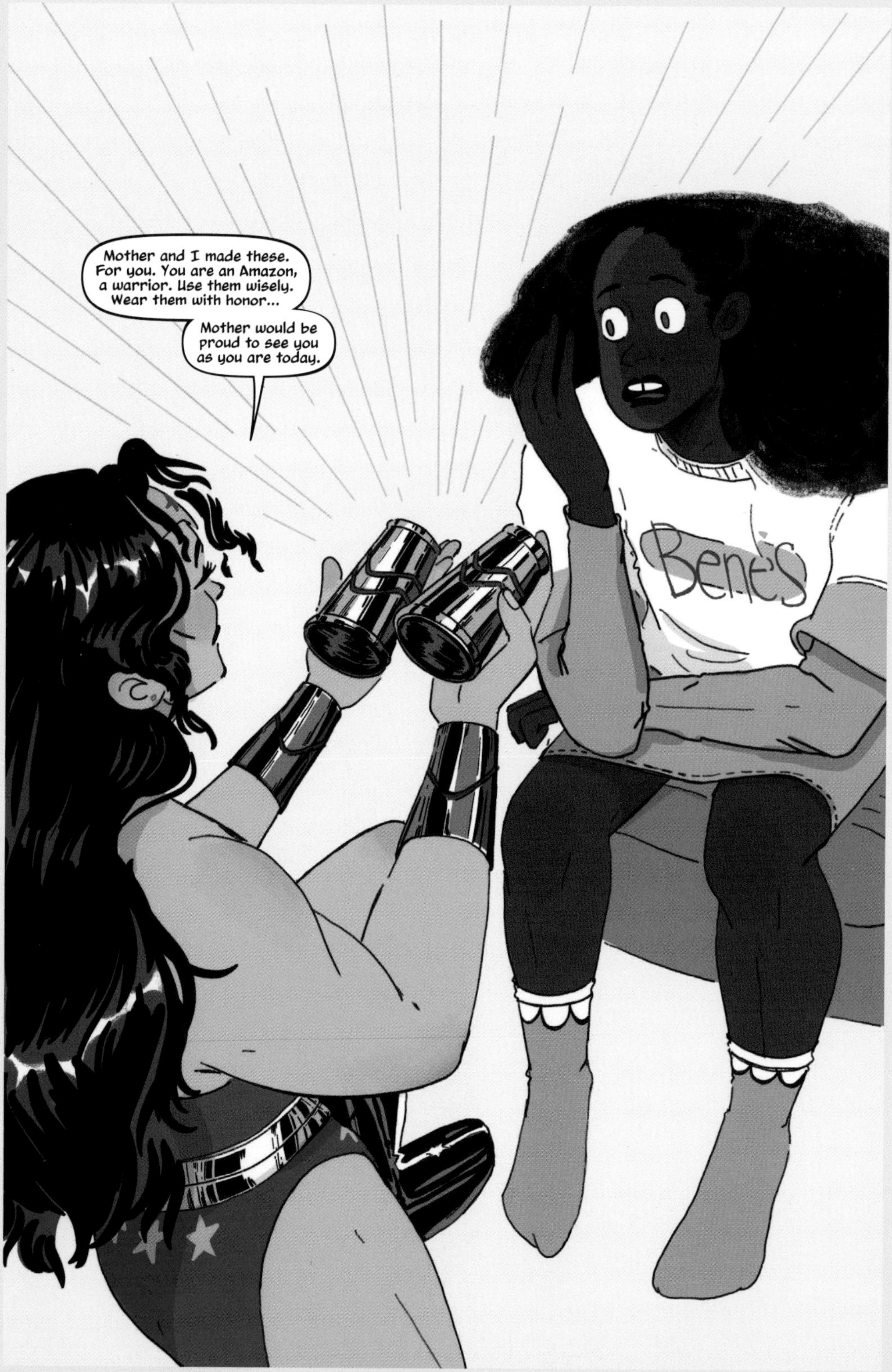
Mother and I made these. For you. You are an Amazon, a warrior. Use them wisely. Wear them with honor...
Mother would be proud to see you as you are today.
Bene's

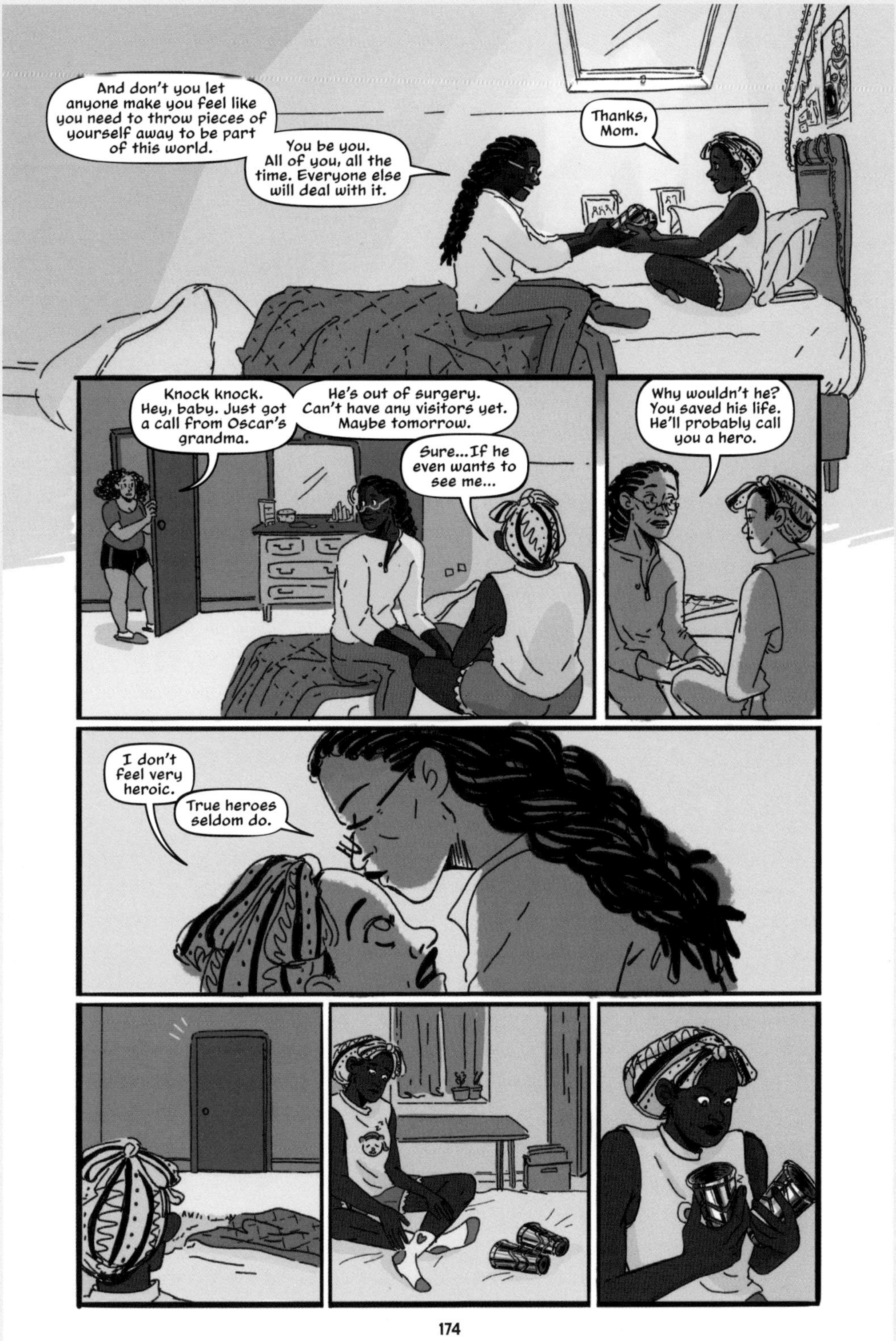
And don't you let anyone make you feel like you need to throw pieces of yourself away to be part of this world.
You be you. All of you, all the time. Everyone else will deal with it.
Thanks, Mom.
Knock knock. Hey, baby. Just got a call from Oscar's grandma.
He's out of surgery. Can't have any visitors yet. Maybe tomorrow.
Sure...If he even wants to see me...
Why wouldn't he? You saved his life. He'll probably call you a hero.
I don't feel very heroic.
True heroes seldom do.

Nubia: Real One
Draft artwork for
p. 115

Nubia: Real One
Draft artwork for
p. 48

Nubia: Real One
Draft artwork for
p. 126

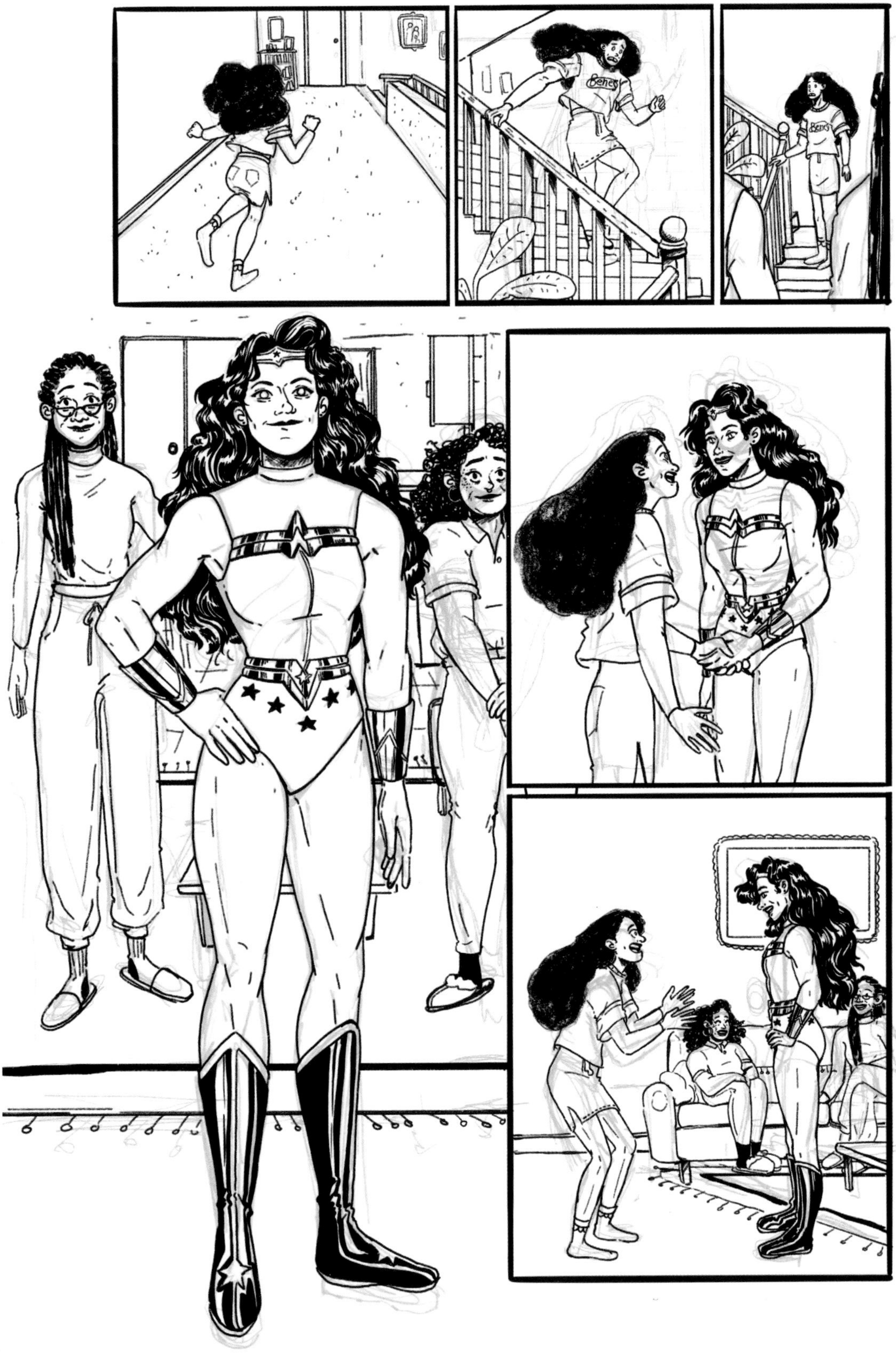

SHAPING THE HERO

A REFLECTION ON SUPERMAN AND LONG-TERM FOSTERING

YAO NKRUMAH ADU

SUPERMAN EPITOMISES THE idealistic comic book hero: a man who is both incredibly powerful, yet humble and single-minded in his quest to protect the most vulnerable. He is also well known for living a double life as the 'mild-mannered' journalist Clark Kent, whose personality presents a stark and often humorous juxtaposition to his mighty alter-ego. Although Superman arrives from a distant planet named Krypton, his sense of humility and steely moral compass are very much of this world. For this, Clark owes much to his adoptive parents, John and Martha Kent – the kind, Midwestern couple who discover a seemingly abandoned child on the side of the road and bring him home to care for as their son. We see the important influence of John and Martha Kent throughout Clark's life, whom he regularly relies upon for guidance and support.

The Kents' loving and unflinching approach to caring for Clark can easily be caricatured as common sense, perhaps even a cliché. However, when contrasted with the experiences of children cared for in the English foster care system, we see this is unfortunately not the case at all. By combining insights from the *Superman* comics, child development theory and current research on the English foster care system, I will provide a unique illustration of how the Kent's approach to raising Clark throughout his childhood directly contributes to shaping the hero he becomes. Drawing upon the lessons from the example set by the Kents also helps to uncover the significant role that foster carers, as well as local authorities, play in shaping the lived experiences of children in care. We shall now turn to comic book lore for Clark's origin story, which brings the Kent's love for him sharply into focus.

JOHN AND MARTHA KENT

Clark's story begins in *Action Comics* #1 (1938), where we discover how the Kents initially come to find Clark and decide to adopt him. The premier issue depicts the Kents' first encounter with 'the Boy', who they find encased in a strange vessel. The Kents take the Boy to an 'orphan asylum', but later return and ask to adopt him, explaining to staff that they could not get him out of their minds. Staff at the 'asylum' are all too ready to see the Boy leave, due to their fear of his super strength, which they perceive to be destructive in nature. The Kents, however, are unperturbed by the Boy's superpowers and decide to adopt him as their own, naming him Clark. The issue then shows the Kents guiding Clark throughout his childhood, helping him to understand his powers, the fearful ways in which others may perceive him, and his potential for assisting humanity.

> 'The love and guidance of his kindly foster parents was to become an important factor in the shaping of The Boy's future.'
> (*Action Comics* Vol. 1, #1, 1938)

In *Superboy* Vol. 1, #8 (1950), we see how the Kents conceal the truth about Clark's superpowers during his early years as a 'toddling infant'. In this issue, Clark uses his superhuman strength to pull a lamppost from the ground and throw it on to a road, unwittingly stopping a criminal car from escaping the scene of a crime. As the criminals are apprehended, John tells Clark to return the lamppost to its original spot before he is seen by police. Clark does as he is told. The early influence of John Kent on shaping Superman's identity comes to the fore when he explicitly identifies Clark's potential to use his powers for good:

> '... We can use this experience to impress something on his mind for all his future life.'
> (*Superboy* Vol. 1, #8, 1950)

Martha Kent is later shown wistfully recounting this story to Clark, who at the time is still a young boy:

> '...You have grown into a Superboy – as we expected, Clark! And some day, I know, you will grow up into a Superman!'
> (*Superboy* Vol. 1, #8, 1950)

As Clark grows up, we see how his famous Superman costume was made. Again, the Kents are central to this story. 'The Superboy Legend' (in *Superboy* Vol. 1, #169, 1970) depicts John and Martha Kent rummaging through their attic, following a

TIME PASSED, AND THE HEALTHY TODDLER DEVELOPED ASTONISHING QUALITIES...
GREAT SCOTT! I CAN'T BELIEVE IT!
I WANTED TO LIFT HIM, BUT INSTEAD HE LIFTED ME!
GOO!
7
OH-HH! HE'S BROKEN ANOTHER TOY!
I NEVER SAW SUCH STRENGTH! HE'S GOING TO BE A HERCULES WHEN HE GROWS UP!

▶ *Superman* Vol. 1, #53
Bill Finger, Wayne Boring, Stan Kaye
Aug. 1948
p. 7 (detail)

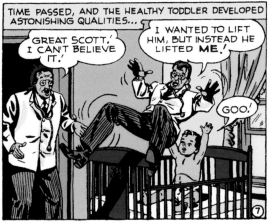

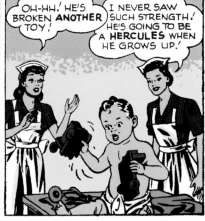

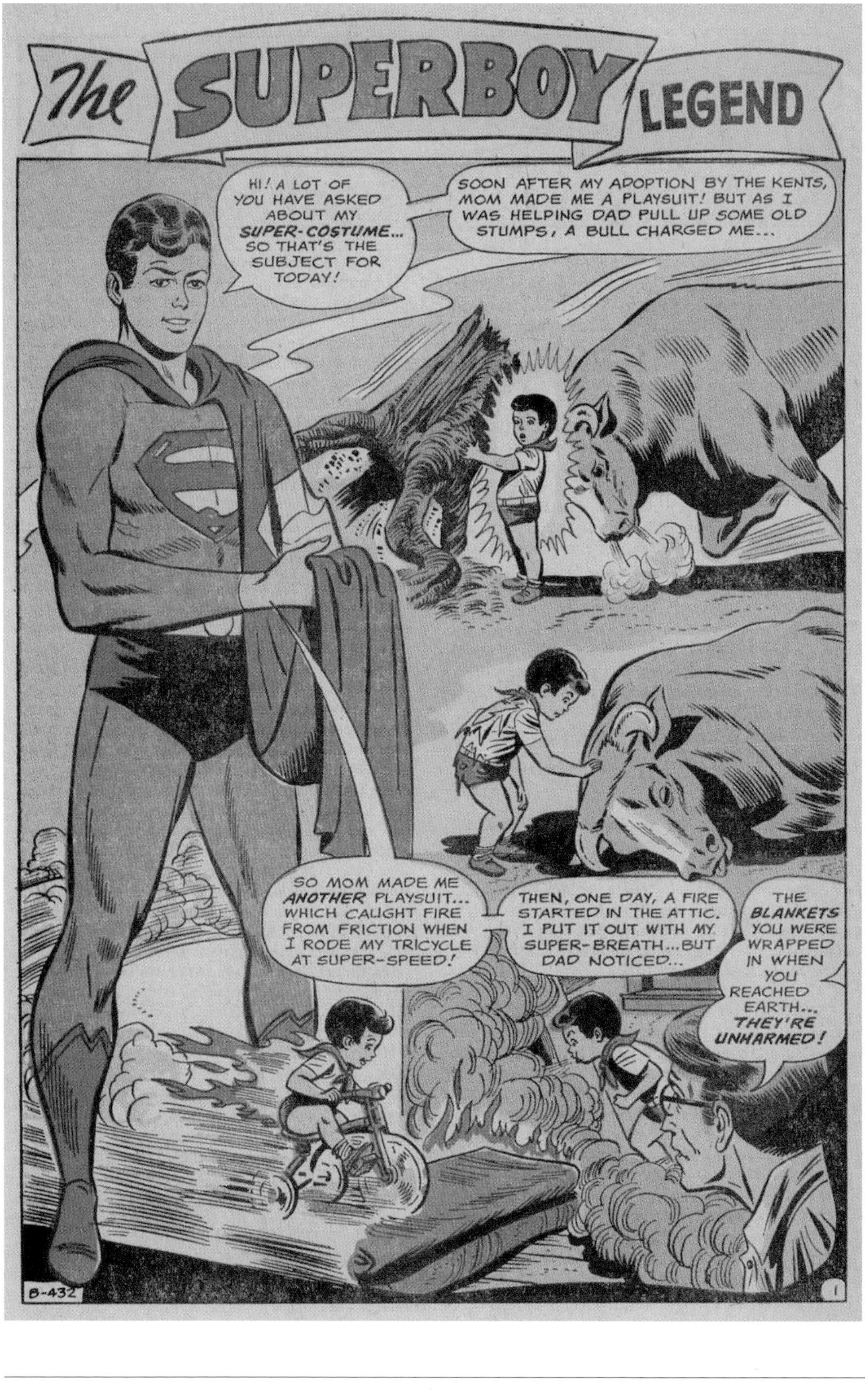
The SUPERBOY LEGEND
HI! A LOT OF YOU HAVE ASKED ABOUT MY SUPER-COSTUME... SO THAT'S THE SUBJECT FOR TODAY!
SOON AFTER MY ADOPTION BY THE KENTS, MOM MADE ME A PLAYSUIT! BUT AS I WAS HELPING DAD PULL UP SOME OLD STUMPS, A BULL CHARGED ME...
SO MOM MADE ME ANOTHER PLAYSUIT... WHICH CAUGHT FIRE FROM FRICTION WHEN I RODE MY TRICYCLE AT SUPER-SPEED!
THEN, ONE DAY, A FIRE STARTED IN THE ATTIC. I PUT IT OUT WITH MY SUPER-BREATH... BUT DAD NOTICED...
THE BLANKETS YOU WERE WRAPPED IN WHEN YOU REACHED EARTH... THEY'RE UNHARMED!
B-432
1

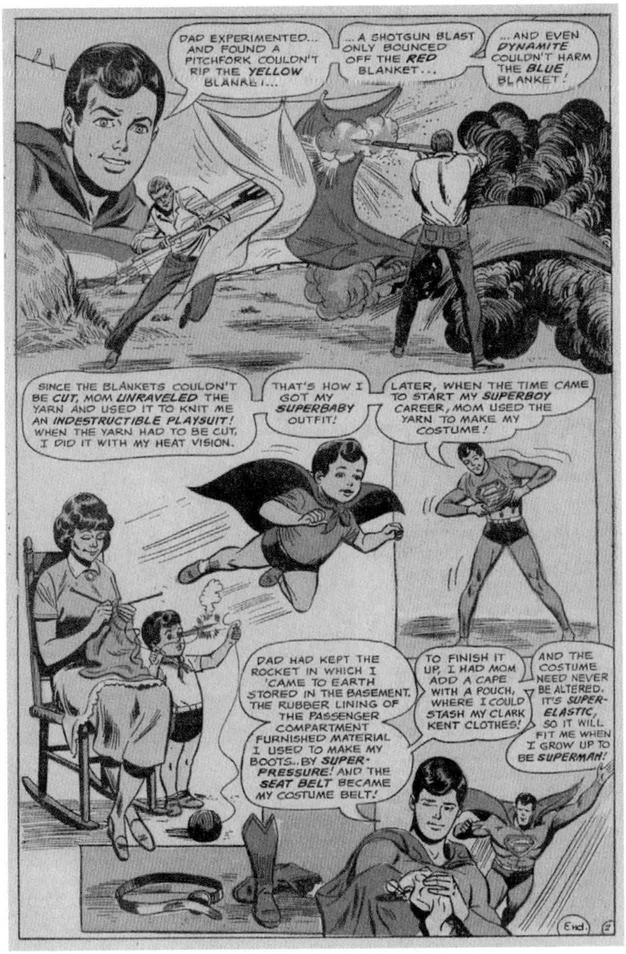
DAD EXPERIMENTED... AND FOUND A PITCHFORK COULDN'T RIP THE YELLOW BLANKET...
...A SHOTGUN BLAST ONLY BOUNCED OFF THE RED BLANKET...
...AND EVEN DYNAMITE COULDN'T HARM THE BLUE BLANKET!
SINCE THE BLANKETS COULDN'T BE CUT, MOM UNRAVELED THE YARN AND USED IT TO KNIT ME AN INDESTRUCTIBLE PLAYSUIT! WHEN THE YARN HAD TO BE CUT, I DID IT WITH MY HEAT VISION.
THAT'S HOW I GOT MY SUPERBABY OUTFIT!
LATER, WHEN THE TIME CAME TO START MY SUPERBOY CAREER, MOM USED THE YARN TO MAKE MY COSTUME!
DAD HAD KEPT THE ROCKET IN WHICH I CAME TO EARTH STORED IN THE BASEMENT. THE RUBBER LINING OF THE PASSENGER COMPARTMENT FURNISHED MATERIAL I USED TO MAKE MY BOOTS...BY SUPER-PRESSURE! AND THE SEAT BELT BECAME MY COSTUME BELT!
TO FINISH IT UP, I HAD MOM ADD A CAPE WITH A POUCH, WHERE I COULD STASH MY CLARK KENT CLOTHES!
AND THE COSTUME NEED NEVER BE ALTERED. IT'S SUPER-ELASTIC, SO IT WILL FIT ME WHEN I GROW UP TO BE SUPERMAN!
End

◀ *Superboy* Vol. 1, #169 Frank Robbins, Bob Brown, Murphy Anderson Oct. 1970, p. 32

▲ *Superboy* Vol. 1, #169 p. 33

house fire that Clark inadvertently started, and put out, using his powers. The capsule Clark was found in, which had been safely kept in the attic by the Kents, was the only object to survive the fire and remained completely unharmed. Realising the materials in the capsule were indestructible, Martha hand-knits Clark his Superman costume using material from the blankets. John also contributes to the costume by forging a pair of boots from the capsule lining.

When Clark reaches his early adult years, he is confronted with the deaths of his adoptive parents, a formative experience that profoundly shapes the adult he eventually grows to become. In *Superman* #53 (1948), John Kent is depicted in his final moments on a hospital bed with Clark at his side (Martha Kent having already passed some years ago). With his last words, John reminds Clark of the following:

To use his powers for good:

> 'No man on Earth has the amazing powers you have. You can use them to become a powerful force for good!'

To use his powers to fight crime in accordance with the law:

> 'There are evil men in this world ... criminals and outlaws who prey on decent folk! You must fight them ... in cooperation with the law!'

To hide his identity in order to fight crime most effectively:

> 'To fight those criminals best, you must hide your true identity! They must never know Clark Kent is a... a Superman! Remember, because that's what you are ... a Superman!' (*Superman* Vol. 1, #53, 1948)

John's advice is crucial in shaping Clark's identity as Superman and the direction his life will take thereafter. Standing at the graves of John and Martha Kent, Clark decides that he will take a job as a reporter at a big newspaper to keep abreast of news about people who may need help. Clark also decides to conceal his identity as Superman by adopting his trademark meek persona as 'Clark', wearing glasses and affecting his speech by stammering. Finally, he states that when he is needed, he will wear his famous costume, stitched and forged by hand for him by John and Martha Kent, revealing his true identity to the world.

Clark's life is punctuated by instances in which his very sense of self is shaped and moulded by the love, care and guidance of his adoptive parents. The Kents learn about Clark's powers as he develops them and teach him ways to manage them. They help him to understand his powers and how to navigate the feelings of confusion and fear that arise when his powers are revealed to others. Importantly, the Kents identify Clark's intrinsic will to use his powers for good, and hone this by encouraging him to use his powers to help vulnerable humans.

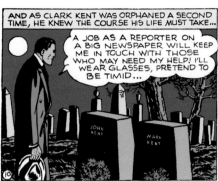

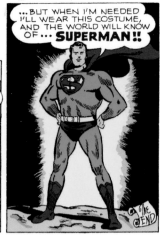

BECOMING SUPERMAN – IDENTITY AND 'SELF-ACTUALISATION'

The Kents play a crucial role in Clark's upbringing by providing him with love and guidance, and an understanding about his origins, his powers and his potential. When examined through the prism of two key child development theories – Abraham Maslow's 'Hierarchy of Needs', and Carl Rogers' 'Unconditional Positive Regard' – we see the important role the Kents play in providing the building blocks for the adult Clark becomes. Both theories belong to a school of thought referred to as 'Humanistic Psychology', which begins with a fundamental belief that every human has an innate desire to realise their true potential and be a 'good person'. The quality of environment a person is raised in is seen as a consequential and largely determining factor in achieving this outcome. According to such theories, development is likely to become skewed in undesirable ways if an environment is sub-optimal, whereas an optimal environment is likely to provide a greater chance for a person's development to flourish. The key thing to note about theories from this perspective is their emphasis on a child's *environment* as the key determinant of their eventual personal and social development, over and above any intrinsic characteristic arising from the child themselves.

Maslow argued that all humans have a specific hierarchy of needs, ranging from basic needs, such as food, sleep and shelter, to more intricate needs, such as love, belonging and self-fulfilment. He suggested that the significance of these needs to an individual is dependent on the nature and quality of their environments. For example, if an individual's need for food and shelter is met, they are more likely to be able to address their need for belonging, love and creativity. The contrary would also be true: if a person is hungry or without shelter, they will naturally find it difficult to prioritise more abstract needs such as the need for creativity. Maslow explained that the satisfaction of fundamental needs provides the secure basis for addressing more complex

AND AS CLARK KENT WAS ORPHANED A SECOND TIME, HE KNEW THE COURSE HIS LIFE MUST TAKE...
A JOB AS A REPORTER ON A BIG NEWSPAPER WILL KEEP ME IN TOUCH WITH THOSE WHO MAY NEED MY HELP! I'LL WEAR GLASSES, PRETEND TO BE TIMID...
JOHN KENT
MARY KENT
...BUT WHEN I'M NEEDED I'LL WEAR THIS COSTUME, AND THE WORLD WILL KNOW OF... SUPERMAN!!
THE END

▲ *Superman* Vol. 1, #53 p. 10 (detail)

needs thereafter. This ideally results in an individual addressing the ultimate need to 'self-actualise' – to realise one's full potential in alignment with their 'true' self.

Rogers also believed that humans are motivated by what he called the 'actualising-tendency'; the desire to self-develop and self-actualise. Rogers argued that children construct their view of who they are as they grow, piece by piece, from a combination of their own experiences of 'good' and 'bad' (placing their hand in a fire or eating a particularly salty olive). Children also have a keen perception of the behaviours that attract 'good' or 'bad' responses from others – for example, receiving a smile when they smile at others. Rogers believed the experiences that help a child achieve self-actualisation should be valued, and from this notion he developed the concept of 'unconditional positive regard'.

Unconditional positive regard is the idea that a caregiver should always communicate with their child in a way that conveys a sense of love, care and acceptance for them. The opposite of unconditional positive regard is described as 'conditional positive regard', a dynamic in which the caregiver only provides the child with positive regard *on the condition* that the child complies with their expectations. In this dynamic, positive regard is withdrawn from the child when they behave in a way perceived as non-compliant by their caregiver. Expressions of love, care and acceptance (positive regard) are then quickly substituted for expressions of hatred, indifference and rejection (negative regard) towards the child. Rogers argued that raising a child within a context of 'unconditional positive regard' is crucially important for helping the child establish a secure and well-rounded sense of identity, as the child is reassured throughout their life that they are accepted and loved, even when faced with expressions of displeasure or reprimand from their caregiver.

Maslow's and Rogers' theories provide useful insights into the ways in which the Kents nurture Clark's sense of belonging, identity and potential for self-actualisation. The Kents attend to Clark's basic physiological needs by taking him into their home as their own child, and foster Clark's sense of belonging by providing him with love, affection and kinship within a family. The Kents also provide Clark with esteem and knowledge of himself by guiding him through his powers and nurturing his potential to help humanity. When seen through Maslow's hierarchy of needs, Clark is provided with the optimal environment in which to 'self-actualise' and establish a secure, well-rounded identity in keeping with the tutelage of his adoptive parents.

Superman Vol. 1, #53 p. 9 (detail) ▼

YEARS PASSED, AND CERTAIN INCIDENTS MADE THE GROWING BOY REALIZE HE WAS DIFFERENT FROM OTHER YOUNGSTERS! THERE WAS THE TIME...
LOOK OUT, CLARK! THAT TRACTOR! OHHH!
GOOD GOSH! YOU'RE NOT EVEN HURT!
BUT LOOK AT THE TRACTOR!

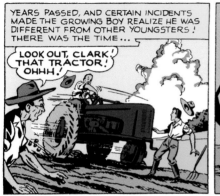

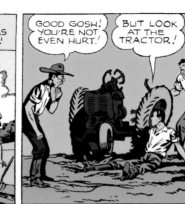

The Kents care for Clark within a context of unconditional positive regard, in the sense that they understand and accept Clark when others (like the 'asylum' staff) do not. Even in circumstances where the Kents could understandably be frightened by the inadvertent destructiveness of Clark's powers, they regularly affirm their love for him and their belief in his inherent desire to do good. Throughout his childhood, Clark is never in doubt about the Kents' love for him nor how he is seen in their eyes – as a *Superboy*, never a naughty one. By the time his adoptive parents pass away, Clark's identity is clearly established, and he is able to explore the world as a confident adult.

LESSONS FROM PRACTICE

Insights about Clark's upbringing can also be gleaned from current research on England's foster care system, which highlights the beneficial impact of secure, long-term and empowering care on the experiences of children growing up in foster care.

England's foster care system is currently blighted by three main issues:

1. Chronic placement instability
2. The use of 'Out of Approval Range' placements: unsuitable placements of sub-optimal quality.
3. The use of 'Next Best Placements': good quality placements that, nonetheless, do not cater to the particular needs of the child referred there.
(Oakley, 2021)

The current system does not meet the needs of children in care and pressure on the system is increasing, to the extent that foster care placements will need to grow by a projected 2.9% each year to meet demand. The use of unsuitable and inconsistent foster care placements has a detrimental impact on the lives of children raised in these environments, and young care leavers continue to face significant difficulties navigating their way through important aspects of independent adult life, such as education, employment and their mental health.

An insightful study by Dinithi Wijedasa (2017) reveals that children in care are one of the most likely cohorts to hold an implicit belief that events in their life are determined by external forces – such as fate or luck – rather than by internal factors (their own thoughts or behaviours). In contrast, a UK study of adults in further and higher education shows this group is much more likely to believe that events in their lives are determined by internal factors than adults educated up to secondary level. According to Wijedasa, such beliefs can become entrenched for children in care due to repeat experiences of impermanence and change, which leave children with a sense of not having much input into the decisions made about their lives. Local authorities can play a vital role, through the foster care system, in supporting children with cultivating a greater sense of control over their own lives, by providing the appropriate conditions to establish meaningful and lasting relationships with long-term care givers:

'Children may feel more empowered and build a sense of control through close positive

▶
Superman
Vol. 1, #53
p. 8

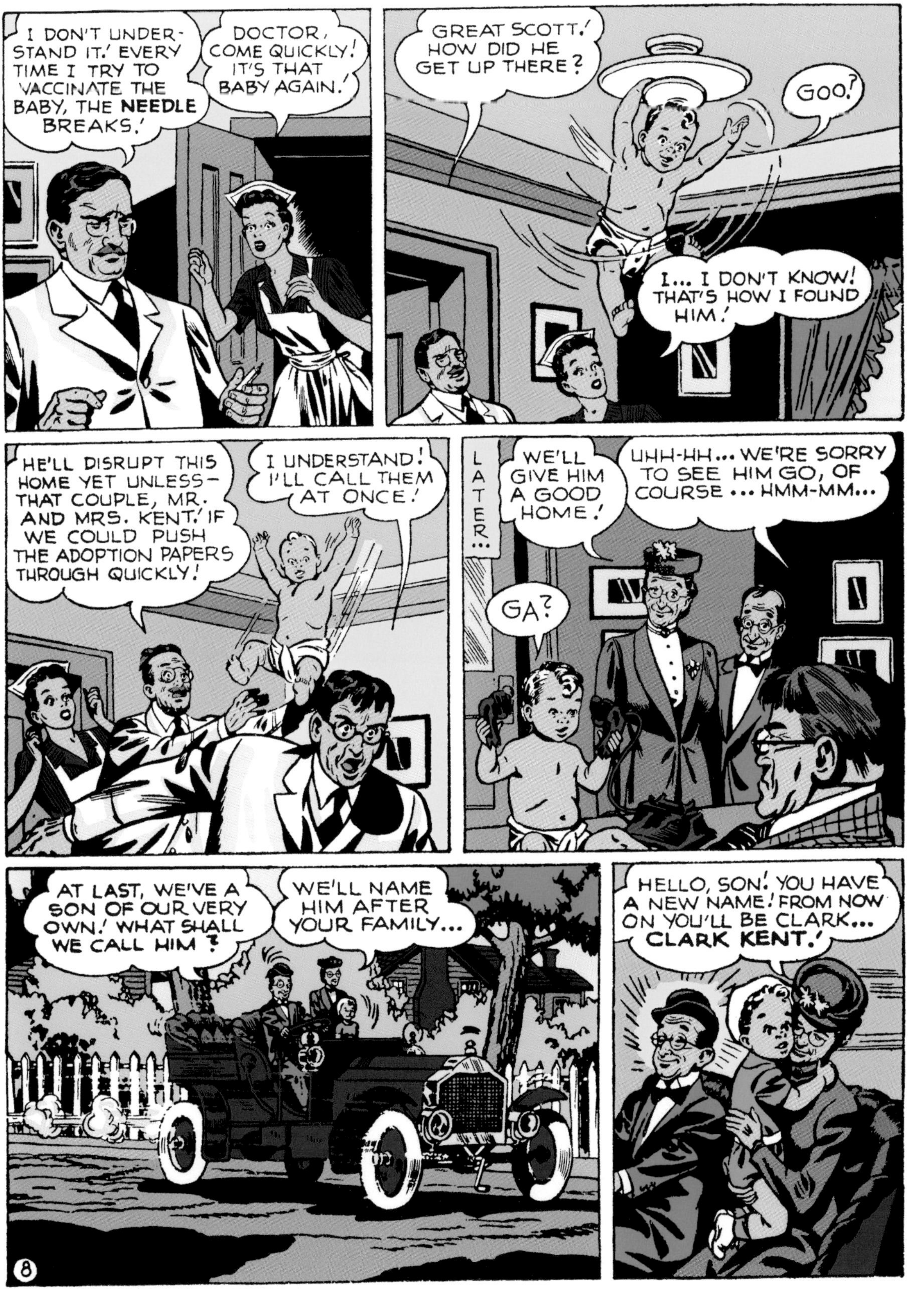

I DON'T UNDERSTAND IT! EVERY TIME I TRY TO VACCINATE THE BABY, THE **NEEDLE** BREAKS!
DOCTOR, COME QUICKLY! IT'S THAT BABY AGAIN!
GREAT SCOTT! HOW DID HE GET UP THERE?
GOO?
I... I DON'T KNOW! THAT'S HOW I FOUND HIM!
HE'LL DISRUPT THIS HOME YET UNLESS— THAT COUPLE, MR. AND MRS. KENT! IF WE COULD PUSH THE ADOPTION PAPERS THROUGH QUICKLY!
I UNDERSTAND! I'LL CALL THEM AT ONCE!
LATER...
WE'LL GIVE HIM A GOOD HOME!
UHH-HH... WE'RE SORRY TO SEE HIM GO, OF COURSE... HMM-MM...
GA?
AT LAST, WE'VE A SON OF OUR VERY OWN! WHAT SHALL WE CALL HIM?
WE'LL NAME HIM AFTER YOUR FAMILY...
HELLO, SON! YOU HAVE A NEW NAME! FROM NOW ON YOU'LL BE CLARK... **CLARK KENT!**

association with adults who are empowered; by nurturing their sense of identity ... and by participating in the decisions that affect them.' (Wijedasa, 2017, p. 14)

This recommendation highlights the importance of a close relationship with a consistent and empowering caregiver as a counterbalance to the disadvantages faced by children in care. Furthermore, having someone to rely on is shown to be an important precursor to ensuring children and young people feel confident and supported during their transition to adulthood. Clark is fortunate to have been raised by the Kents, who bring him from a perilous and uncertain environment into a nurturing and secure family home. Clark benefits from his close association with the Kents, whose guidance both shapes his identity as Superman and provides the tools for him to establish his mild-mannered day-to-day persona. Ultimately, the tight-knit and lasting bond shared between Clark and his adoptive parents proves to be key in empowering Clark with the belief that he is not just in control of his powers, but his life as a whole.

CONCLUSION

Jonathan and Martha Kent are the quintessential comic representation of the ideal adoptive parents. They embody a model of approaching long-term foster care with the intent to love, care for, protect and guide a child throughout their life. The Kents' approach to Clark's care highlights the significant impact of the presence of a benevolent, wise and trustworthy presence in the life of a developing child.

Clark is loved and cared for by the Kents, who encourage and guide him in understanding his powers. Clark's fundamental needs are duly attended to, which provides the optimal conditions to develop a secure sense of identity and eventually self-actualise. From a theoretical perspective, we see that the Kents' approach to raising Clark is very much in keeping with key child development principles. Also, close association with a consistent, reliable and empowering caregiver is shown to be a key component in enabling children in care to develop secure beliefs about their ability to affect their own lives. Clark's close and lasting bond with the Kents is crucial for instilling him with the knowledge that he is in control of his powers, his identity and his life.

Analysing the Kents' approach to Clark's care through the dual prisms of child development theory and social work best practice helps us to understand the significance of a child's environment (specifically their main caregivers) on shaping their sense of identity, belonging, core beliefs and purpose. We see the Kents' significant influence in shaping the hero we know as Superman. Similarly, we see the important role that foster carers, and local authorities, can play in shaping the prospects of children in their care: by providing security and stability, responding appropriately to the child's needs, and empowering them to realise their innate potential.

Joe Shuster and Jerry Siegel, children of Jewish immigrants to Canada and the United States respectively, created a character in Superman in which they could identify aspects of themselves.

Superman reflected their own experience of crafting their identities and establishing themselves in a world unfamiliar to them. Their story highlights the importance of amplifying the voices of people with lived experience of a particular circumstance, be it immigration or foster care, by providing them the platform to tell their stories and provide their expertise. People with care experience already provide unique and powerful contributions to discussion and thinking around social work policy (Jackson et al., 2020). Therefore, the continued promotion of such voices remains an important piece of the puzzle for engendering responsive and meaningful change in social work practice.

BIBLIOGRAPHY

Dubois-Comtois, K., Bussières, E., Cyr, C., St-Onge, J., Baudry, C., Milot, T. and Labbé, A. (2021), 'Are children and adolescents in foster care at greater risk of mental health problems than their counterparts? A meta-analysis', *Children and Youth Services Review*, Vol. 127:106100

Häggman-Laitila, A., Salokekkilä, P. and Karki, S. (2019), 'Young People's Preparedness for Adult Life and Coping After Foster Care: A Systematic Review of Perceptions and Experiences in the Transition Period', *Child Youth Care Forum*, Vol. 48, pp. 633–661

Jackson, R., Brady, B., Forkan, C., Tierney, E. and Danielle, K. (2020), 'Influencing Policy and Practice for Young People in Foster Care: Learning from a Model of Collective Participation', *Children and Youth Services Review*, Vol. 113(4):104901

Jackson, S. and Martin, P. Y. (1998), 'Surviving the care system: education and resilience', *Journal of Adolescence*, Vol. 21(5): pp. 569–583

Oakley, M. (2021), 'Fostering the future: Helping local authorities to fulfil their legal duties', *Social Market Foundation*, 25 June 2021

Sudbury, J. and Whittaker, A., *Human Growth and Development: An introduction for social workers*. London: Routledge (2018), pp. 304-310

Wijedasa D. (2017), '"People like me don't have much of a chance in life": comparing the locus of control of young people in foster care with that of adoptees, children from disadvantaged backgrounds and children in the general population', *Adoption & Fostering*, Vol. 41(1), pp. 5-19

COMICS REFERENCED

Bridwell, E. Nelson (writer), 'The Superboy Legend,' in *Superboy*, Vol. 1, #169. DC: October 1970

Dorfman, Leo (writer), *Superman*, Vol. 1, #161. DC: May 1963

Finger, Bill (writer), *Superboy*, Vol. 1, #8. DC: May 1950

Finger, Bill (writer), *Superman*, Vol. 1, #53. DC: August 1948

Siegel, Jerry (writer), *Superman*, Vol. 1, #1. DC: June 1938

ABOUT YAO NKRUMAH ADU:

Yao is a registered social worker currently working in child safeguarding at the London Borough of Newham. He has over ten years' experience working in local authority settings in roles related to children's education. Yao holds a Development Studies MSc, Social Work PGDip and Politics & International Relations BA. Yao is passionate about relationship-based practice and the use of emerging technologies in social work.

A TOOL FOR ACTIVISM

AN INTERVIEW WITH LISA WOOL-RIM SJÖBLOM

INTERVIEWED BY LAURA CHASE

WHEN AND HOW did the idea of *Palimpsest* first come about?

I had the idea for quite a long time, and originally planned for *Palimpsest* to take the form of a novel. The title came to me early on, and I knew that I wanted to write something about being adopted. I've always wanted to be a writer and never really had ambitions to be a comic artist. I started to write the novel and realised early on that I didn't have enough of the story to tell. At the time I was also taking a drawing class – which didn't go very well! – and for the final project I made a comic strip about being adopted. One of the examiners told me about the Comic Art School in Malmö (in southern Sweden) and recommended that I apply. I then decided to make *Palimpsest* into comic strips and began working on the project while studying in Malmö.

I restarted the project as a series of 'punch line' comic strips, which were more focused on the 'comical' side of being adopted but quickly ran out of

ideas. I started researching and reading about adoptees and adoption, and soon realised that I had oversimplified what being adopted means. I had also taken a self-deprecating approach to my own experience, which was a bit crushing. It wasn't the story I wanted to tell, and so I took some time away from the project. It was helpful that I had spent many years working in publishing and had a degree in literature, which gave me the self-awareness to realise that this wasn't what I wanted it to be.

A couple of years passed, and I had children. I started to approach my own adoption experience in a completely different way when my son started asking questions about the way we looked and specifically why we looked different from his grandparents and other people in Sweden. I realised that I needed to start searching for our Korean roots after the birth of my second child. Along the way, I discovered problems with my adoption documents and also started connecting with other adoptees, asking if they had also experienced issues with their documents. This experience introduced me to an entirely new side of adoption, which is a billion-dollar industry fuelled by dodgy interests and a market for children. I realised that my story was not unique, and that's when I hit upon the story that I needed to tell. Coinciding with all of this activity is that I started speaking up a little bit about my experience and findings and subsequently incurred the anger of adoptive parents, who told me that I shouldn't speak about these issues. I realised then that we don't only have the problem with the industry, but that the voices of adoptees are also marginalised and told to be quiet. There aren't that many adoptee voices to begin with, but there are certainly very few critical voices. *Palimpsest* became both a way for me to tell my own story, as well as a way to add to a narrative that was missing: a critical adoption story from the perspective of an adoptee.

I first heard the word *Palimpsest* in Jeanette Winterson's book, *Written on the Body* and realised that it was also the perfect metaphor for both adoption and having your experience erased.

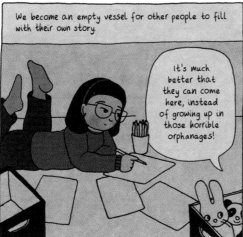

◀ Original artwork for *Palimpsest* cover, Lisa Wool-Rim Sjöblom

▶ *Palimpsest* Lisa Wool-Rim Sjöblom, 2019 p. 14 (detail)

We become an empty vessel for other people to fill with their own story.
It's much better that they can come here, instead of growing up in those horrible orphanages!
Eventually, we start retelling those myths we've been fed ourselves.
Since my parents couldn't have children of their own, they turned to adoption.

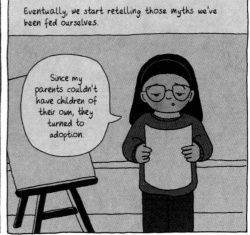

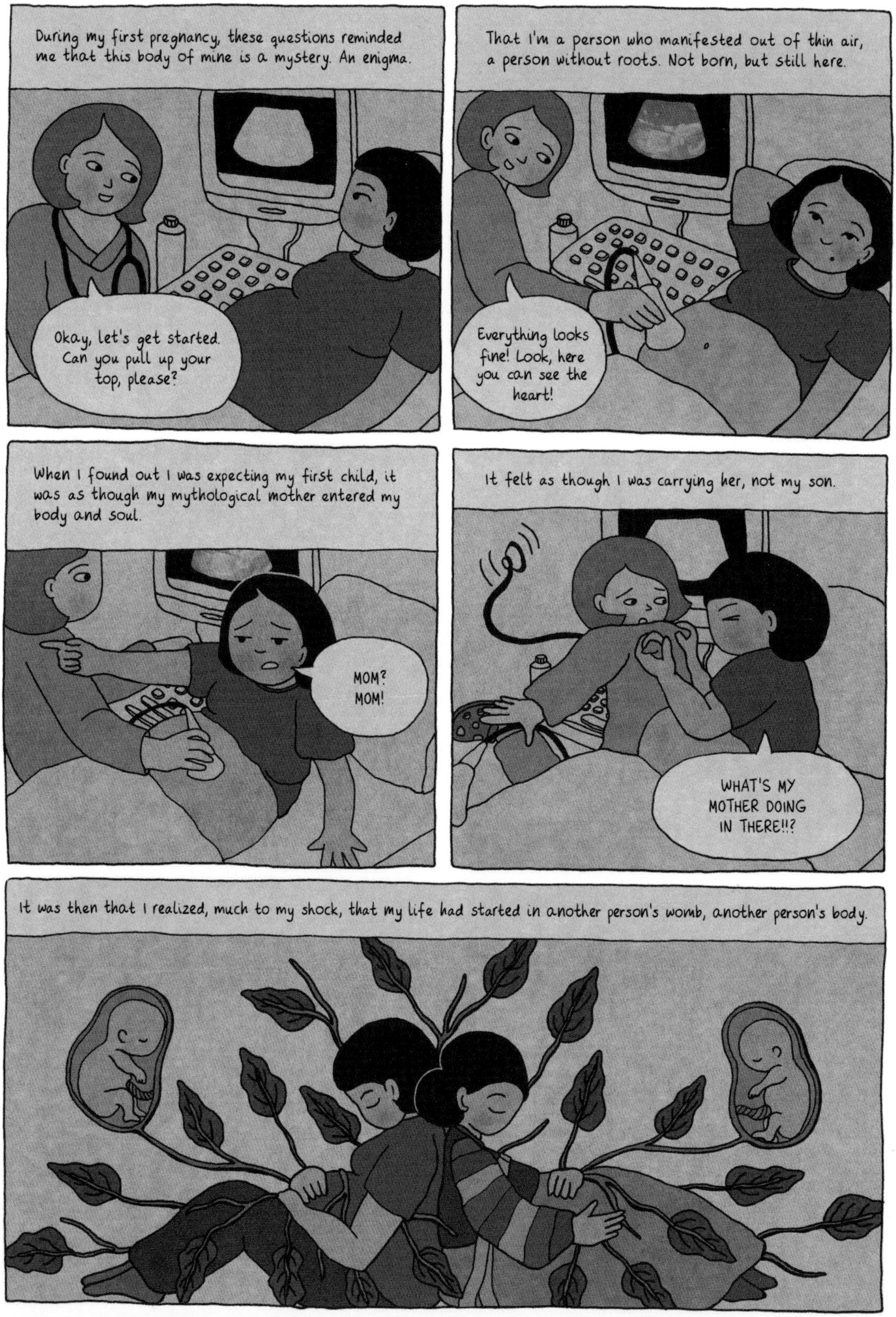
During my first pregnancy, these questions reminded me that this body of mine is a mystery. An enigma.
Okay, let's get started. Can you pull up your top, please?
That I'm a person who manifested out of thin air, a person without roots. Not born, but still here.
Everything looks fine! Look, here you can see the heart!
When I found out I was expecting my first child, it was as though my mythological mother entered my body and soul.
MOM? MOM!
It felt as though I was carrying her, not my son.
WHAT'S MY MOTHER DOING IN THERE!!?
It was then that I realized, much to my shock, that my life had started in another person's womb, another person's body.

There are so many layers that you can explore, including an origin story that is overwritten. Historically, palimpsests were not simply used to recycle paper but also as a way of overwriting pagan texts with sacred texts. It was a method used by the Church to improve the existing message. This can be connected to adoption, as adoptees are told that they have been given a better life and that the place where you have been brought to is better than the place from which you came. There is also the fraudulent aspect of forging documents, which many of the adoptees I have spoken with have experienced. In my case, new documents were created. It's such a perfect – and beautiful – word, on so many levels.

> Had you previously used drawing as a means of recording your own experiences and memories?

Not much, although I did keep a daily diary where I drew pictures for a time. As a child, I wanted to be an artist and was drawing all the time. I think that when you are a child, you are a natural comic book artist because you add text and speech bubbles to your drawings without thinking of it as a comic. I've always loved reading comics, but the idea that you could become an illustrator or comic artist wasn't introduced to me until much later on. When I started drawing comic strips, something fell into place. I had a lot of role models (like Art Spiegelman) who transformed my whole view on comics. I had read [Spiegelman's] *Maus* many years before I started making [autobiographical] comic strips and was completely blown away, like most people. I think you could say that *Maus* was the

◄
Palimpsest
p. 11

turning point when people realised that you could tell incredibly meaningful stories but also portray really dark moments and subjects in a comic book. Spiegelman presented a really deeply personal narrative, and no one was left untouched by it. *Persepolis* [by Marjane Satrapi] was also a transformative reading experience for me and convinced me that you can tell deeply personal and violent stories in a comic book form.

> The visual style that you employ in *Palimpsest* is very unique. How does the novel's style relate to its content?

Before working on *Palimpsest*, I mainly worked on comics for children, one of which focused on a pair of bunnies (Sleepybones and Lazyhead) who lived in the woods. It was while I working on this children's comic that I experimented with the colour palette that I subsequently used in *Palimpsest*. I grew up in northern Sweden, where these colours are really prominent. This colour palette has been with me for my whole life, and so it wasn't so much a stylistic choice as much as it simply felt like me and something I felt comfortable using.

When it came to drawing the people, this was also new territory for me, partly because I am terrible at life drawing. I had specifically never before drawn Asian people because, in my experience as an adoptee, I didn't really understand what I looked like. The only pictures I was ever shown were racist stereotypes: yellow skin, squinty eyes, buck teeth, thick glasses, rice hats, mock traditional clothing and so on. I had never really seen any beautiful drawings of Asian people, so I had no idea how to draw myself. One of the big jokes that people tell in the comics profession is that comic artists always end up drawing themselves (even when we're drawing animals, etc.). You can always see the artist in the characters. A great example of this is Don Rosa, who draws Scrooge McDuck. I had mainly drawn white people and subsequently drawn myself as white. When I decided to make this book, I had to learn how to draw myself and other Asian characters without falling into racist stereotypes. It was a bit of a challenging process and, again, I didn't really think or plan too far ahead, instead trying different techniques as I went along.

> *Palimpsest* illustrates some deeply personal and painful experiences. How did it feel to experience those moments again in the process of drawing yourself?

I think it was quite healing. When it comes to drawing something that is inherently political, it's a liberating process, especially when it's clear that many people will react negatively to the message you are drawing. When you know you are drawing in resistance, it feels like you are reclaiming something that's yours and that you have the power to shape it.

Just the act of drawing Asian people was a radical act for me, and a part of reclaiming the way that I look and not having to talk about myself in terms of difference. One of the most powerful aspects that emerged from making this a comic (rather than a written novel) is that instead of writing sentences such as 'I *don't* look like the majority of Swedes' or 'I am *not* white', I could simply draw myself,

which is a positive and empowering act.

One thing I did struggle with was self-censorship. Since I had started telling my story, I had received a lot of negative backlash and was honestly nervous about releasing this story. For almost an entire year I worked on self-defence strategies, sharpening my arguments, sourcing relevant research to support every claim I made in the book, getting thicker skin and building up the confidence that I had a right to tell this story. I think this process was actually more painful than the act of drawing personal moments on the page. I've always been very sensitive to conflict and disagreements, but [making *Palimpsest*] felt so important. While I was drawing, I could hear the negative comments that the work was going to receive.

> In addition to images, dialogue and narrative text, the reader also encounters formal adoption paperwork and correspondence that you have redrawn in *Palimpsest*. These documents are animated through your annotations and comments, and almost become additional characters in the story. Why do you feel it was important to include this additional layer of text in the novel?

The documents were a way for me to provide proof that the claims and arguments I was making in the book were factual and not made up. When you speak in positive terms – for example, 'most adoptees are happy' – no one asks you for a source. However, if you say one negative statement – for example, 'adoptees are

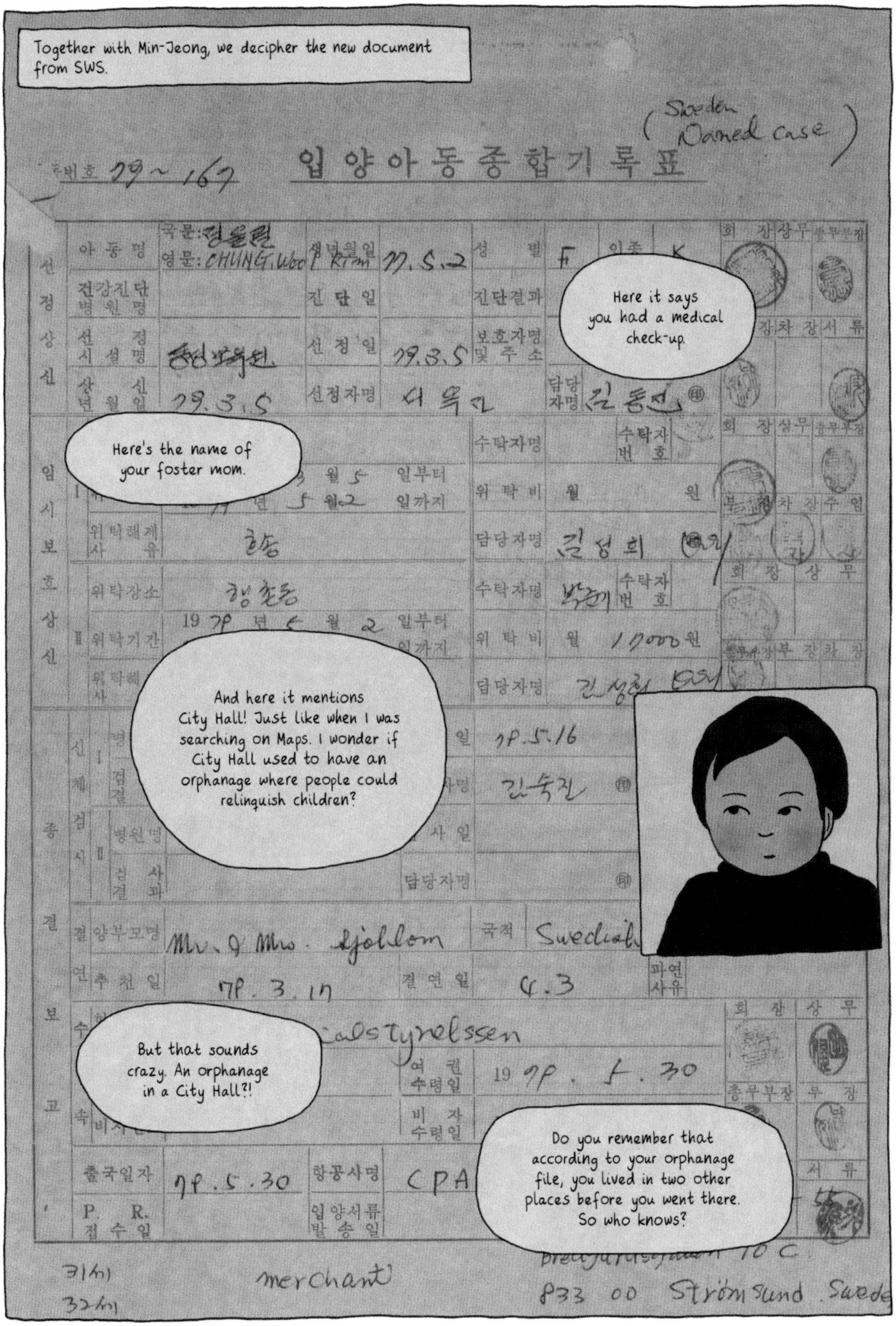
Together with Min-Jeong, we decipher the new document from SWS.
Here it says you had a medical check-up.
Here's the name of your foster mom.
And here it mentions City Hall! Just like when I was searching on Maps. I wonder if City Hall used to have an orphanage where people could relinquish children?
But that sounds crazy. An orphanage in a City Hall?!
Do you remember that according to your orphanage file, you lived in two other places before you went there. So who knows?

▶ *Palimpsest* p. 59

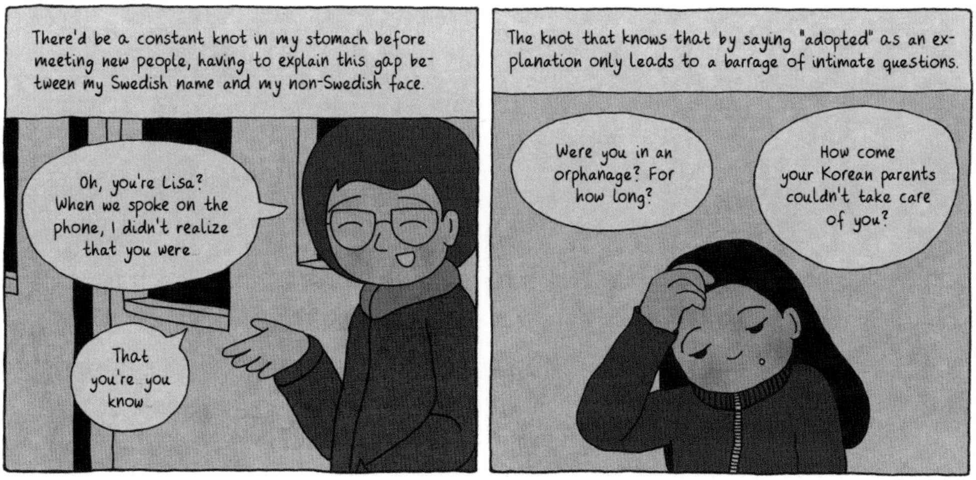
There'd be a constant knot in my stomach before meeting new people, having to explain this gap between my Swedish name and my non-Swedish face.
Oh, you're Lisa? When we spoke on the phone, I didn't realize that you were...
That you're... you know...
The knot that knows that by saying "adopted" as an explanation only leads to a barrage of intimate questions.
Were you in an orphanage? For how long?
How come your Korean parents couldn't take care of you?

◀ *Palimpsest* p. 20 (detail)

over-represented when it comes to suicide attempts' – people immediately demand the source behind that statement. By putting my own documents in the story, it felt like the story became increasingly real.

As much as I am frustrated by these documents, they are also really beautiful, and I felt that they needed to be included. I feel that they also contribute to the 'layering' effect that is also conveyed in the title.

> What aspects of the comic strip do you think make it a suitable space for the issues of identity, memory and social justice that you raise in *Palimpsest*?

Comics serve as the primary tool for my activism. When people are presented with difficult topics through visual imagery, they tend to respond more empathetically. You tend to sympathise with the character more easily because of the use of pictures – even if it's a cartoon face. Most of my characters are really cute and a bit childlike, so you sort of have to sympathise with them. I've noticed – particularly on Instagram – how incredibly efficient it is to have drawings accompany a complicated and heavy text. When you add a picture [to a difficult piece of text] – even if it's fictional – it makes the whole topic more approachable. I've also noticed that when you write comments [on social media], people can be incredibly vicious. When you write the same thing with a picture, something happens with the person who is looking at it.

I think [a comic is] a really beautiful and brilliant way to communicate controversial topics – or just heavy things in general – because it makes the information accessible. The sharp edges became a little bit more round. It's not like I'm making the topic any easier or less violent than it really is, but when information is processed through a speech bubble, it softens the message.

> You are working on a book that focuses on the experiences of Chilean first mothers whose children were taken from them and sold for adoption in Sweden. How have you found the process of telling another person's story (as opposed to your own)?

▶ *Palimpsest* p. 21

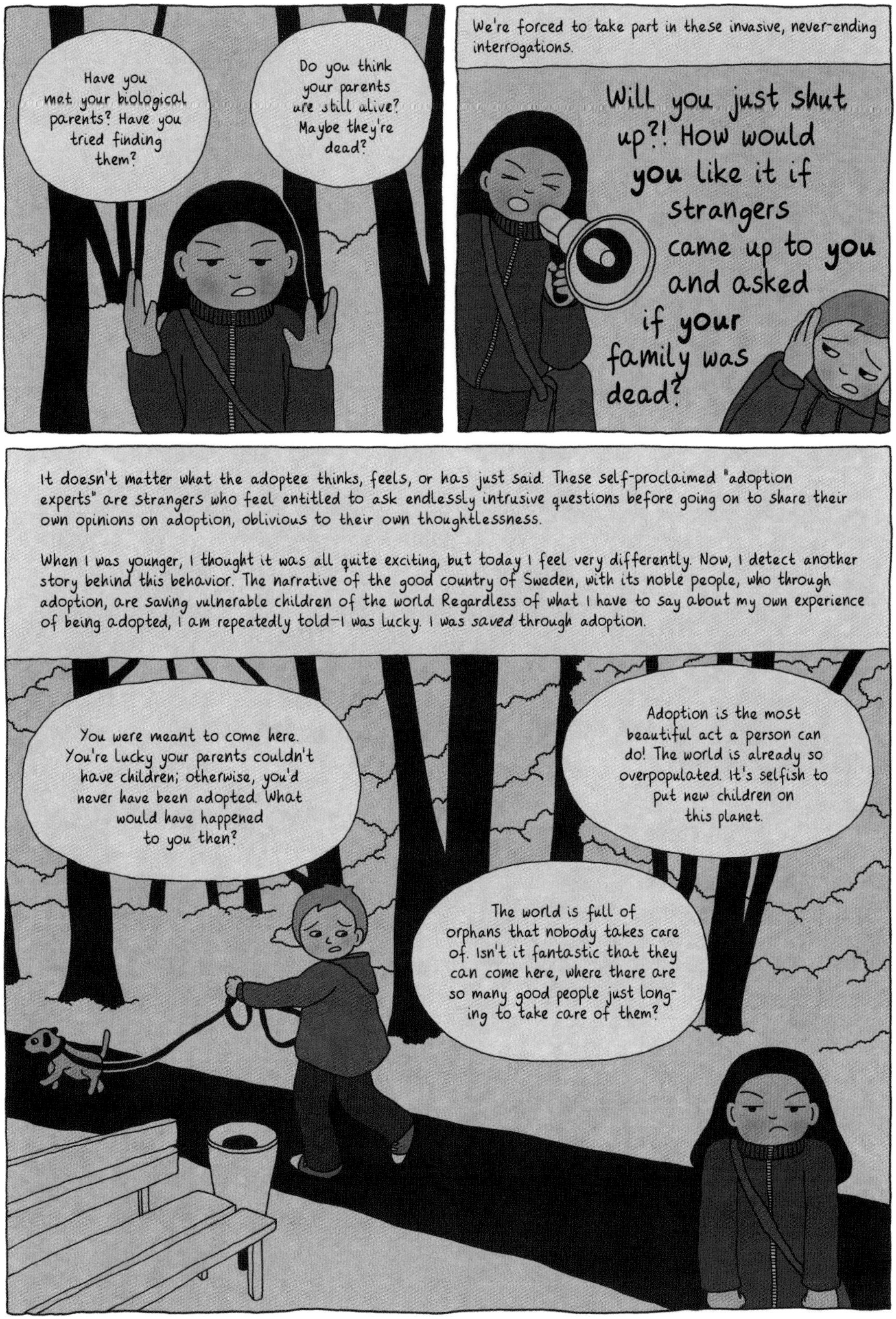
Have you met your biological parents? Have you tried finding them?
Do you think your parents are still alive? Maybe they're dead?
We're forced to take part in these invasive, never-ending interrogations.
Will you just shut up?! How would you like it if strangers came up to you and asked if your family was dead?
It doesn't matter what the adoptee thinks, feels, or has just said. These self-proclaimed "adoption experts" are strangers who feel entitled to ask endlessly intrusive questions before going on to share their own opinions on adoption, oblivious to their own thoughtlessness.
When I was younger, I thought it was all quite exciting, but today I feel very differently. Now, I detect another story behind this behavior. The narrative of the good country of Sweden, with its noble people, who through adoption, are saving vulnerable children of the world. Regardless of what I have to say about my own experience of being adopted, I am repeatedly told—I was lucky. I was *saved* through adoption.
You were meant to come here. You're lucky your parents couldn't have children; otherwise, you'd never have been adopted. What would have happened to you then?
Adoption is the most beautiful act a person can do! The world is already so overpopulated. It's selfish to put new children on this planet.
The world is full of orphans that nobody takes care of. Isn't it fantastic that they can come here, where there are so many good people just longing to take care of them?

It's such a huge – and nerve-racking! – responsibility. I know these women have felt quite used by the media, after having been approached by several journalists over the past few years [since this particular news story was picked up by the international media]. One thing that has helped is the fact that I am adopted and can show them *Palimpsest* and explain how I put my own story out there. I understand what it means to have been taken from your mother, and what this did to my own mother. I keep in close contact with everyone I portray in the book and ask for permission and approval for everything that I write. I consult them throughout the process and try to be as respectful as I possibly can. The process of creating a visual representation of their history is a bit tricky because most of them don't have any photographs from this period. I have hardly any reference photos, but I've been listening to a lot of biographical filmmakers (film and comics are quite linked, in my opinion). One filmmaker talks about what is the most important element of the film, and agrees that the *story* is the most important. You should tell the story, make sure that the facts are correct, and other details are secondary. Some of the mothers I have spoken to have blocked out certain memories and details of their past experiences as a result of trauma, and so it becomes my responsibility to fill in the blanks.

What is the most critical message that you would like to communicate for readers to better understand the experience and identity of an adoptee?

I think that what drives me the most is the fight for justice. I think that the most important message for me to communicate is that 'this is what has been done to human beings'. We have been stolen, our identities have been removed for the purpose of then selling us to satisfy other people's needs. My main focus is always on the industry and its players, as well as how the needs of adults [in the West, mainly] – who can't have children themselves, or want to save children, or for whatever reason – and their interests are the ones guarded by this industry, and not the children's rights. This is the main focus with my activism and comics.

I tell the stories through human beings' experiences because I think that if you just present the big picture, no one is going to listen, because it's so vast and there's so much money involved. If you just give the numbers, it's unfathomable. The most important thing for me is to educate people about an industry that is constantly portrayed as beautiful. I add the personal stories to make the big picture accessible.

I'm not really interested in talking about how it was when I was growing up in my adoptive family. I also don't really portray adoptive parents' voices at all in my work, which people are always asking me about. There are *so many* stories about adoptive parents, and many more than there are about adoptees, even happy adoptees – whose stories are often by their adoptive parents. There are definitely not enough stories about adoptees who have been abused by the industry, nor are there enough stories about first mothers. If there are stories about first mothers, they're usually embedded in classist and racist

The focus is always on the adoptive parents.
"In the beginning the cat was born in a land far away. He didn't have a Mom
or Dad who could take care of him."*
What about this one?
Maybe it's because everything is written by adoptive parents.
"You thought her eyes were the kindest eyes you'd ever seen yourself reflected in. She whispered to you in a strange language that she was your mother and that she would never, ever leave you."*
No wonder it comes as such a huge shock when you start to see the cold reality of how an adoption works, as an adult.
Being chosen for adoption is actually dependent on fulfilling the right criteria. That we are cute enough, and that we have been picked out by a social worker.
And one thing no one ever mentions is how many times we were rejected, how many times we didn't meet the expectations of these potential parents.

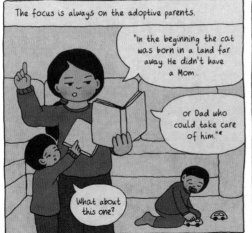

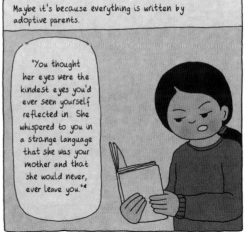

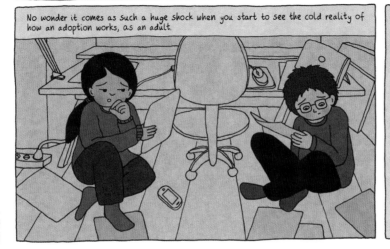

▶ *Palimpsest* p. 36 (detail)

ideas about who is fit to be a parent and who is not. Adoption doesn't just happen because we are nurturing the needs of children. Adoption happens because there are *some* children who are wanted for adoption by others. The entire structure would be very different if adoption was centred around the child in mind.

What does Korea mean to you?

I still feel this tremendous loss when I think of Korea. I mourn that I can't speak the language and that Korea is a foreign place to me still. I hate that it is. When I see other people appropriate Korean culture as their own, I feel really angry because it feels like something I can't do as an adoptee. I can't claim Korea as mine because I was sold, and I had my mother tongue removed from me. I can't relate culturally with Korea. When I try, I always feel loss and grief. For example, every time I eat Korean food, I think, 'Oh, I love this food so much; this is so wonderful!', and then I feel sadness. It's always there, lurking, this sadness. But I can also feel defensive when someone is criticising

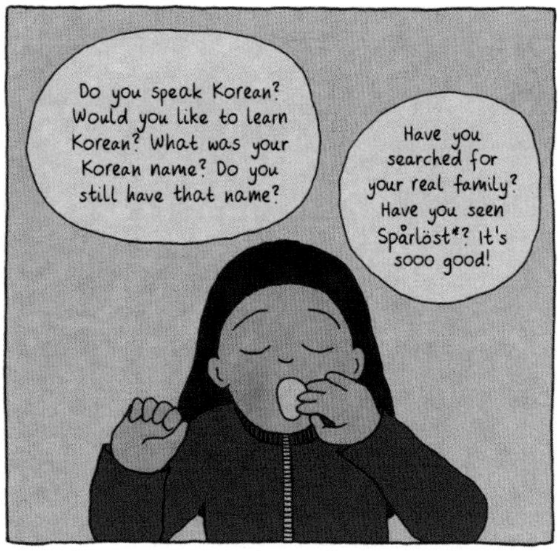
Do you speak Korean? Would you like to learn Korean? What was your Korean name? Do you still have that name?
Have you searched for your real family? Have you seen Spårlöst*? It's sooo good!

◂
Palimpsest
p. 20 (detail)

Korea because I do have some sense that this is my country.

What does Sweden mean to you?

Sweden is becoming more and more complicated these days. I haven't lived there for five years and from what I understand from my friends who are still there, it's getting worse and worse in terms of racism. One of Sweden's most racist political parties is gaining support, and other parties are taking on similar racist rhetoric. Since the pandemic, there have been racist attacks targeting Asian communities, and it's become more dangerous to be Asian in Sweden.

I feel this disappointment and anger with Sweden. I feel betrayed. They promised me through adoption – or rather the 'contract' was – that I was supposed to get 'a better life'. Instead, I was fed food that my digestive system can't take, and I can't speak to my [birth] mother now. In Sweden, I have always been treated as a stranger or a lesser human being, and in turn I internalised racist ideas for so many years. But I still need to have a relationship [with Sweden]. I am a Swedish citizen, and it's still the language I'm the most fluent in. I have family members there, and that's where I grew up. It's upsetting that Sweden has done so little to help its adoptees, even though we are the biggest adopting country in the world.

Looking ahead, how do you see comics evolving as a space for autobiographical stories? How about as a vehicle and/or tool for adoptee rights activism?

I think we're already there and have been there for some time! There are so many wonderful comics – one of my absolute favourites is *Grass* [by Keum Suk Gendry-Kim], which focuses on the Korean 'comfort women' who were trafficked into sexual slavery by the Japanese military during the occupation. It's one of the most horrific things that anyone can write about, and it's beautifully done through the medium of comics.

There are more and more comics coming out… There are so many Vietnamese-American artists in America writing about the Vietnam War, and every single one is really fascinating. Artists are writing about the Israeli-Palestinian conflict, as well as deeply personal experiences, like abortion, alcoholism, domestic abuse and rape. Comics anthologies have been produced in response to the #MeToo movement. It feels like [the comics genre] is just exploding right now with brutally honest, complex, autobiographical stories, and people are doing so many creative things to tell these stories.

I think the fight that remains is not so much about what comics can do, but rather how they are seen. I still think that comics are considered a lesser art form, and that [comics practitioners] need to fight to be recognised as artists – and get paid accordingly. There are so many incredibly beautiful comic books out there that should be considered 'high art'. Maybe this is the fight that remains? As an illustrator you are paid a lot more for a single illustration than a comics artist is for a comics page that may consist of several 'illustrations'. This reflects on how comics are seen.

> Can you describe how you went about finding and connecting with other adoptees/support networks?

Adoptees speak a lot about their feelings of isolation. We're isolated, not just because we may be adopted into white communities where we aren't that many, but also – maybe on a subconscious level – because we're taught to see ourselves with the view that adoption doesn't mean anything and that it's just a way to form a family. We're told that adoption is something that doesn't follow us around later in life and that we're just like other people. So, in a way we are taught not to seek out other adoptees, because what would we have in common?

As a result, a lot of adoptees look at each other with a bit of suspicion. In Sweden, when I was growing up, you always knew if there was another adoptee in the room. If you met an Asian person who spoke perfect Swedish, you knew they were adopted. This is very different than in the UK and America, where of course there are lots of different types of immigrant communities. In Sweden, adoptees spot

each other. I was always a bit scared of other adoptees until I started digging into my own adoption story. Today, it is the complete opposite dynamic, and most of my friends are adoptees because it's such an important thing. There is so much about the adoptee experience that you just can't talk about with anyone else.

> What would you say to someone who wants to document their personal experience through comics?

Don't get stuck in the drawings. I've had a few workshops with young people, and the first thing they say happens to be the same thing that I say, which is 'I can't draw, so I can't do this.' But don't get stuck in the drawings. The most important thing is to have something to say. The rest will follow.

ABOUT LISA WOOL-RIM SJÖBLOM:
Lisa Wool-Rim Sjöblom is an illustrator, cartoonist and graphic designer living in Auckland, New Zealand, with her partner and two children. She has a Master's degree in literature from Södertörn University and has studied at the Comic Art School in Malmö. Palimpsest is her first graphic novel. She is an adoptee rights activist whose work comments on issues of adoption, racism, representation and identity.

Overleaf:
Palimpsest
p. 55; p. 73;
p. 150; p. 151

Back then, when I embarked on my first search, I believed my adoption was proof that I was never supposed to exist.

I'd grown up with the feeling that I was a mistake. Who gives up a wanted child?

These emotions were difficult to process. The people I confided in tended to translate my thoughts into their versions of my life. The only thing that belonged to me was my wish for death. I wanted the intense yearning for my roots to vanish like magic. It only resulted with me locked up in a psychiatric ward.

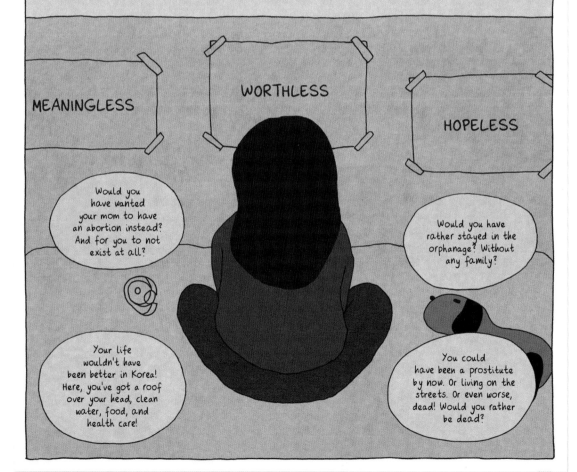

MEANINGLESS

WORTHLESS

HOPELESS

Would you have wanted your mom to have an abortion instead? And for you to not exist at all?

Would you have rather stayed in the orphanage? Without any family?

Your life wouldn't have been better in Korea! Here, you've got a roof over your head, clean water, food, and health care!

You could have been a prostitute by now. Or living on the streets. Or even worse, dead! Would you rather be dead?

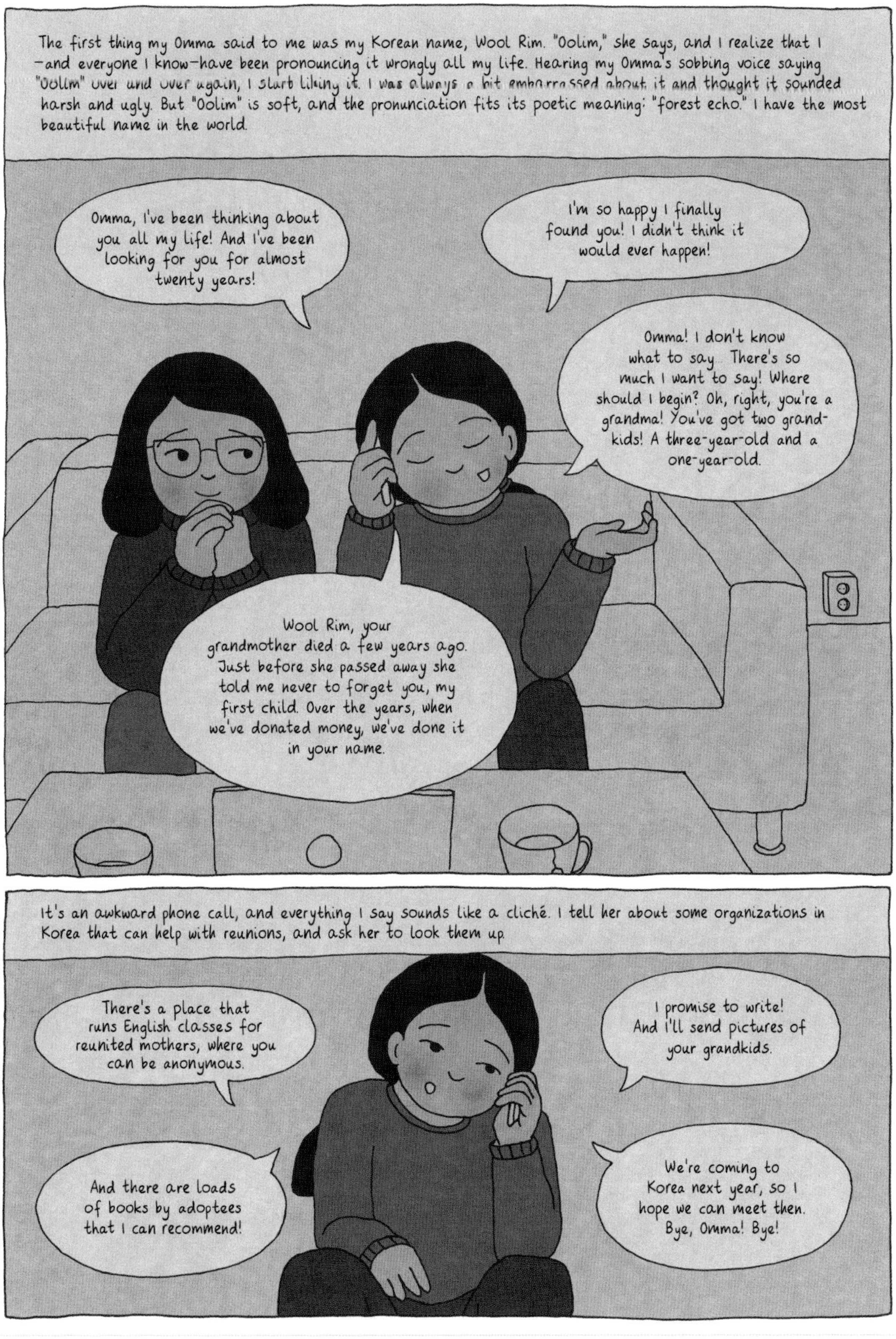
The first thing my Omma said to me was my Korean name, Wool Rim. "Oolim," she says, and I realize that I—and everyone I know—have been pronouncing it wrongly all my life. Hearing my Omma's sobbing voice saying "Oolim" over and over again, I start liking it. I was always a bit embarrassed about it and thought it sounded harsh and ugly. But "Oolim" is soft, and the pronunciation fits its poetic meaning: "forest echo." I have the most beautiful name in the world.
Omma, I've been thinking about you all my life! And I've been looking for you for almost twenty years!
I'm so happy I finally found you! I didn't think it would ever happen!
Omma! I don't know what to say... There's so much I want to say! Where should I begin? Oh, right, you're a grandma! You've got two grandkids! A three-year-old and a one-year-old.
Wool Rim, your grandmother died a few years ago. Just before she passed away she told me never to forget you, my first child. Over the years, when we've donated money, we've done it in your name.
It's an awkward phone call, and everything I say sounds like a cliché. I tell her about some organizations in Korea that can help with reunions, and ask her to look them up.
There's a place that runs English classes for reunited mothers, where you can be anonymous.
I promise to write! And I'll send pictures of your grandkids.
And there are loads of books by adoptees that I can recommend!
We're coming to Korea next year, so I hope we can meet then. Bye, Omma! Bye!

어기는 3층 출발층 입니다
You are here on the Departures Hall (3rd Floor)

Our trip to the airport feels surreal. I want the bus to turn around, or for something to happen that forces us to spend another night in Korea. Anything for one more day in this wonderful country. I don't want this to be my only trip to Korea; yet, the country slowly disappears behind us.

I have unanswered questions and I'm returning to Sweden with many more. I have a hopeless longing for my unknown siblings.

When will Omma feel comfortable enough to open up about the past? Will my siblings ever know they have an older sister? Will my dad ever want to meet me? The quest for your past is usually viewed as the end of a painful journey where an adoptee can finally find peace when they reunite with their family. For me, though, this is just the beginning of an uprising, of a rebellion.

It's been 35 years since I was adopted to Sweden. How little I was. How little I knew.

And now, I leave Korea once more.

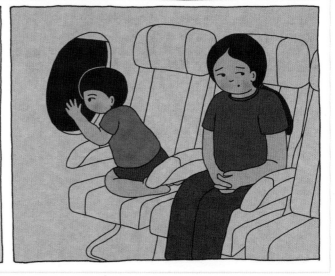

to once again arrive in a country where I'm a stranger.
Ni hao? Konichiwa? Where are you from?
At home, an e-mail from KAS awaits me.
Hi! We've got the result from the DNA test for Lisa and Lisa's birth mother. It shows with 99,997% accuracy that they are mother and daughter.
Congratulations!
And an e-mail from Mrs. Kim.
Dear Wool Rim,
Because of the language barrier, your mother can't express her deep feelings for you. She wishes you the best of luck in life, and acknowledges you as her blood daughter. However, she does not want any more contact at this time. She feels that the two of you need more time before you can meet and have an understanding of one another.
UNKNOWN SISTER
UNKNOWN BROTHER
OMMA
DAD
TEDDY
UNKNOWN BROTHER
POPPY
UNKNOWN BROTHER
There is a word in Korean culture—한/HAN—which describes the bottomless sorrow people feel after an enduring suffering, after having been wronged, persecuted, and oppressed. 한 is a part of Korea's cultural identity, and it comprises hope, despair, acceptance, and a resilient desire for revenge. At this very moment, another vulnerable family is currently being torn apart, another child is being dispatched to a distant country with faked papers, under false pretenses. For them we must bear witness.

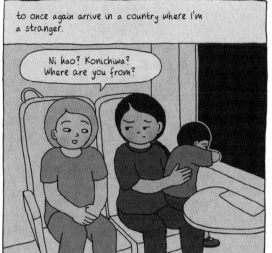

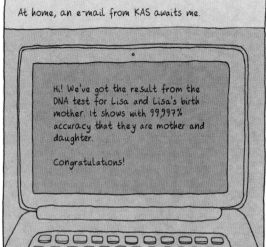

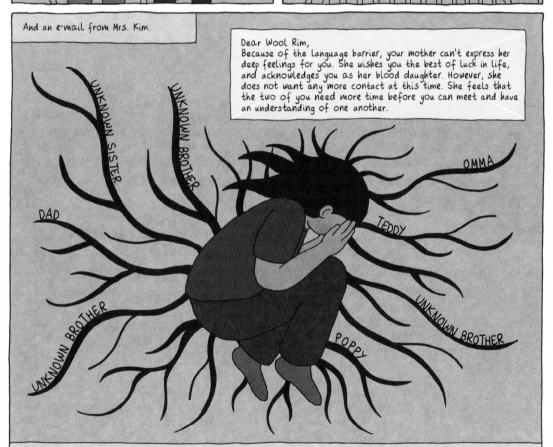

ASIA ALFASI

BASEERAH IS A sci-fi adventure about an Orphaned Oracle who, following her birth, is delivered into the care of The Custodian. From this moment, she is instantly set on the path to inheriting The Custodian's vital role as she sacrifices her own eyes in her quest to open a thousand more.

Baseerah is a character and story concept that have been very close to me for many years. I've grown up with my feet in two distinctly different cultures, making it necessary for me to continually explore and push past boundaries and preconceptions set in front of me. I remember feeling surprised and shocked at each turn as I found my previously held convictions to be swayed, and my perspective grew and morphed to accommodate each new point of view.

In exploring my heritage, I was struck by how many – if not most – prophets and agents of great change and influence in history *were* foundlings. This experience gives them an extremely unique point of view on the world and a resilience that lends itself to them exploring the world in unparalleled ways.

And so, I set to craft a story moulding the different ingredients of thought, influence, history, culture, folklore, philosophy, superheroes and manga into a cohesive story. This is its beginning, and I'll continue to weave all the above and more into it as I explore the topic and push it to its maximum potential.

ASIA ALFASI is an award-winning British-Libyan graphic novelist. Born in Libya in 1984, she spent her formative years first in Tripoli and then in Glasgow, Scotland where she migrated with her family.

After discovering and falling in love with comics and manga, she realised their immense potential at humanising issues and bringing forth the plight of often marginalised peoples to the fore, therefore furthering understanding.

Ever since, she has represented the Muslim and Arab voice through her work, with the ultimate aim of harnessing the medium as a tool for cross-cultural dialogue, understanding and societal creative exchange.

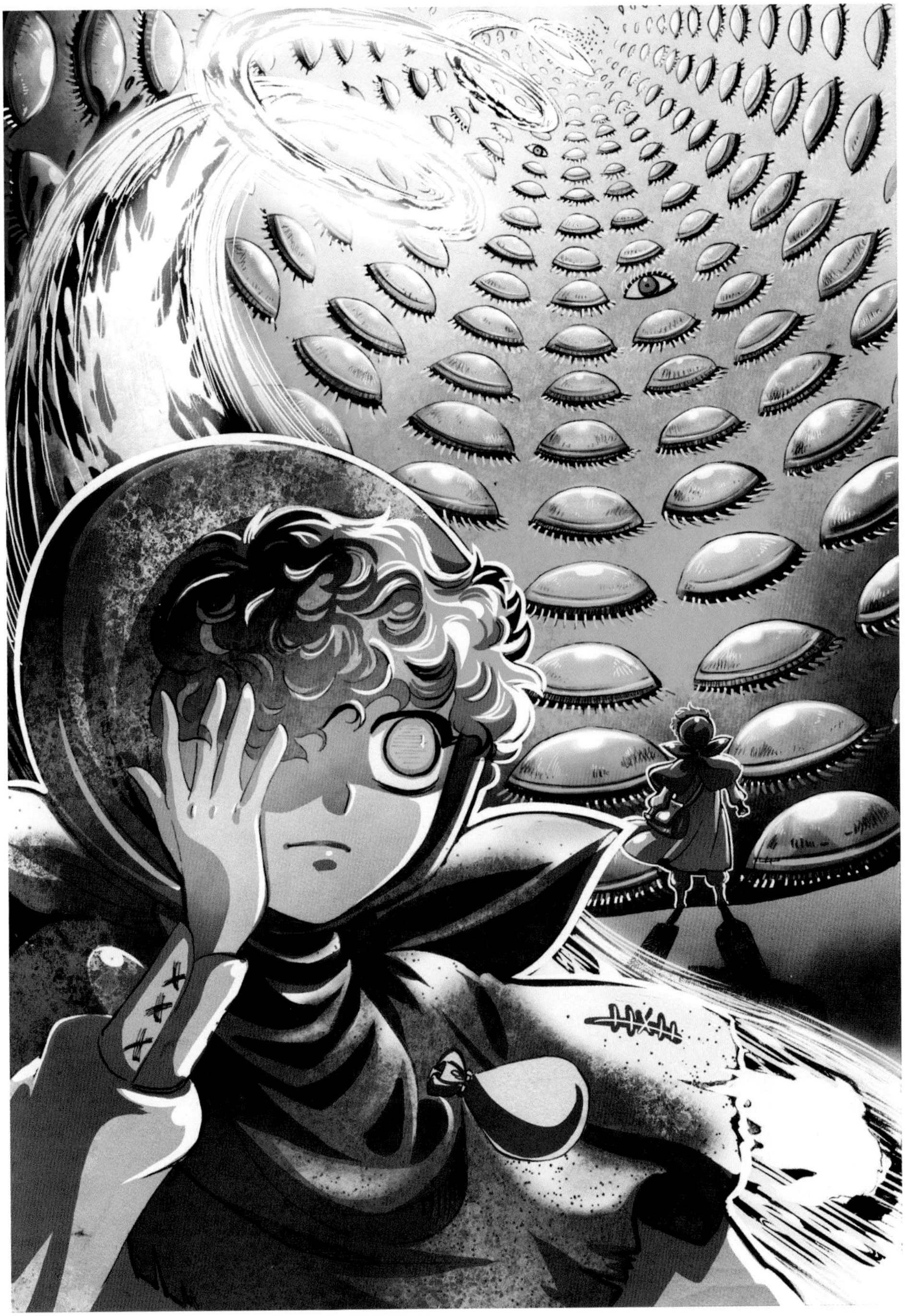

Title: *Baseerah*
Date: 2021
Size: 297 x 420 mm
Description: Cartridge paper; drawn and inked on paper; finished digitally: tones, effects, text and speech bubbles added digitally using Clip Studio Paint and Photoshop

▶
Cover from *Baseerah*

Overleaf: selected spreads from *Baseerah*

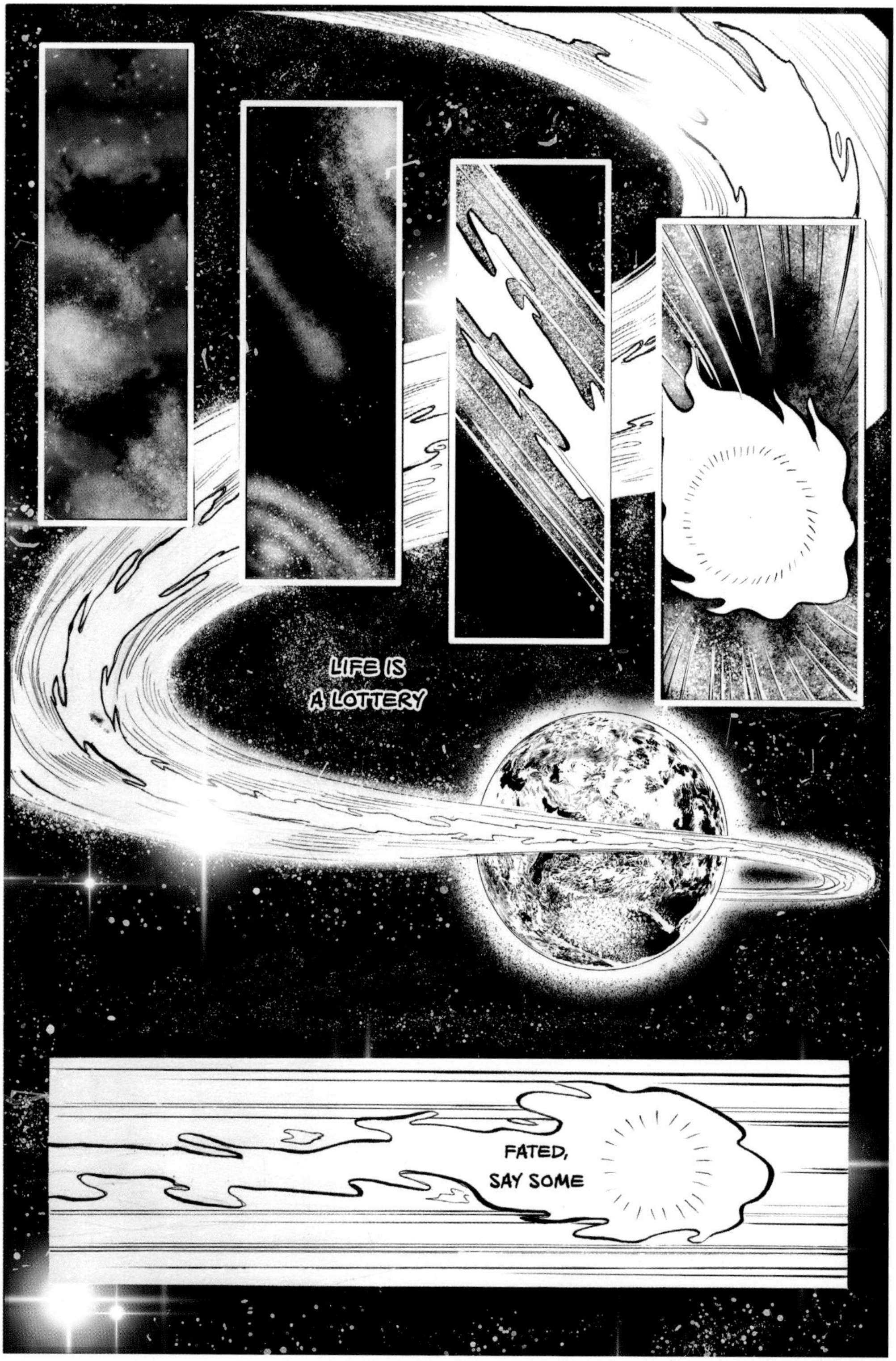
LIFE IS
A LOTTERY
FATED,
SAY SOME

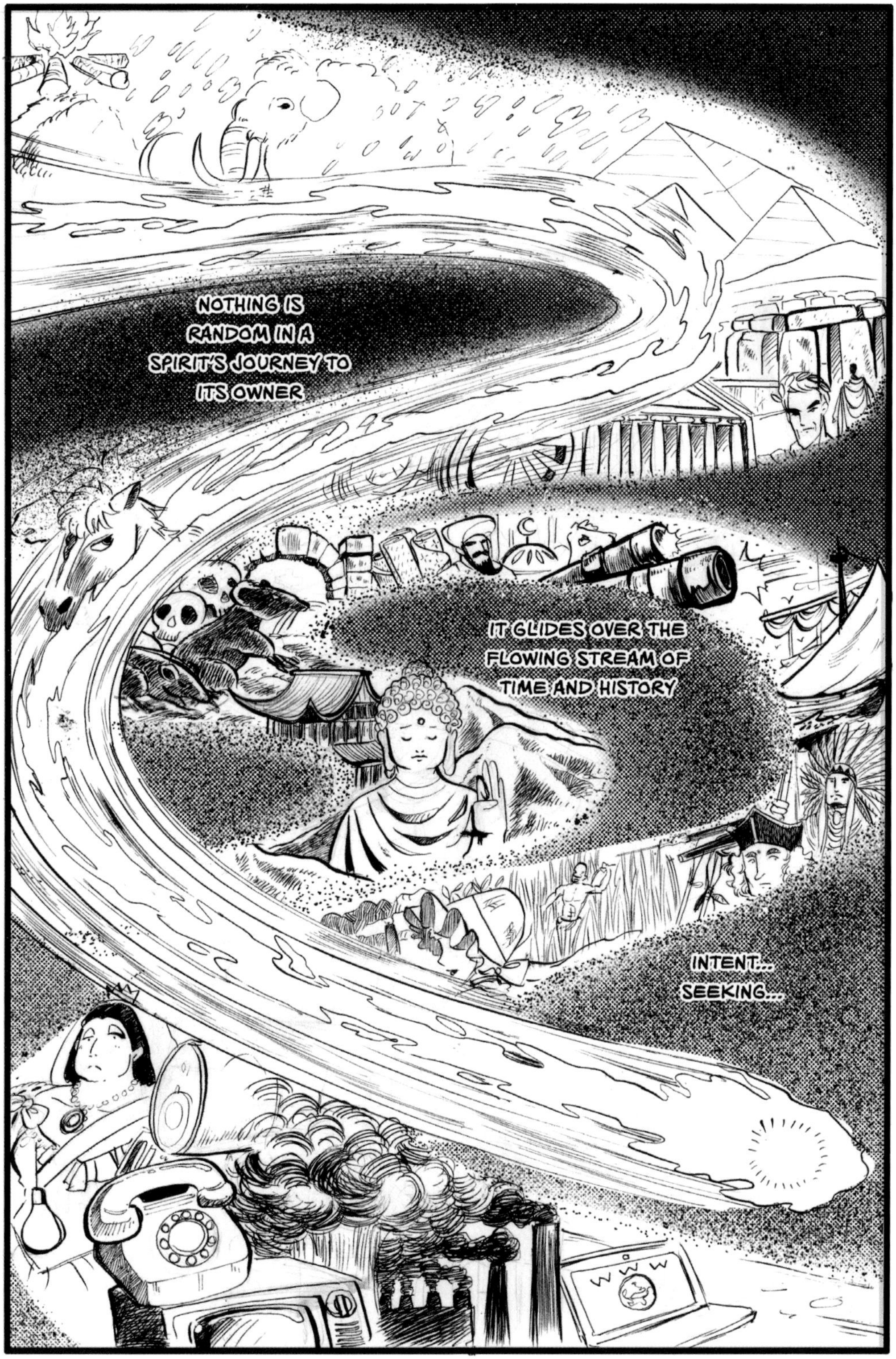
NOTHING IS RANDOM IN A SPIRIT'S JOURNEY TO ITS OWNER
IT GLIDES OVER THE FLOWING STREAM OF TIME AND HISTORY
INTENT... SEEKING...

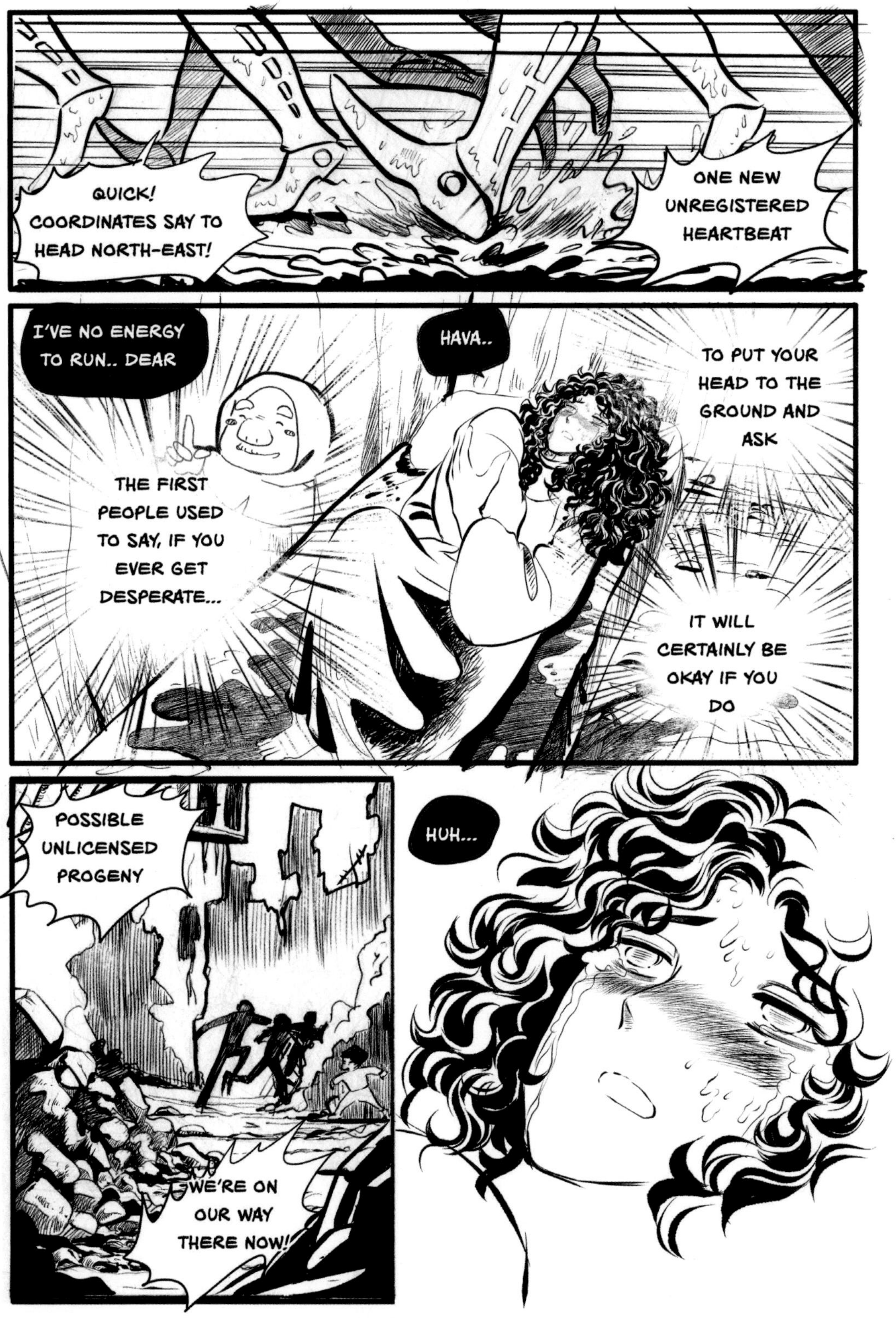
QUICK! COORDINATES SAY TO HEAD NORTH-EAST!
ONE NEW UNREGISTERED HEARTBEAT
I'VE NO ENERGY TO RUN.. DEAR
HAVA..
THE FIRST PEOPLE USED TO SAY, IF YOU EVER GET DESPERATE...
TO PUT YOUR HEAD TO THE GROUND AND ASK
IT WILL CERTAINLY BE OKAY IF YOU DO
POSSIBLE UNLICENSED PROGENY
WE'RE ON OUR WAY THERE NOW!
HUH...

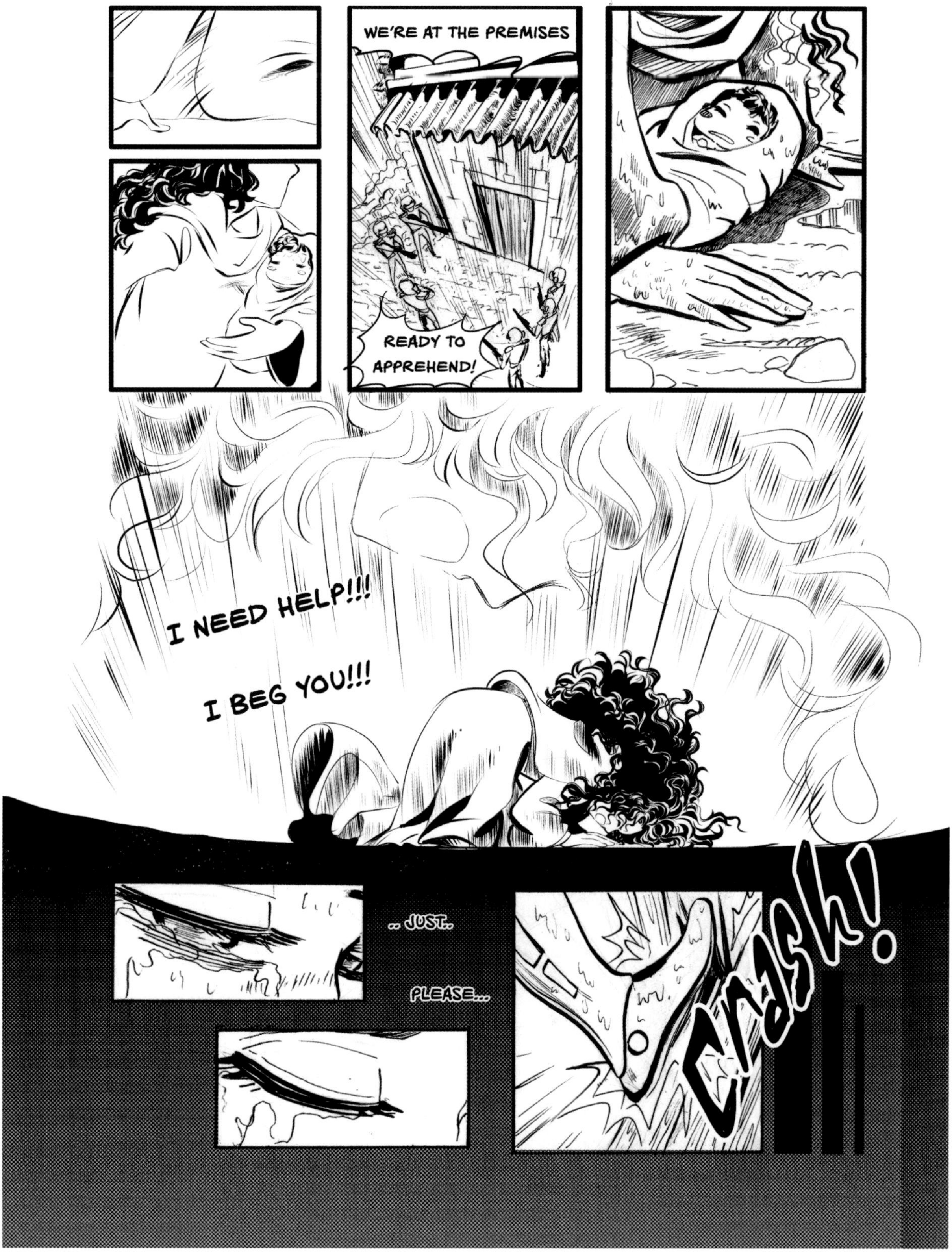
WE'RE AT THE PREMISES
READY TO APPREHEND!
I NEED HELP!!!
I BEG YOU!!!
.. JUST..
PLEASE...
Crash!

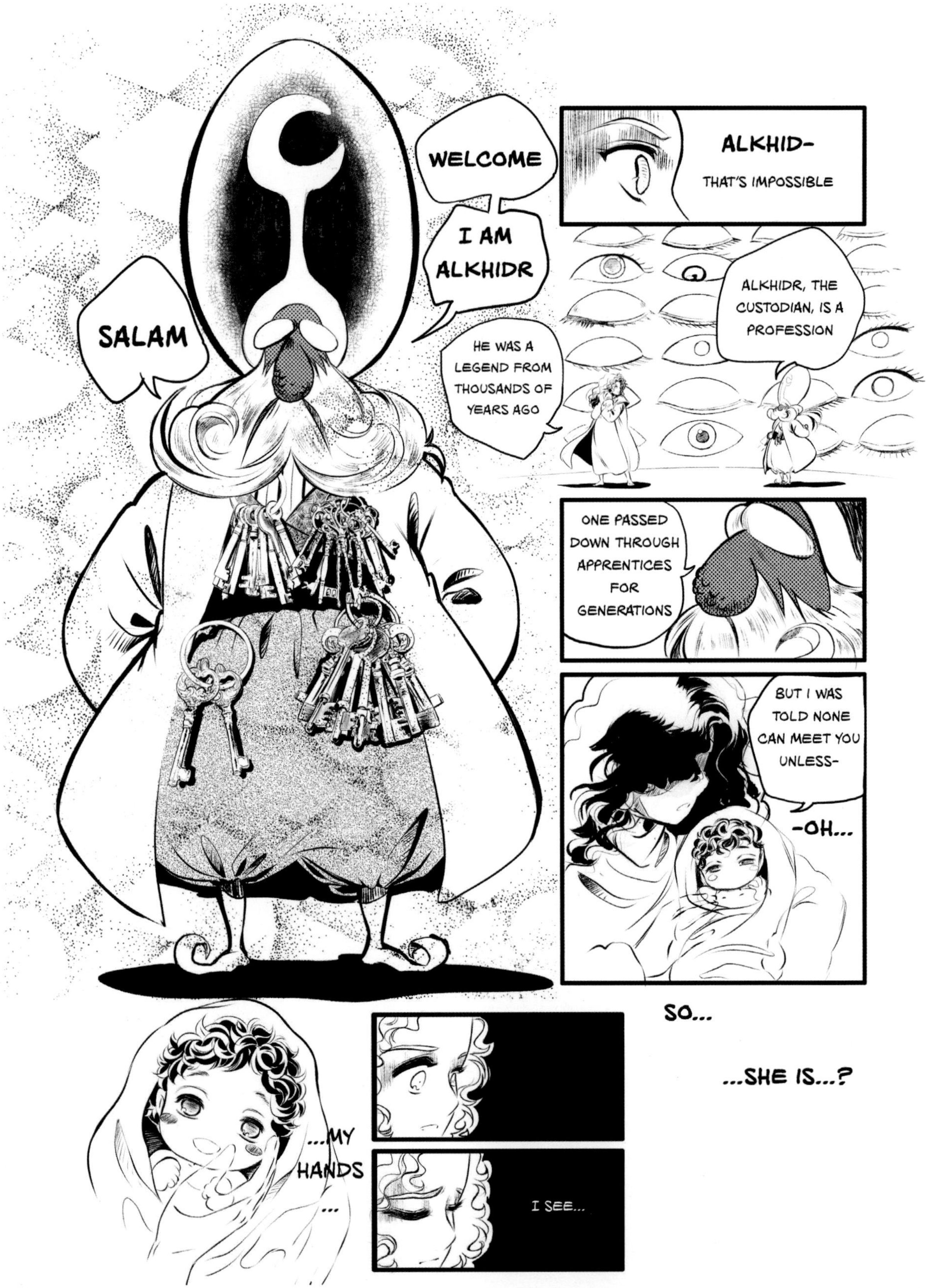
SALAM
WELCOME
I AM ALKHIDR
ALKHID-
THAT'S IMPOSSIBLE
HE WAS A LEGEND FROM THOUSANDS OF YEARS AGO
ALKHIDR, THE CUSTODIAN, IS A PROFESSION
ONE PASSED DOWN THROUGH APPRENTICES FOR GENERATIONS
BUT I WAS TOLD NONE CAN MEET YOU UNLESS-
-OH...
SO...
...SHE IS...?
...MY HANDS
...
I SEE...

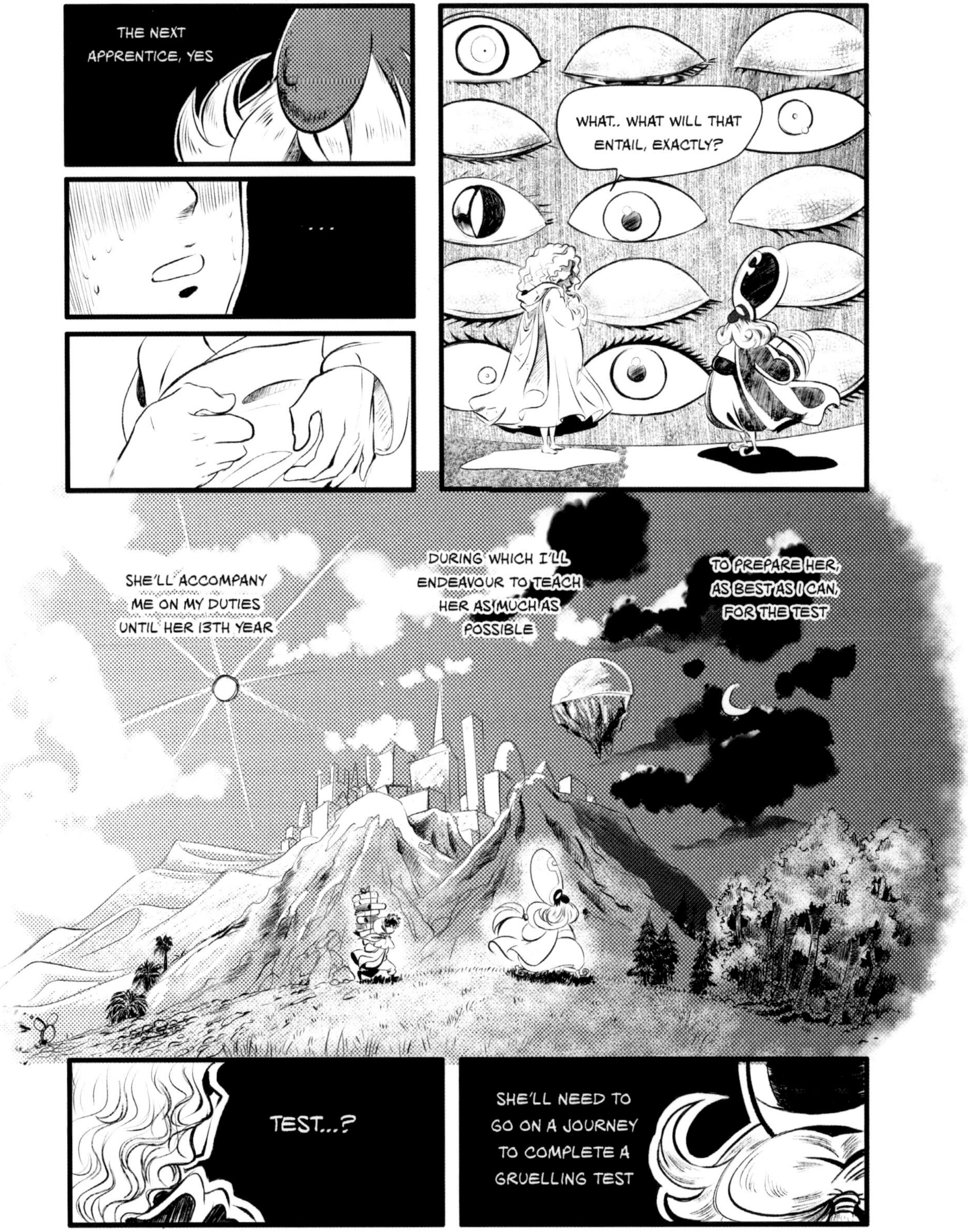
THE NEXT APPRENTICE, YES
...
WHAT.. WHAT WILL THAT ENTAIL, EXACTLY?
SHE'LL ACCOMPANY ME ON MY DUTIES UNTIL HER 13TH YEAR
DURING WHICH I'LL ENDEAVOUR TO TEACH HER AS MUCH AS POSSIBLE
TO PREPARE HER, AS BEST AS I CAN, FOR THE TEST
TEST...?
SHE'LL NEED TO GO ON A JOURNEY TO COMPLETE A GRUELLING TEST

BEX GLENDINING

INSPIRED BY SUPERMAN'S origins, *Begin Again* explores the idea of growth and discovery of self in a new environment, alongside aspects of isolation, loneliness and puzzlement. Featuring both snapshots from the character's new life and abstract snippets representing negative and sometimes overwhelming emotions, the story flows in a non-linear pattern that can be read in any order with the viewer revisiting panels to change or repeat the story. I also wanted to explore themes of queerness and queer love, which is shown through the use of colours, and gender-fluidity of the main character. I hope this piece brings forward a sense of comfort and peace through difficult times, and an acknowledgement that there can be happiness and light within even the darkest of times.

BEX GLENDINING (she/they) is a biracial queer, UK-based illustrator, comic artist and colourist. Bex has worked as a cover artist, colourist and interior artist on projects such as *Seen: Edmonia Lewis*, *Penultimate Quest*, *Rolled & Told*, *Lupina* and multiple covers for Penguin Random House.

▶
Title: *Begin Again*
Date: 2021
Size: 297 x 420 mm
Description: Digital illustration using Photoshop and a Wacom tablet

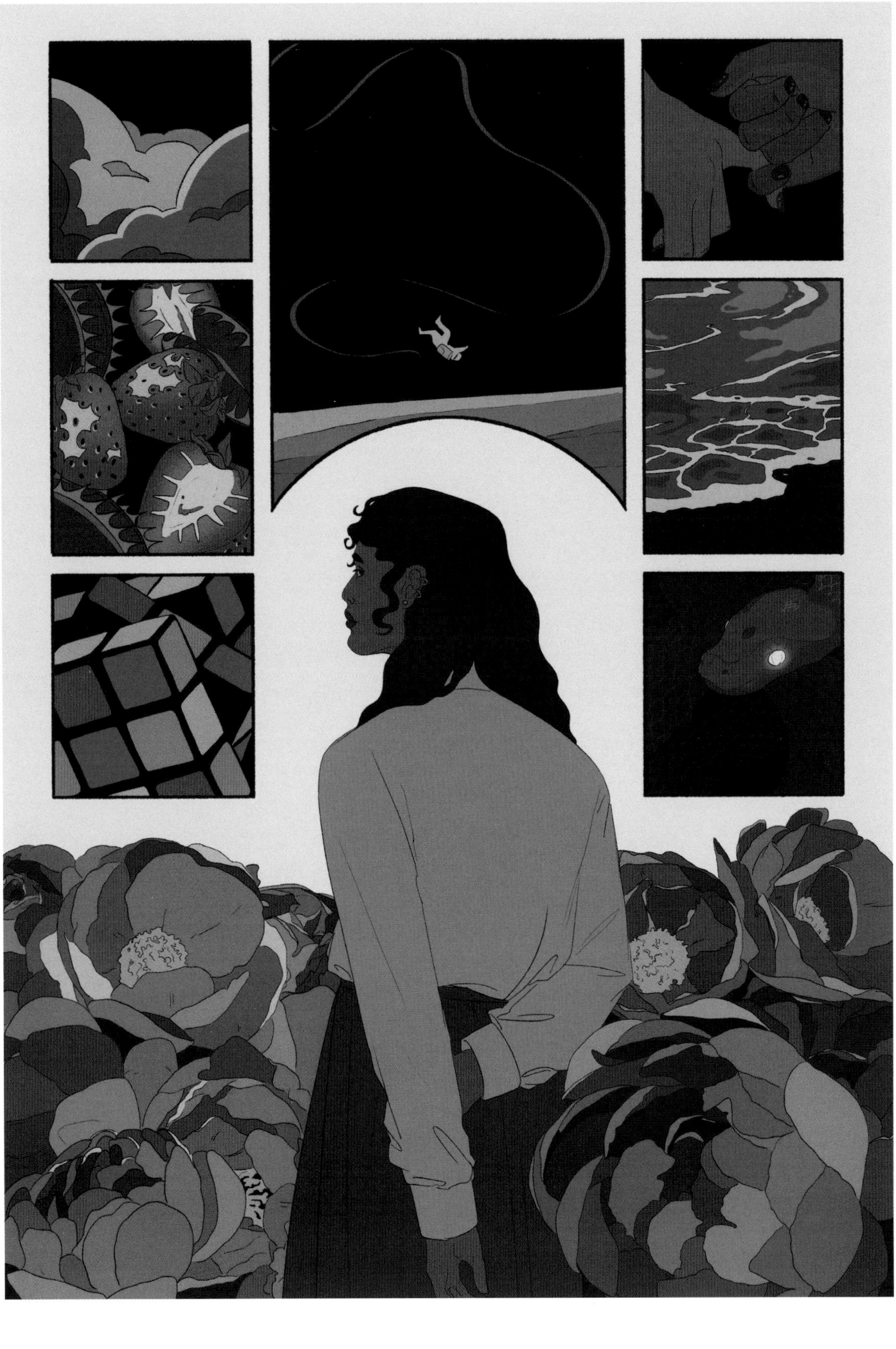

WOODROW PHOENIX

UP IN FLAMES woodrow phoenix

ALMOST ALL CHILD heroes have back stories that begin with trauma; disastrous circumstances that end up with both parents dying and a child left all alone.

In fiction – and in life – we measure heroism in a protagonist by the depth of difficulties they have to rise above. A happy, untroubled life of loving comfort does not make for compelling stories and celebrated victories. To test our heroes and make them prove their mettle, they have to endure the worst possible challenges. And what could be more dreadful for a child than having their entire world destroyed?

There is also another very practical reason for taking support away from a child protagonist. If there are parents, then there is someone to say no. Most of the challenging and dangerous adventures that children embark on in fictional narratives would never happen if there was a sensible adult around. For the action to happen at all, the first thing we have to do is kill the parents. This powerful beginning for our story also gives our unfortunate protagonist a spur to torment them and drive them forward. They need answers. They need justice. Perhaps they need revenge. They definitely need to build a new world to replace the one they lost. Can they do it? Will they overcome all odds to dispel the darkness and emerge into the light? Yes, they will. We need them to win and their story won't be over until they do.

These situations are exaggerated, operatic, melodramatic, oversimplified, but

in a way they have to be; the emotional devastation of a real orphan is so huge it can only be expressed in the heightened dramatic language of comics imagery. *Up in Flames* is a look at all those inciting incidents, distilled into one long disaster poem.

WOODROW PHOENIX is a writer, artist and graphic designer based in London and Cambridge. His constant experiments with form and style in the comic strip medium have resulted in an extremely varied output of narratives in national UK newspapers, including the *Guardian*, the *Independent* and the *London Evening Standard*, in magazines, newspapers and comics across Europe, the USA and Japan, and in television projects for Walt Disney and the Cartoon Network.

His books include *SugarBuzz!*, *Plastic Culture*, the critically acclaimed *Rumble Strip* and its sequel *Crash Course*, the award-winning anthology *Nelson*, and the experimental *She Lives*, a gallery installation that is also a giant graphic novel. Woodrow is a visiting lecturer at the University of Middlesex, teaching on the MA course in Children's Book Illustration and Graphic Novels. His most recent book for children, *Donny Digits*, was published in October 2021.

▲

Title: *Up in Flames*
Date: 2021
Size: 1730 x 330mm
Description: Graphite pencil, India ink, Tombo Fudenosuke brush pen on card

PLATES

GASOLINE ALLEY

Frank O. King (1918-64), 1918–present

On 14 February 1921, Walt Wallet discovers an infant (Skeezix) left on his doorstep, who he eventually adopts. *Gasoline Alley* stands apart from other comics by having its characters age in real time. Skeezix attends university, serves in The Second World War and creates a family of his own before eventually taking over his adoptive father's business. Skeezix is now a grandfather in what is currently the longest-running strip in the United States.

    NB: This comic includes negative depictions of cultural stereotypes that are both inaccurate and harmful.

▶
Gasoline Alley
Frank King
31 Dec. 1922
*Chicago
Sunday Tribune*

COMIC SECTION

Chicago Sunday Tribune.

THE WORLD'S GREATEST NEWSPAPER

COMIC SECTION

DECEMBER 31, 1922

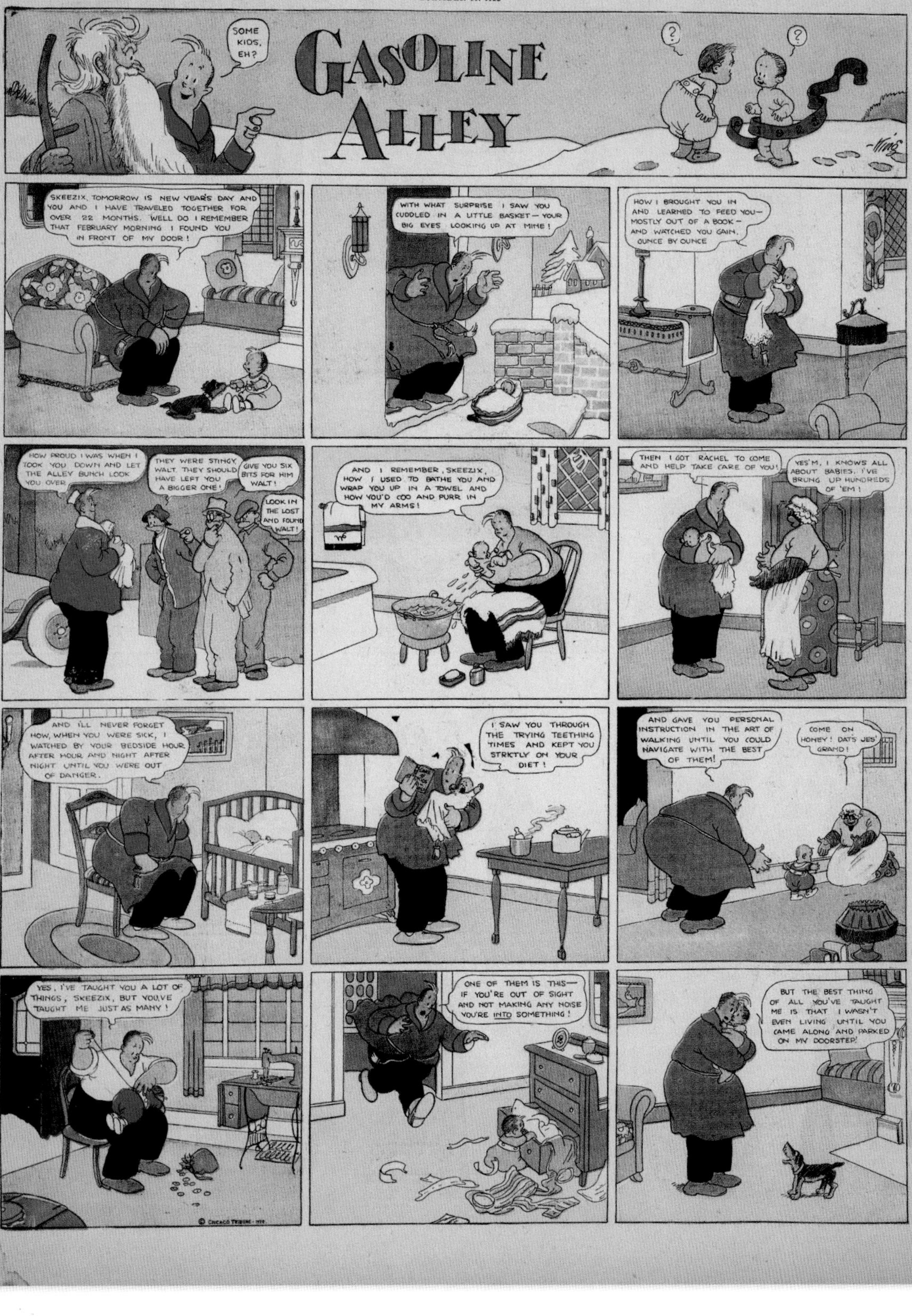
SOME KIDS, EH?
GASOLINE ALLEY
?
?
SKEEZIX, TOMORROW IS NEW YEAR'S DAY AND YOU AND I HAVE TRAVELED TOGETHER FOR OVER 22 MONTHS. WELL DO I REMEMBER THAT FEBRUARY MORNING I FOUND YOU IN FRONT OF MY DOOR!
WITH WHAT SURPRISE I SAW YOU CUDDLED IN A LITTLE BASKET — YOUR BIG EYES LOOKING UP AT MINE!
HOW I BROUGHT YOU IN AND LEARNED TO FEED YOU — MOSTLY OUT OF A BOOK — AND WATCHED YOU GAIN, OUNCE BY OUNCE
HOW PROUD I WAS WHEN I TOOK YOU DOWN AND LET THE ALLEY BUNCH LOOK YOU OVER
THEY WERE STINGY, WALT. THEY SHOULD HAVE LEFT YOU A BIGGER ONE!
GIVE YOU SIX BITS FOR HIM WALT!
LOOK IN THE LOST AND FOUND WALT!
AND I REMEMBER, SKEEZIX, HOW I USED TO BATHE YOU AND WRAP YOU UP IN A TOWEL AND HOW YOU'D COO AND PURR IN MY ARMS!
THEN I GOT RACHEL TO COME AND HELP TAKE CARE OF YOU!
YES'M, I KNOWS ALL ABOUT BABIES. I'VE BRUNG UP HUNDREDS OF 'EM!
AND I'LL NEVER FORGET HOW, WHEN YOU WERE SICK, I WATCHED BY YOUR BEDSIDE HOUR AFTER HOUR AND NIGHT AFTER NIGHT UNTIL YOU WERE OUT OF DANGER.
I SAW YOU THROUGH THE TRYING TEETHING TIMES AND KEPT YOU STRICTLY ON YOUR DIET!
AND GAVE YOU PERSONAL INSTRUCTION IN THE ART OF WALKING UNTIL YOU COULD NAVIGATE WITH THE BEST OF THEM!
COME ON HONEY! DATS JES' GRAND!
YES, I'VE TAUGHT YOU A LOT OF THINGS, SKEEZIX, BUT YOU'VE TAUGHT ME JUST AS MANY!
ONE OF THEM IS THIS — IF YOU'RE OUT OF SIGHT AND NOT MAKING ANY NOISE YOU'RE INTO SOMETHING!
BUT THE BEST THING OF ALL YOU'VE TAUGHT ME IS THAT I WASN'T EVEN LIVING UNTIL YOU CAME ALONG AND PARKED ON MY DOORSTEP!

LITTLE ORPHAN ANNIE

Harold Gray (1924-68), 1924-2010

Little Orphan Annie introduced the world to Annie, a child living in an orphanage and dreaming of a family to call her own. Annie's trademark toughness and quick wit help her cope with the challenges of the orphanage and continue to prove useful after she is fostered by wealthy businessman Daddy Warbucks. Although they form a familial bond, Annie is never formally adopted. Her 'orphan' status becomes an important signifier of her resilience, giving her the courage to help strangers and organise war support efforts, among other adventures.

▶
Little Orphan Annie
Harold Gray
2 Nov. 1924
Chicago Tribune

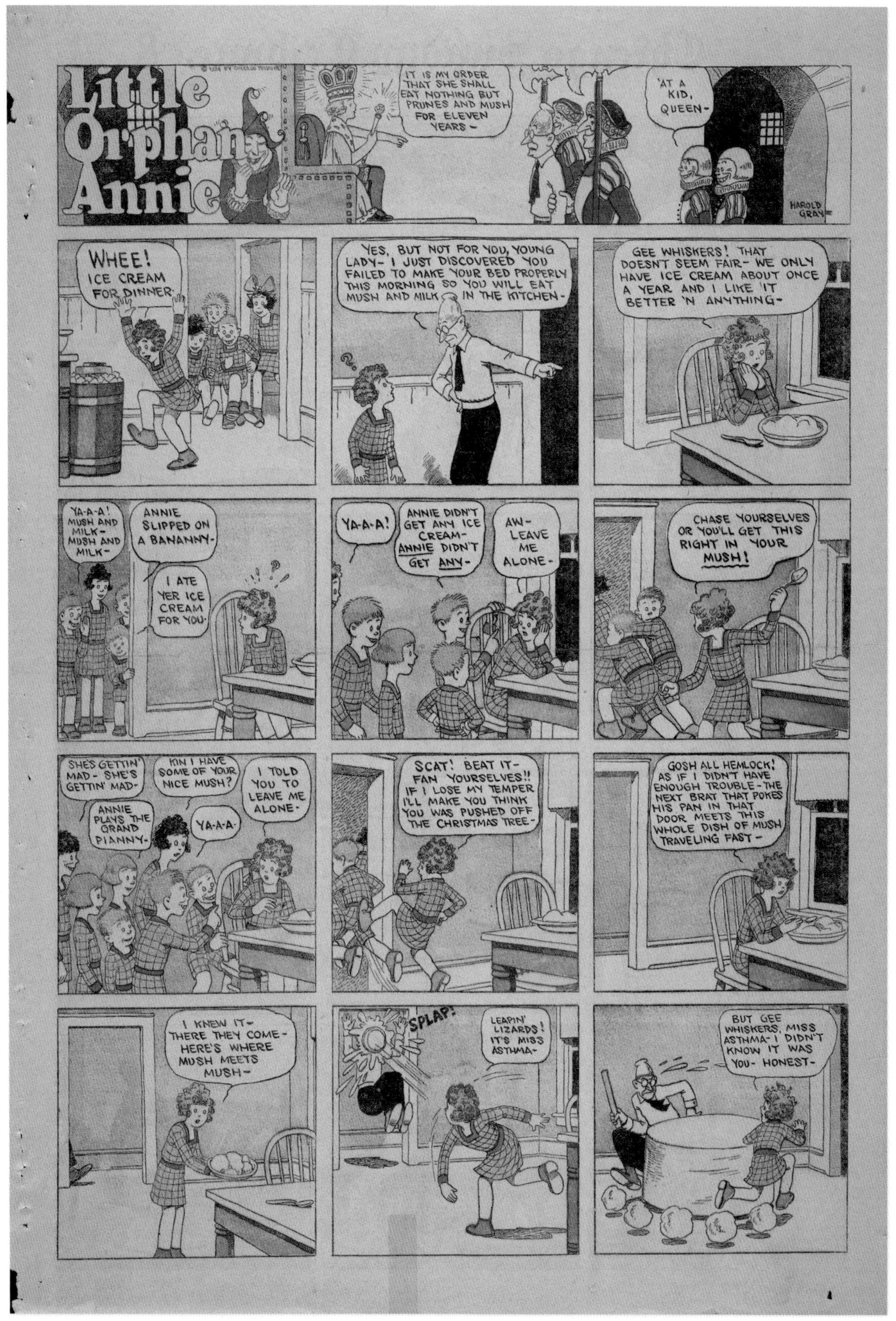
Little Orphan Annie
IT IS MY ORDER THAT SHE SHALL EAT NOTHING BUT PRUNES AND MUSH FOR ELEVEN YEARS -
'AT A KID, QUEEN -
HAROLD GRAY
WHEE! ICE CREAM FOR DINNER.
YES, BUT NOT FOR YOU, YOUNG LADY - I JUST DISCOVERED YOU FAILED TO MAKE YOUR BED PROPERLY THIS MORNING SO YOU WILL EAT MUSH AND MILK IN THE KITCHEN -
GEE WHISKERS! THAT DOESN'T SEEM FAIR - WE ONLY HAVE ICE CREAM ABOUT ONCE A YEAR AND I LIKE 'IT BETTER 'N ANYTHING -
YA-A-A! MUSH AND MILK - MUSH AND MILK -
ANNIE SLIPPED ON A BANANNY -
I ATE YER ICE CREAM FOR YOU.
YA-A-A!
ANNIE DIDN'T GET ANY ICE CREAM - ANNIE DIDN'T GET ANY -
AW - LEAVE ME ALONE -
CHASE YOURSELVES OR YOU'LL GET THIS RIGHT IN YOUR MUSH!
SHE'S GETTIN' MAD - SHE'S GETTIN' MAD -
KIN I HAVE SOME OF YOUR NICE MUSH?
I TOLD YOU TO LEAVE ME ALONE -
ANNIE PLAYS THE GRAND PIANNY -
YA-A-A.
SCAT! BEAT IT - FAN YOURSELVES!! IF I LOSE MY TEMPER I'LL MAKE YOU THINK YOU WAS PUSHED OFF THE CHRISTMAS TREE -
GOSH ALL HEMLOCK! AS IF I DIDN'T HAVE ENOUGH TROUBLE - THE NEXT BRAT THAT POKES HIS PAN IN THAT DOOR MEETS THIS WHOLE DISH OF MUSH TRAVELING FAST -
I KNEW IT - THERE THEY COME - HERE'S WHERE MUSH MEETS MUSH -
SPLAP!
LEAPIN' LIZARDS! IT'S MISS ASTHMA -
BUT GEE WHISKERS, MISS ASTHMA - I DIDN'T KNOW IT WAS YOU - HONEST -

DC

Various artists, 1934–present

Superman was created by two teenagers, Joe Shuster and Jerry Siegel. While Superman's extraordinary powers entertained the masses, his internal struggle to understand his origins introduced a new emotional and psychological depth to comics. Superman's sense of displacement also reflected the challenges faced by immigrants living in America. As sons of Jewish immigrants, Shuster and Siegel drew a superhero in which they could also see aspects of themselves.

In *Batman*, Bruce Wayne is only a child when he witnesses both his parents' murders in a deserted alleyway. This traumatic experience inspires Wayne to devote his life to the pursuit of bringing criminals to justice. However, Wayne's desire for retribution leaves Batman always teetering on the edge of darkness. When facing off against villains like the Penguin (also orphaned) and the Joker, Batman's own inner turmoil becomes even more apparent.

▶
World's Best Comics
Vol. 1, # 1
Fred Ray
Mar. 1941

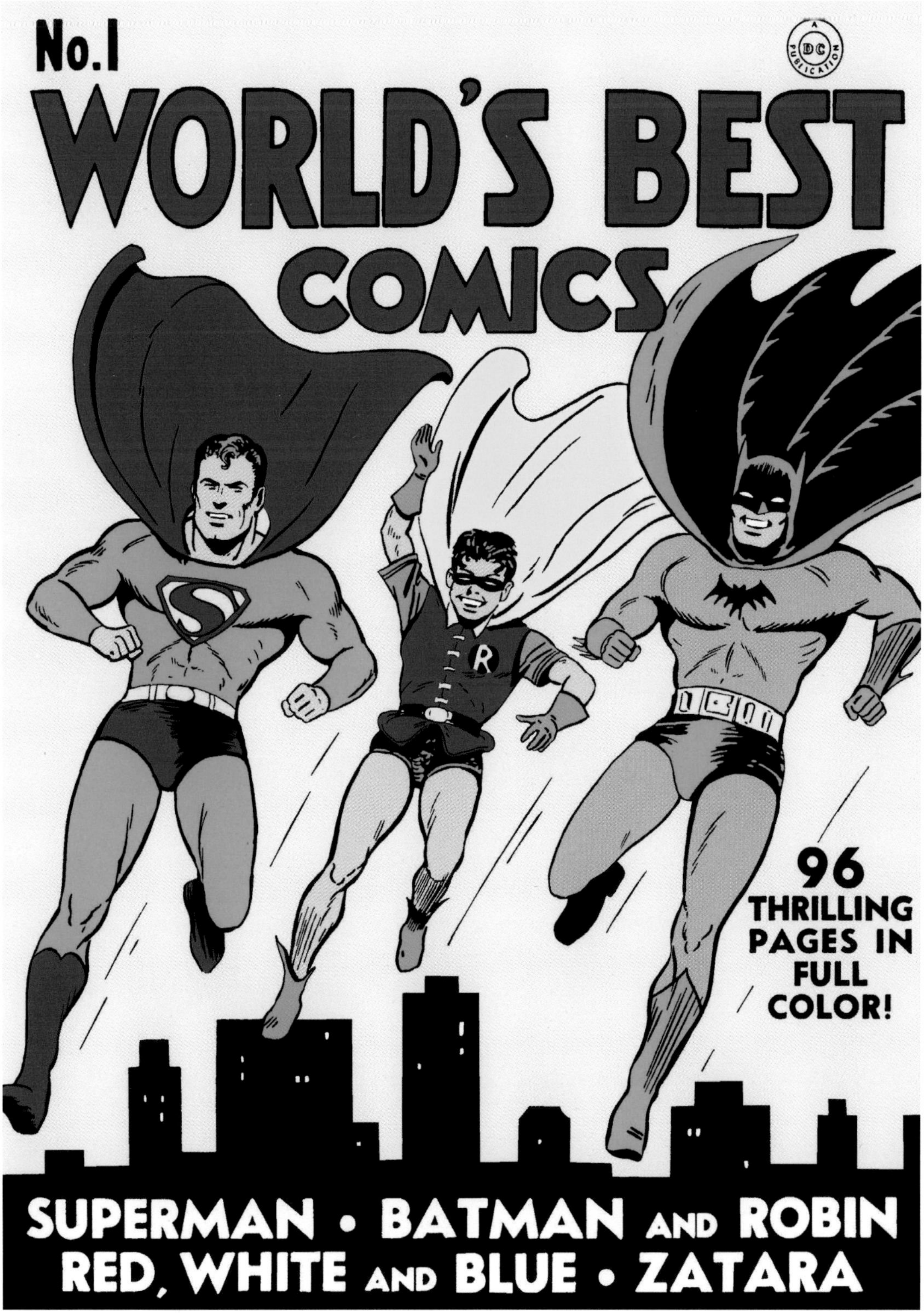
No. 1
A DC PUBLICATION
WORLD'S BEST COMICS
96 THRILLING PAGES IN FULL COLOR!
SUPERMAN • BATMAN AND ROBIN
RED, WHITE AND BLUE • ZATARA

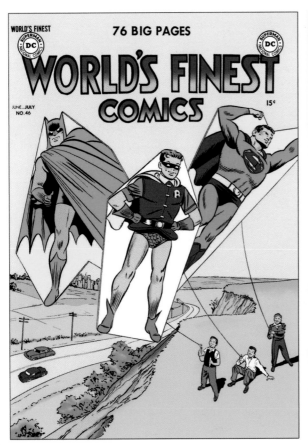

WORLD'S FINEST
76 BIG PAGES
SUPERMAN
DC
NATIONAL COMICS
WORLD'S FINEST
COMICS
JUNE...JULY
NO.46
15¢

▲
World's Finest Comics
Vol. 1, #46
Win Mortimer
Jun. 1950

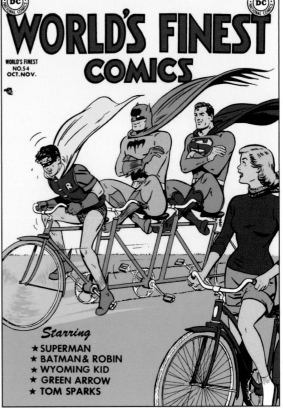

76 BIG PAGES
15c
SUPERMAN
DC
NATIONAL COMICS
WORLD'S FINEST
COMICS
WORLD'S FINEST
NO.54
OCT.NOV.
Starring
★ SUPERMAN
★ BATMAN & ROBIN
★ WYOMING KID
★ GREEN ARROW
★ TOM SPARKS

▲
World's Finest Comics
Vol. 1, #54
Win Mortimer
Oct. 1951

▶
World's Finest Comics
Vol. 1, #39
Win Mortimer
Mar. 1949

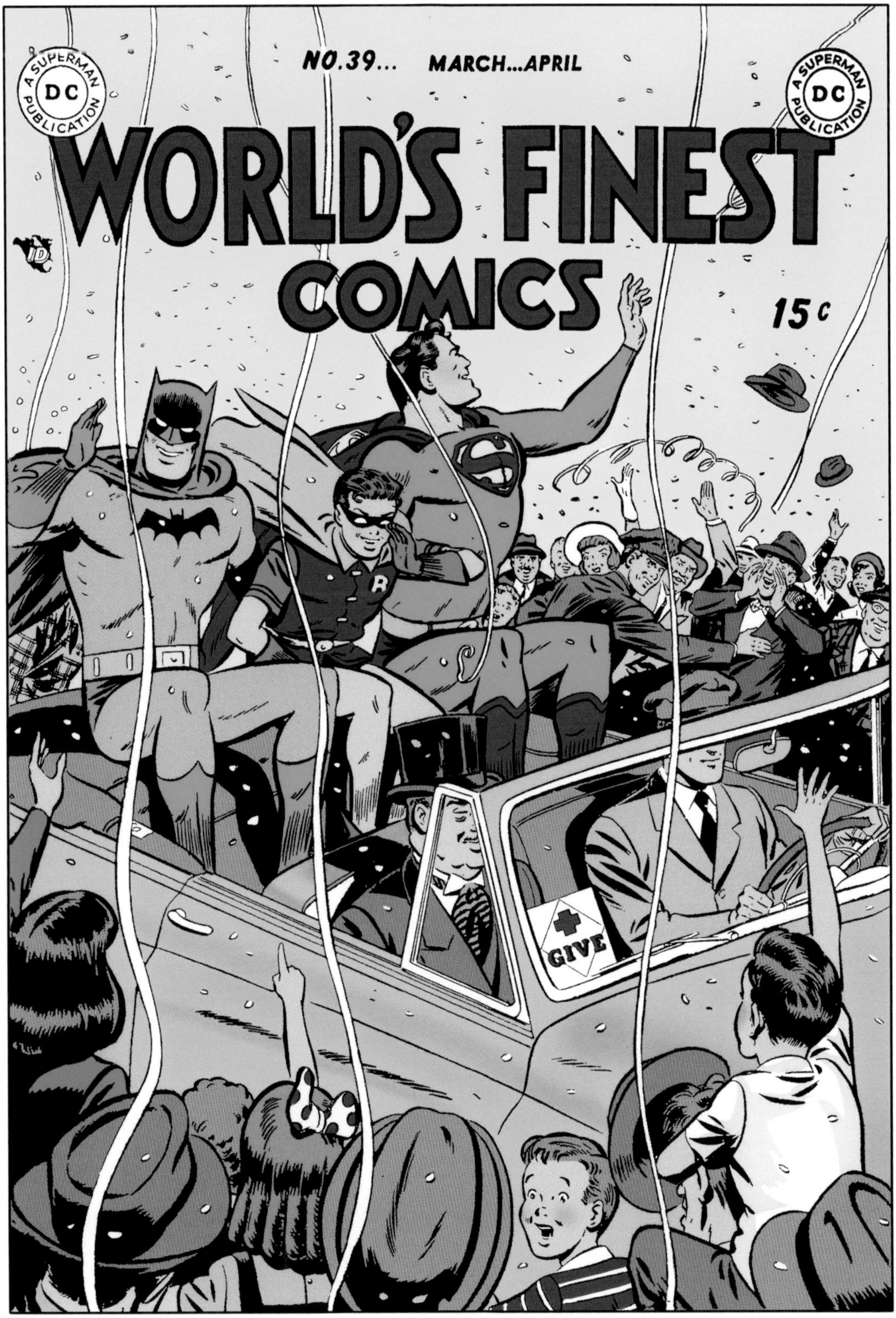

NO.39... MARCH...APRIL
A SUPERMAN DC PUBLICATION
A SUPERMAN DC PUBLICATION
WORLD'S FINEST COMICS
15¢
GIVE

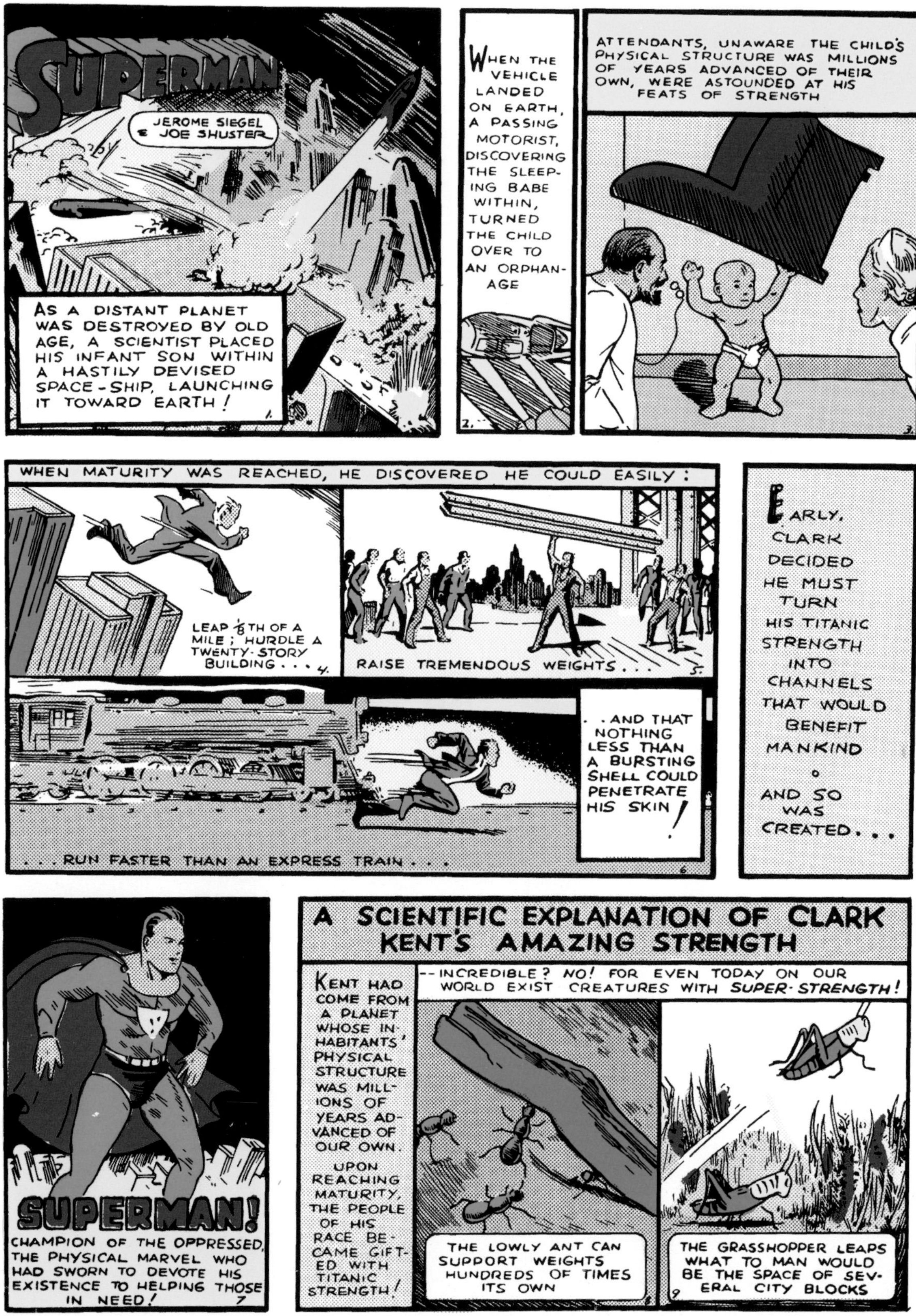
SUPERMAN
JEROME SIEGEL & JOE SHUSTER
AS A DISTANT PLANET WAS DESTROYED BY OLD AGE, A SCIENTIST PLACED HIS INFANT SON WITHIN A HASTILY DEVISED SPACE-SHIP, LAUNCHING IT TOWARD EARTH!
1.
WHEN THE VEHICLE LANDED ON EARTH, A PASSING MOTORIST, DISCOVERING THE SLEEPING BABE WITHIN, TURNED THE CHILD OVER TO AN ORPHANAGE
2.
ATTENDANTS, UNAWARE THE CHILD'S PHYSICAL STRUCTURE WAS MILLIONS OF YEARS ADVANCED OF THEIR OWN, WERE ASTOUNDED AT HIS FEATS OF STRENGTH
3.
WHEN MATURITY WAS REACHED, HE DISCOVERED HE COULD EASILY:
LEAP 1/8TH OF A MILE; HURDLE A TWENTY-STORY BUILDING . . .
4.
RAISE TREMENDOUS WEIGHTS . . .
5.
. . . RUN FASTER THAN AN EXPRESS TRAIN . . .
. . AND THAT NOTHING LESS THAN A BURSTING SHELL COULD PENETRATE HIS SKIN!
6
EARLY, CLARK DECIDED HE MUST TURN HIS TITANIC STRENGTH INTO CHANNELS THAT WOULD BENEFIT MANKIND
AND SO WAS CREATED . . .
SUPERMAN!
CHAMPION OF THE OPPRESSED, THE PHYSICAL MARVEL WHO HAD SWORN TO DEVOTE HIS EXISTENCE TO HELPING THOSE IN NEED!
7
A SCIENTIFIC EXPLANATION OF CLARK KENT'S AMAZING STRENGTH
KENT HAD COME FROM A PLANET WHOSE INHABITANTS' PHYSICAL STRUCTURE WAS MILLIONS OF YEARS ADVANCED OF OUR OWN. UPON REACHING MATURITY, THE PEOPLE OF HIS RACE BECAME GIFTED WITH TITANIC STRENGTH!
--INCREDIBLE? NO! FOR EVEN TODAY ON OUR WORLD EXIST CREATURES WITH SUPER-STRENGTH!
THE LOWLY ANT CAN SUPPORT WEIGHTS HUNDREDS OF TIMES ITS OWN
8
THE GRASSHOPPER LEAPS WHAT TO MAN WOULD BE THE SPACE OF SEVERAL CITY BLOCKS
9

◀
Action Comics
Vol. 1, #1
Jerry Siegel,
Joe Shuster
Jun. 1938, p. 1

▶
Superman
Vol. 1, #50
Wayne Boring
Jan. 1948

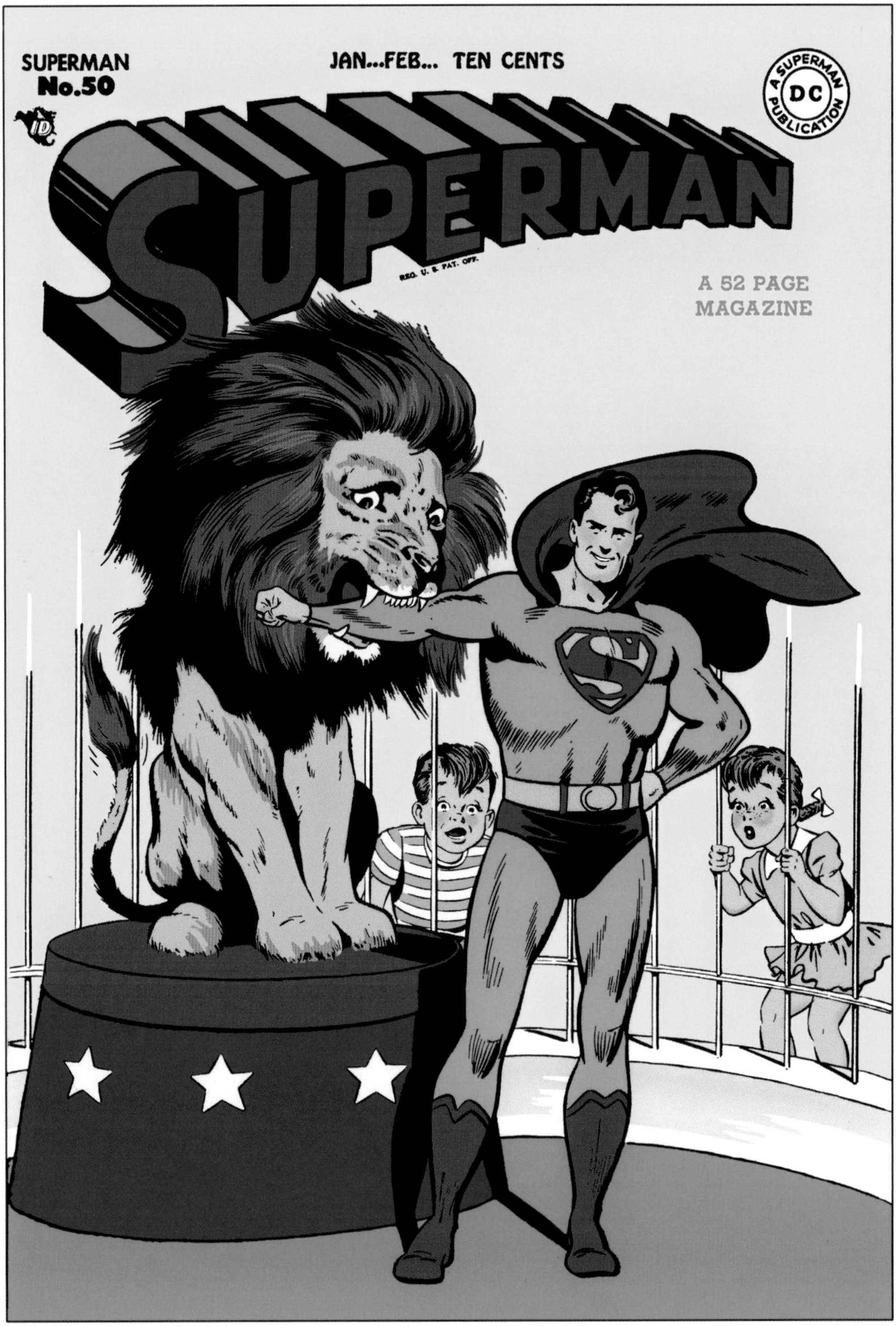
SUPERMAN
No.50
JAN...FEB... TEN CENTS
A SUPERMAN DC PUBLICATION
SUPERMAN
REG. U. S. PAT. OFF.
A 52 PAGE
MAGAZINE

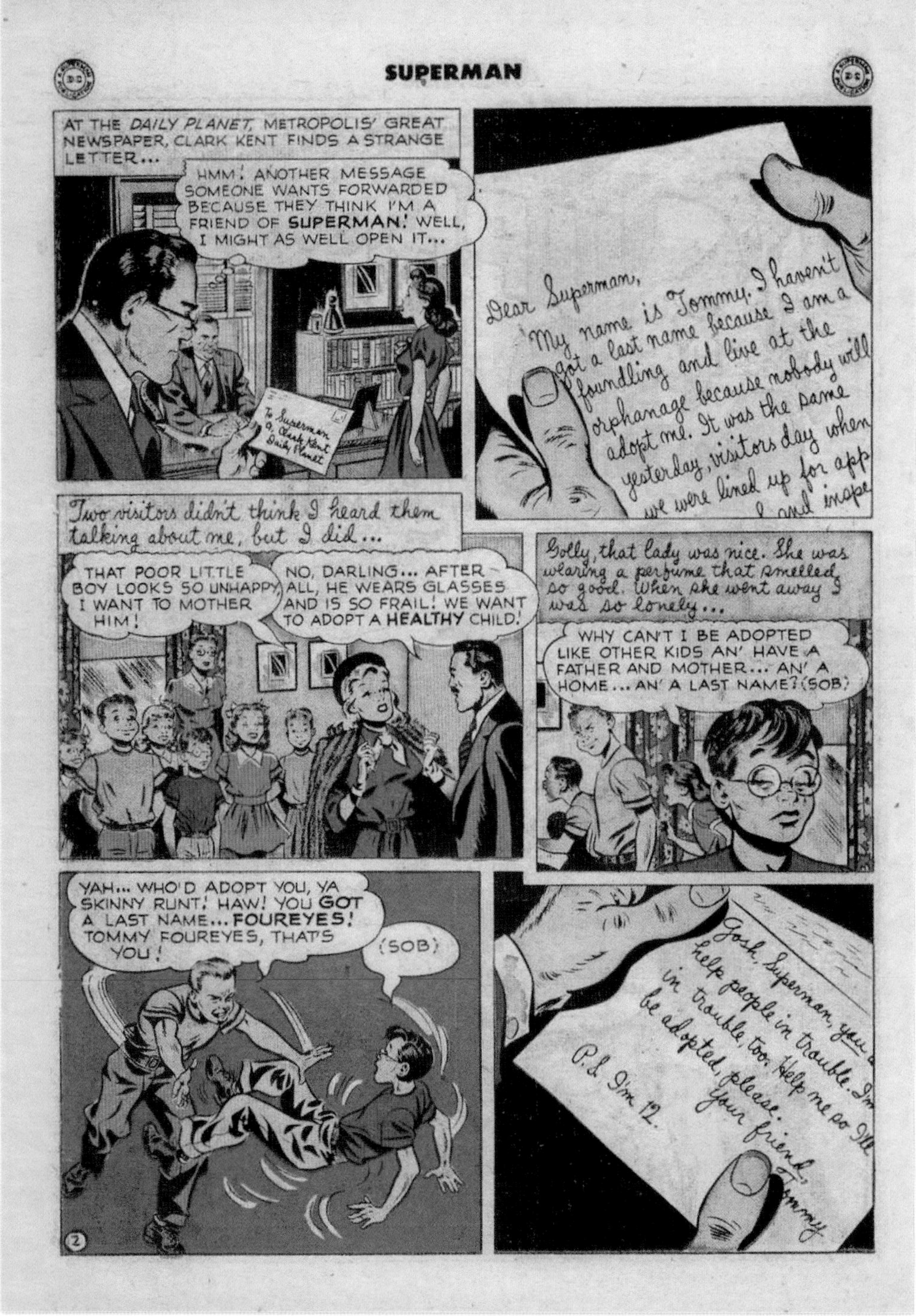
SUPERMAN
AT THE DAILY PLANET, METROPOLIS' GREAT NEWSPAPER, CLARK KENT FINDS A STRANGE LETTER...
HMM! ANOTHER MESSAGE SOMEONE WANTS FORWARDED BECAUSE THEY THINK I'M A FRIEND OF SUPERMAN! WELL, I MIGHT AS WELL OPEN IT...
To Superman c/o Clark Kent Daily Planet
Dear Superman,
My name is Tommy. I haven't got a last name because I am a foundling and live at the orphanage because nobody will adopt me. It was the same yesterday, visitors day when we were lined up for app
Two visitors didn't think I heard them talking about me, but I did...
THAT POOR LITTLE BOY LOOKS SO UNHAPPY. I WANT TO MOTHER HIM!
NO, DARLING... AFTER ALL, HE WEARS GLASSES AND IS SO FRAIL! WE WANT TO ADOPT A HEALTHY CHILD!
Golly, that lady was nice. She was wearing a perfume that smelled so good. When she went away I was so lonely...
WHY CAN'T I BE ADOPTED LIKE OTHER KIDS AN' HAVE A FATHER AND MOTHER... AN' A HOME... AN' A LAST NAME? (SOB)
YAH... WHO'D ADOPT YOU, YA SKINNY RUNT! HAW! YOU GOT A LAST NAME... FOUREYES! TOMMY FOUREYES, THAT'S YOU!
(SOB)
Gosh, Superman, you help people in trouble. I'm in trouble, too. Help me so I'll be adopted, please.
Your friend, Tommy
P.S. I'm 12.
2

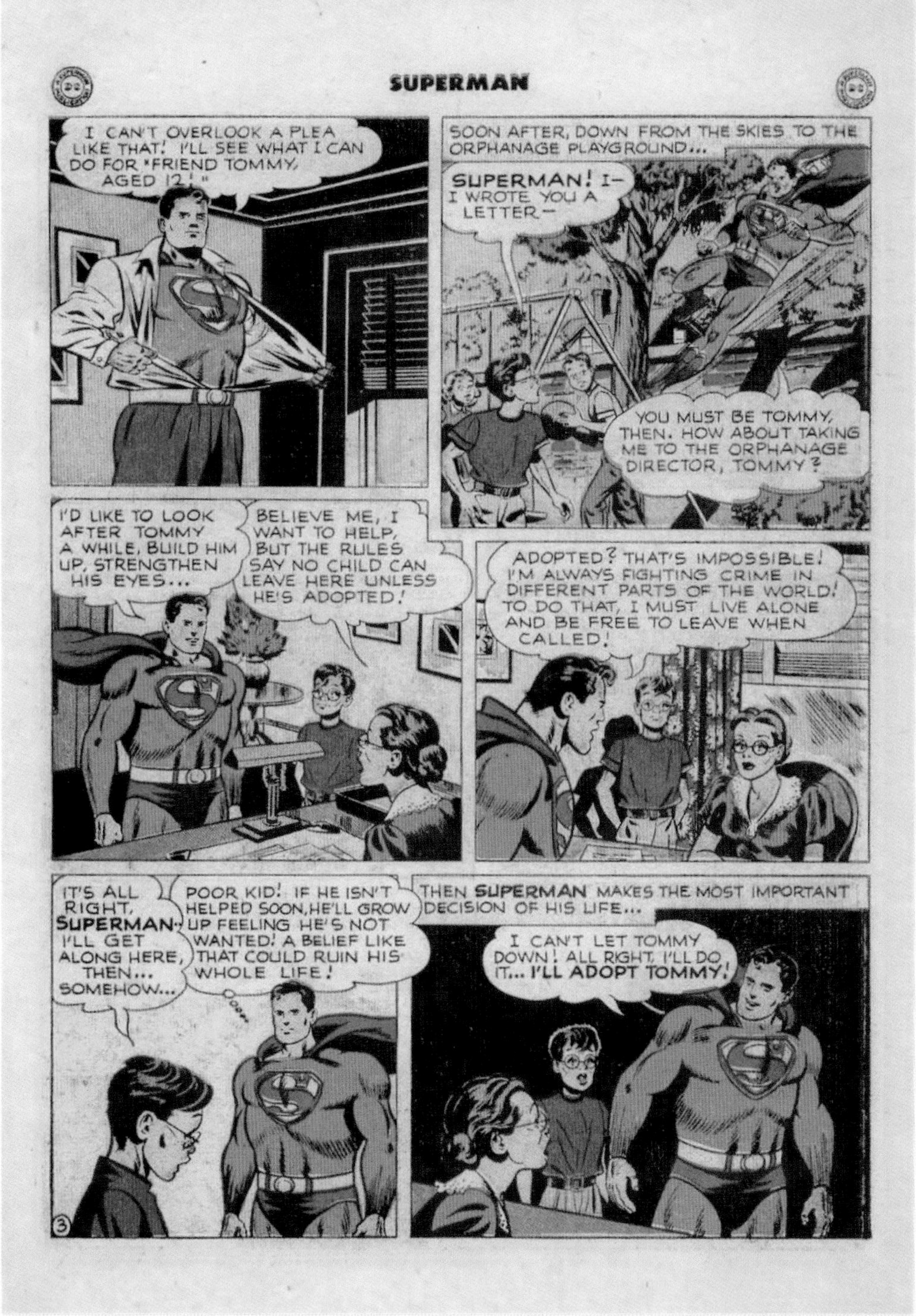
SUPERMAN
I CAN'T OVERLOOK A PLEA LIKE THAT! I'LL SEE WHAT I CAN DO FOR "FRIEND TOMMY, AGED 12!"
SOON AFTER, DOWN FROM THE SKIES TO THE ORPHANAGE PLAYGROUND...
SUPERMAN! I– I WROTE YOU A LETTER–
YOU MUST BE TOMMY, THEN. HOW ABOUT TAKING ME TO THE ORPHANAGE DIRECTOR, TOMMY?
I'D LIKE TO LOOK AFTER TOMMY A WHILE, BUILD HIM UP, STRENGTHEN HIS EYES...
BELIEVE ME, I WANT TO HELP, BUT THE RULES SAY NO CHILD CAN LEAVE HERE UNLESS HE'S ADOPTED!
ADOPTED? THAT'S IMPOSSIBLE! I'M ALWAYS FIGHTING CRIME IN DIFFERENT PARTS OF THE WORLD! TO DO THAT, I MUST LIVE ALONE AND BE FREE TO LEAVE WHEN CALLED!
IT'S ALL RIGHT, SUPERMAN. I'LL GET ALONG HERE, THEN... SOMEHOW...
POOR KID! IF HE ISN'T HELPED SOON, HE'LL GROW UP FEELING HE'S NOT WANTED! A BELIEF LIKE THAT COULD RUIN HIS WHOLE LIFE!
THEN SUPERMAN MAKES THE MOST IMPORTANT DECISION OF HIS LIFE...
I CAN'T LET TOMMY DOWN! ALL RIGHT, I'LL DO IT... I'LL ADOPT TOMMY!
3

◀ ▶
Superman
Vol. 1, #57
Edmond Hamilton,
Wayne Boring
Mar. 1949
pp. 2–3

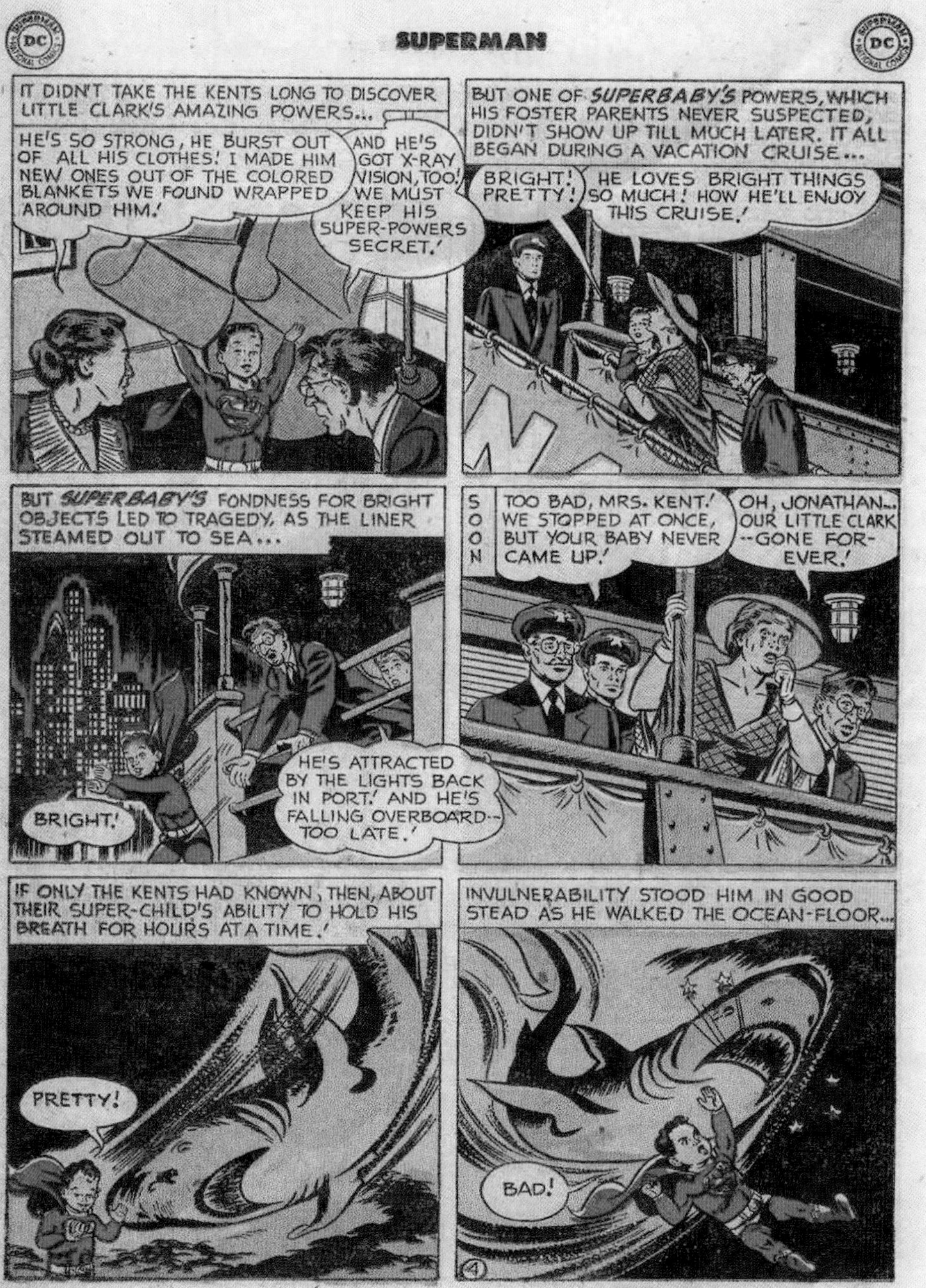
SUPERMAN
IT DIDN'T TAKE THE KENTS LONG TO DISCOVER LITTLE CLARK'S AMAZING POWERS...
HE'S SO STRONG, HE BURST OUT OF ALL HIS CLOTHES! I MADE HIM NEW ONES OUT OF THE COLORED BLANKETS WE FOUND WRAPPED AROUND HIM!
AND HE'S GOT X-RAY VISION, TOO! WE MUST KEEP HIS SUPER-POWERS SECRET!
BUT ONE OF SUPERBABY'S POWERS, WHICH HIS FOSTER PARENTS NEVER SUSPECTED, DIDN'T SHOW UP TILL MUCH LATER. IT ALL BEGAN DURING A VACATION CRUISE...
BRIGHT! PRETTY!
HE LOVES BRIGHT THINGS SO MUCH! HOW HE'LL ENJOY THIS CRUISE!
BUT SUPERBABY'S FONDNESS FOR BRIGHT OBJECTS LED TO TRAGEDY, AS THE LINER STEAMED OUT TO SEA...
BRIGHT!
HE'S ATTRACTED BY THE LIGHTS BACK IN PORT! AND HE'S FALLING OVERBOARD-- TOO LATE!
SOON
TOO BAD, MRS. KENT! WE STOPPED AT ONCE, BUT YOUR BABY NEVER CAME UP!
OH, JONATHAN... OUR LITTLE CLARK --GONE FOR-EVER!
IF ONLY THE KENTS HAD KNOWN, THEN, ABOUT THEIR SUPER-CHILD'S ABILITY TO HOLD HIS BREATH FOR HOURS AT A TIME!
PRETTY!
INVULNERABILITY STOOD HIM IN GOOD STEAD AS HE WALKED THE OCEAN-FLOOR...
BAD!
4

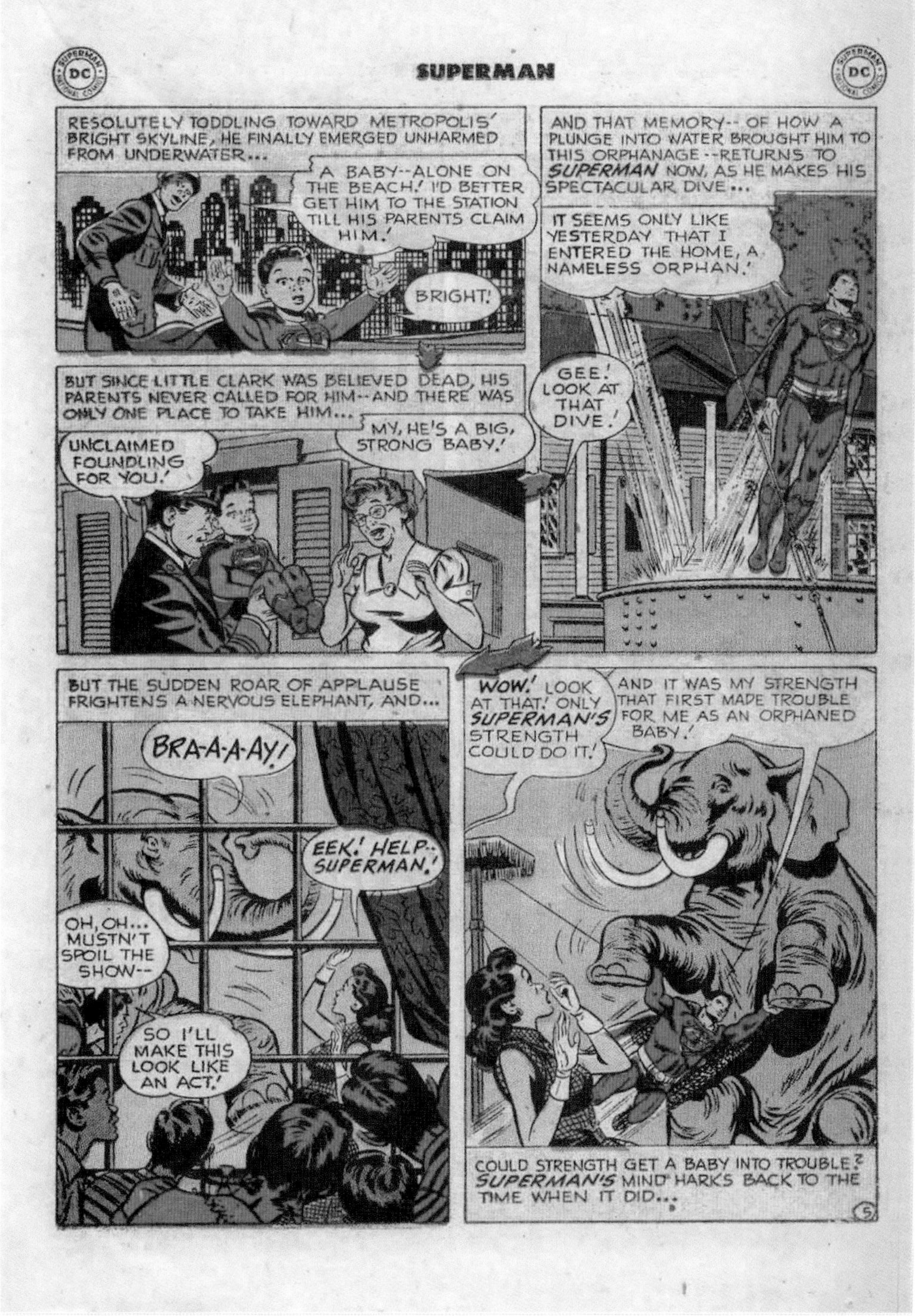
SUPERMAN
RESOLUTELY TODDLING TOWARD METROPOLIS' BRIGHT SKYLINE, HE FINALLY EMERGED UNHARMED FROM UNDERWATER...
A BABY--ALONE ON THE BEACH! I'D BETTER GET HIM TO THE STATION TILL HIS PARENTS CLAIM HIM!
BRIGHT!
AND THAT MEMORY-- OF HOW A PLUNGE INTO WATER BROUGHT HIM TO THIS ORPHANAGE --RETURNS TO SUPERMAN NOW, AS HE MAKES HIS SPECTACULAR DIVE...
IT SEEMS ONLY LIKE YESTERDAY THAT I ENTERED THE HOME, A NAMELESS ORPHAN!
BUT SINCE LITTLE CLARK WAS BELIEVED DEAD, HIS PARENTS NEVER CALLED FOR HIM--AND THERE WAS ONLY ONE PLACE TO TAKE HIM...
MY, HE'S A BIG, STRONG BABY!
UNCLAIMED FOUNDLING FOR YOU!
GEE! LOOK AT THAT DIVE!
BUT THE SUDDEN ROAR OF APPLAUSE FRIGHTENS A NERVOUS ELEPHANT, AND...
BRA-A-A-AY!
EEK! HELP-- SUPERMAN!
OH, OH... MUSTN'T SPOIL THE SHOW--
SO I'LL MAKE THIS LOOK LIKE AN ACT!
WOW! LOOK AT THAT! ONLY SUPERMAN'S STRENGTH COULD DO IT!
AND IT WAS MY STRENGTH THAT FIRST MADE TROUBLE FOR ME AS AN ORPHANED BABY!
COULD STRENGTH GET A BABY INTO TROUBLE? SUPERMAN'S MIND HARKS BACK TO THE TIME WHEN IT DID...
5

◀ ▶
Superman
Vol. 1, #73
Bill Finger,
Al Plastino
Nov. 1951
pp. 4–5

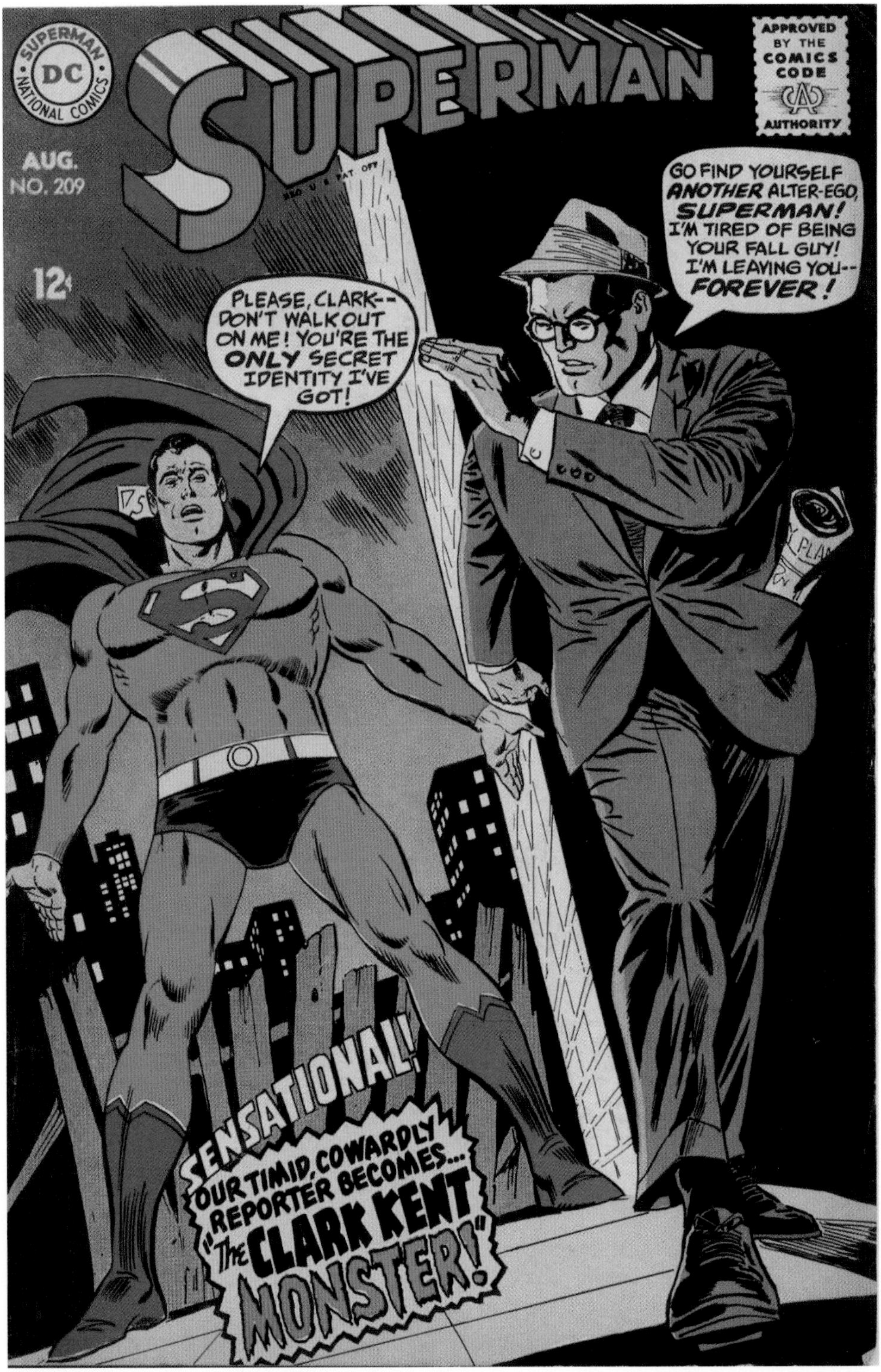
SUPERMAN
SUPERMAN DC NATIONAL COMICS
APPROVED BY THE COMICS CODE AUTHORITY
AUG. NO. 209
12¢
PLEASE, CLARK-- DON'T WALK OUT ON ME! YOU'RE THE ONLY SECRET IDENTITY I'VE GOT!
GO FIND YOURSELF ANOTHER ALTER-EGO, SUPERMAN! I'M TIRED OF BEING YOUR FALL GUY! I'M LEAVING YOU-- FOREVER!
SENSATIONAL! OUR TIMID, COWARDLY REPORTER BECOMES... "The CLARK KENT MONSTER!"

◄
Superman
Vol. 1, #209
Ross Andru,
Mike Esposito
Aug. 1968

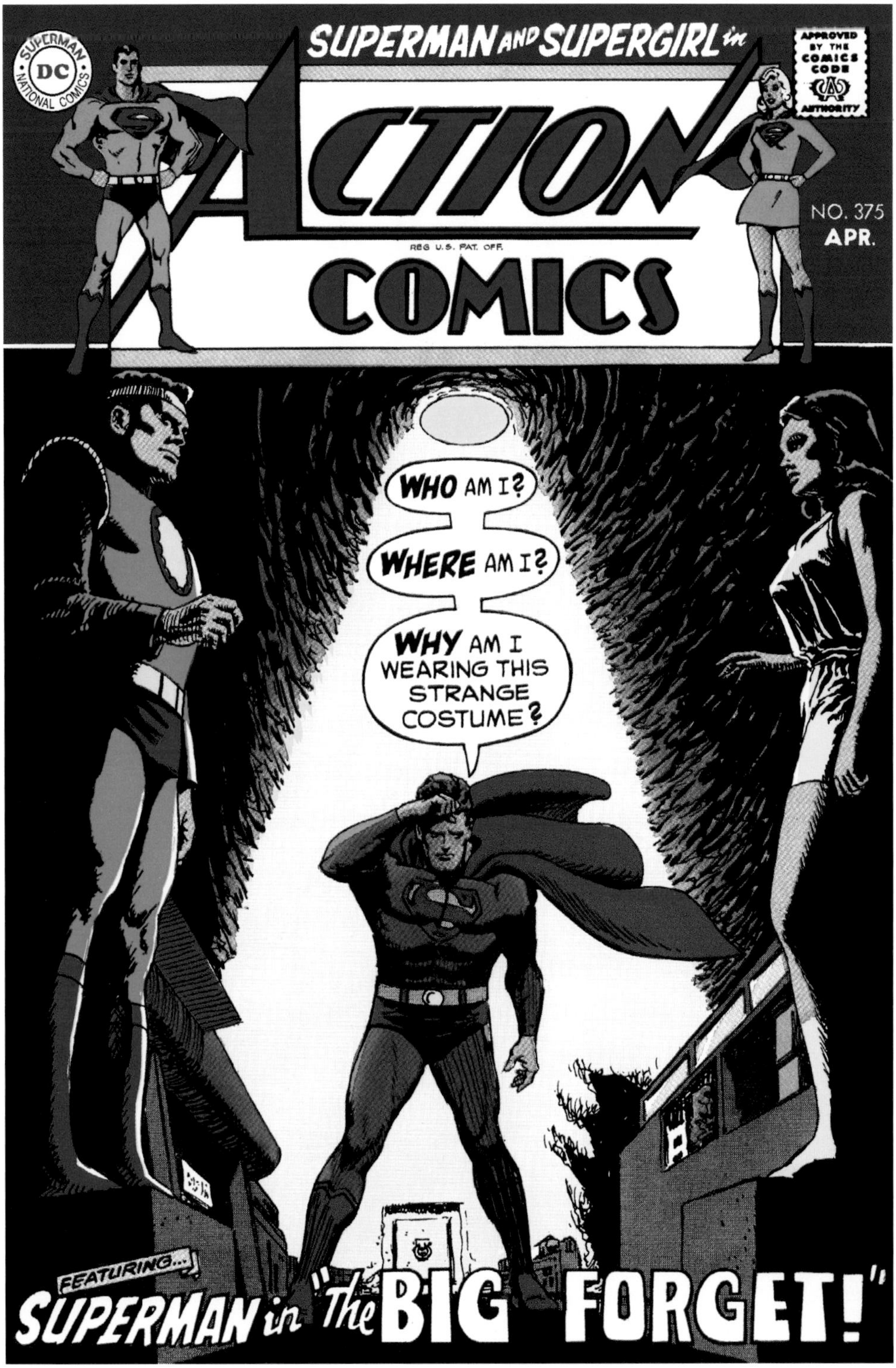
SUPERMAN AND SUPERGIRL in
ACTION COMICS
REG. U.S. PAT. OFF.
NO. 375
APR.
APPROVED BY THE COMICS CODE AUTHORITY
SUPERMAN DC NATIONAL COMICS
WHO AM I?
WHERE AM I?
WHY AM I WEARING THIS STRANGE COSTUME?
FEATURING...
SUPERMAN in "The BIG FORGET!"

Action Comics
Vol. 1, #375
Curt Swan,
Carmine
Infantino
Apr. 1969

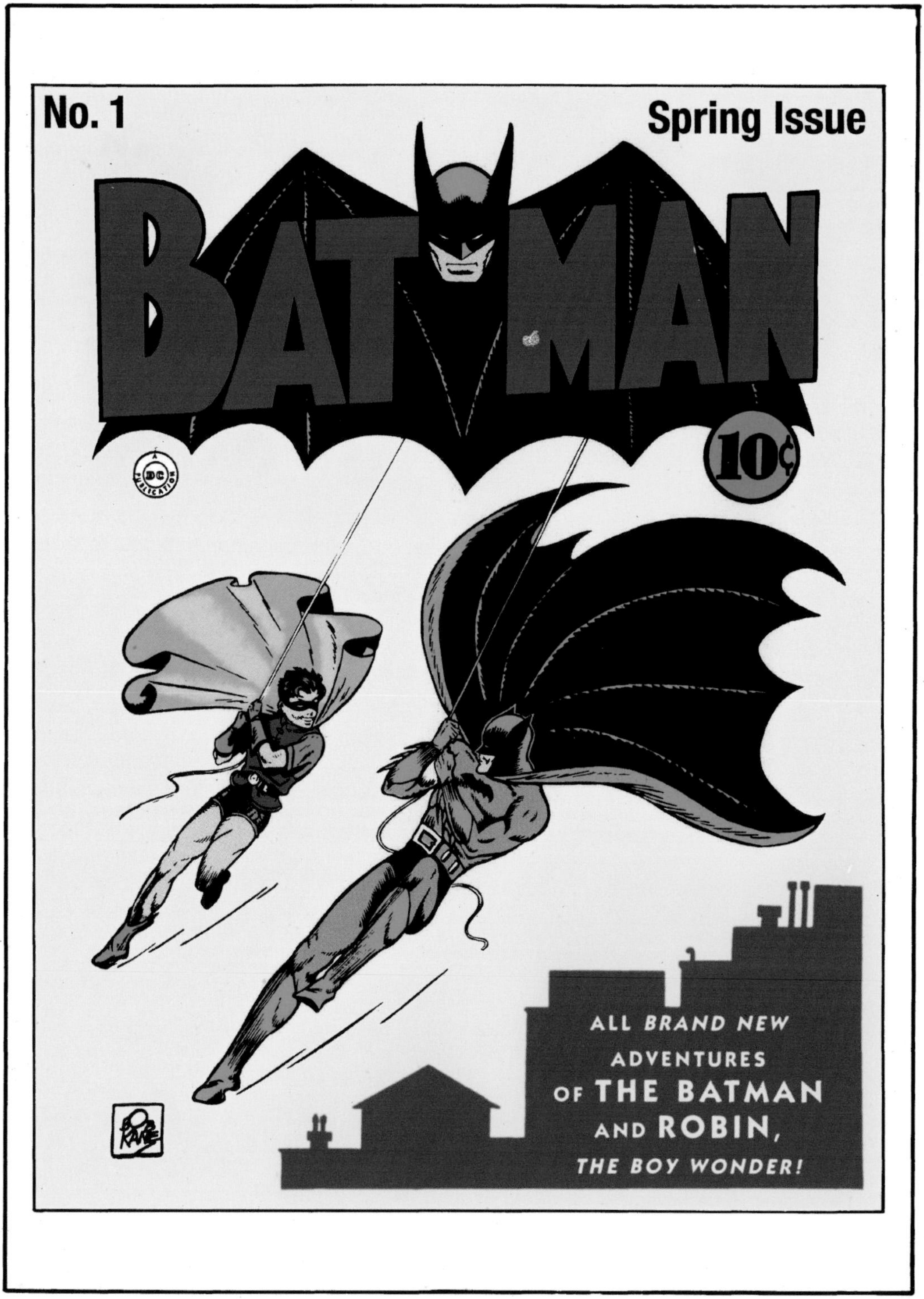
No. 1
Spring Issue
BATMAN
10¢
DC PUBLICATION
KANE
ALL BRAND NEW
ADVENTURES
OF THE BATMAN
AND ROBIN,
THE BOY WONDER!

◄
Batman
Vol. 1, #1
Bob Kane,
Jerry Robinson
Mar. 1940

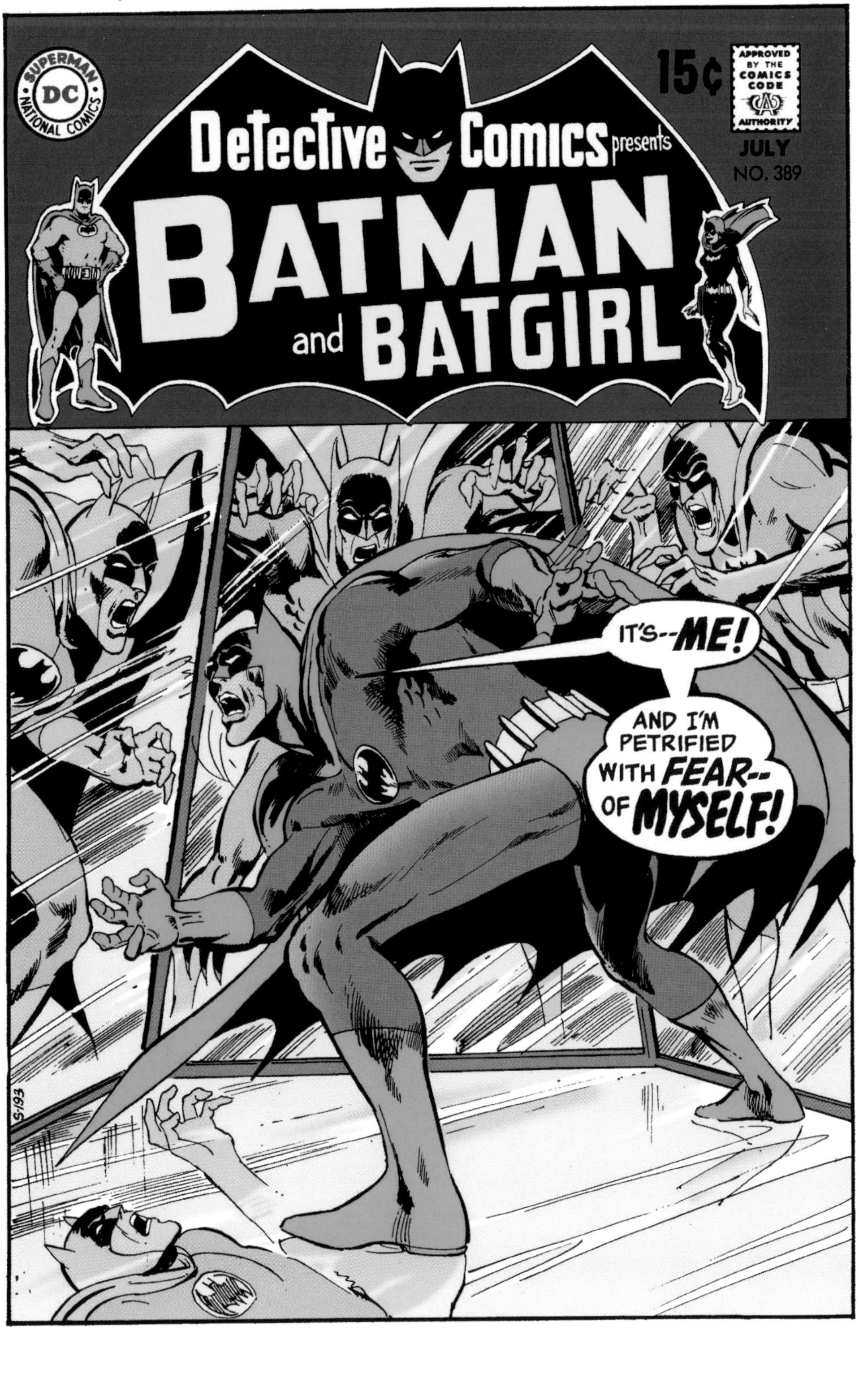
SUPERMAN DC NATIONAL COMICS
15¢
APPROVED BY THE COMICS CODE AUTHORITY
Detective Comics presents
JULY
NO. 389
BATMAN
and BATGIRL
IT'S--ME!
AND I'M PETRIFIED WITH FEAR-- OF MYSELF!
S-193

▶ *Detective Comics*
Vol. 1, #389
Neal Adams,
Gaspar Saladino
Jul. 1969

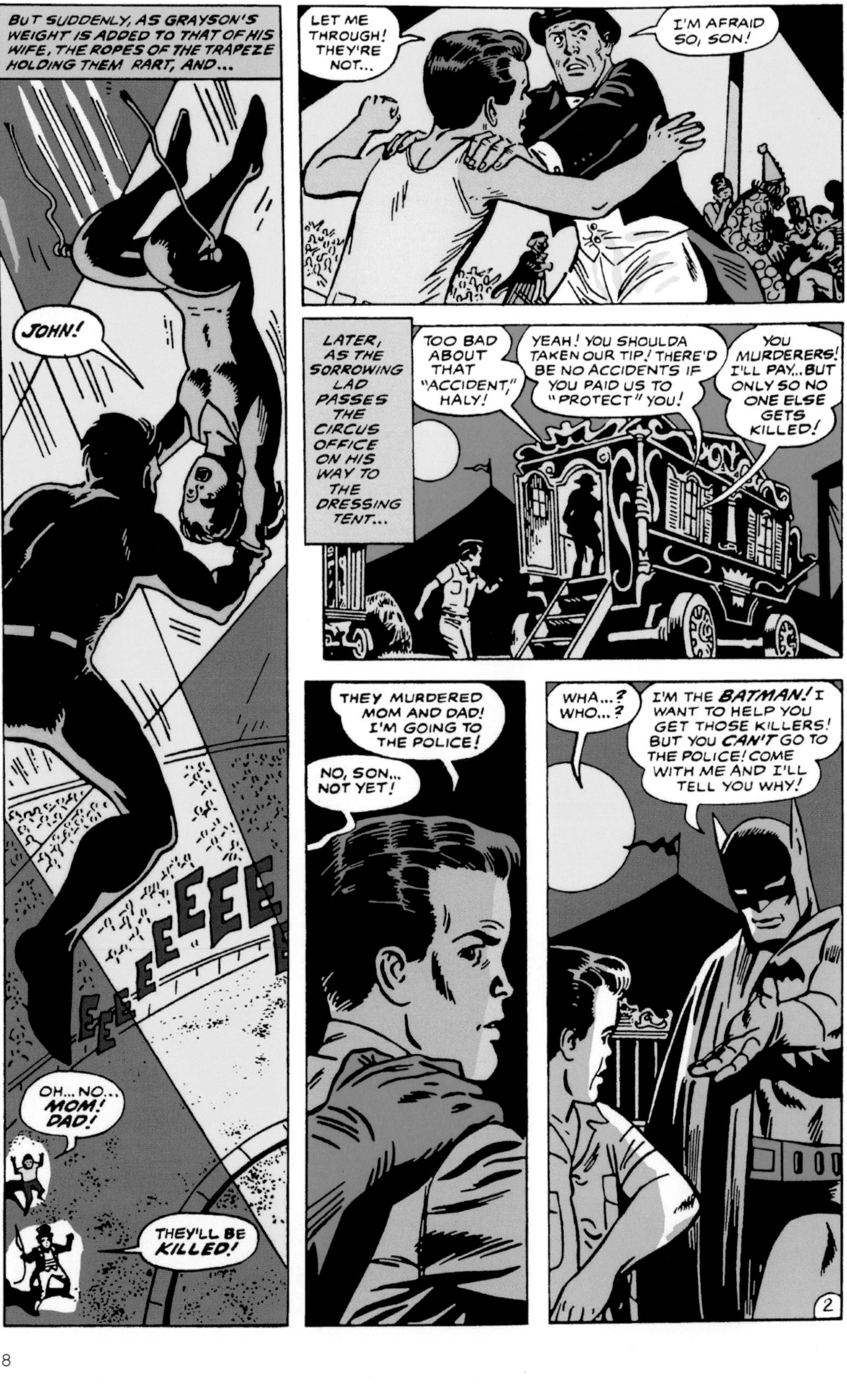

BUT SUDDENLY, AS GRAYSON'S WEIGHT IS ADDED TO THAT OF HIS WIFE, THE ROPES OF THE TRAPEZE HOLDING THEM PART, AND...
JOHN!
EEEEEEEEE
OH...NO... MOM! DAD!
THEY'LL BE KILLED!
LET ME THROUGH! THEY'RE NOT...
I'M AFRAID SO, SON!
LATER, AS THE SORROWING LAD PASSES THE CIRCUS OFFICE ON HIS WAY TO THE DRESSING TENT...
TOO BAD ABOUT THAT "ACCIDENT," HALY!
YEAH! YOU SHOULDA TAKEN OUR TIP! THERE'D BE NO ACCIDENTS IF YOU PAID US TO "PROTECT" YOU!
YOU MURDERERS! I'LL PAY...BUT ONLY SO NO ONE ELSE GETS KILLED!
THEY MURDERED MOM AND DAD! I'M GOING TO THE POLICE!
NO, SON... NOT YET!
WHA...? WHO...?
I'M THE BATMAN! I WANT TO HELP YOU GET THOSE KILLERS! BUT YOU CAN'T GO TO THE POLICE! COME WITH ME AND I'LL TELL YOU WHY!
2

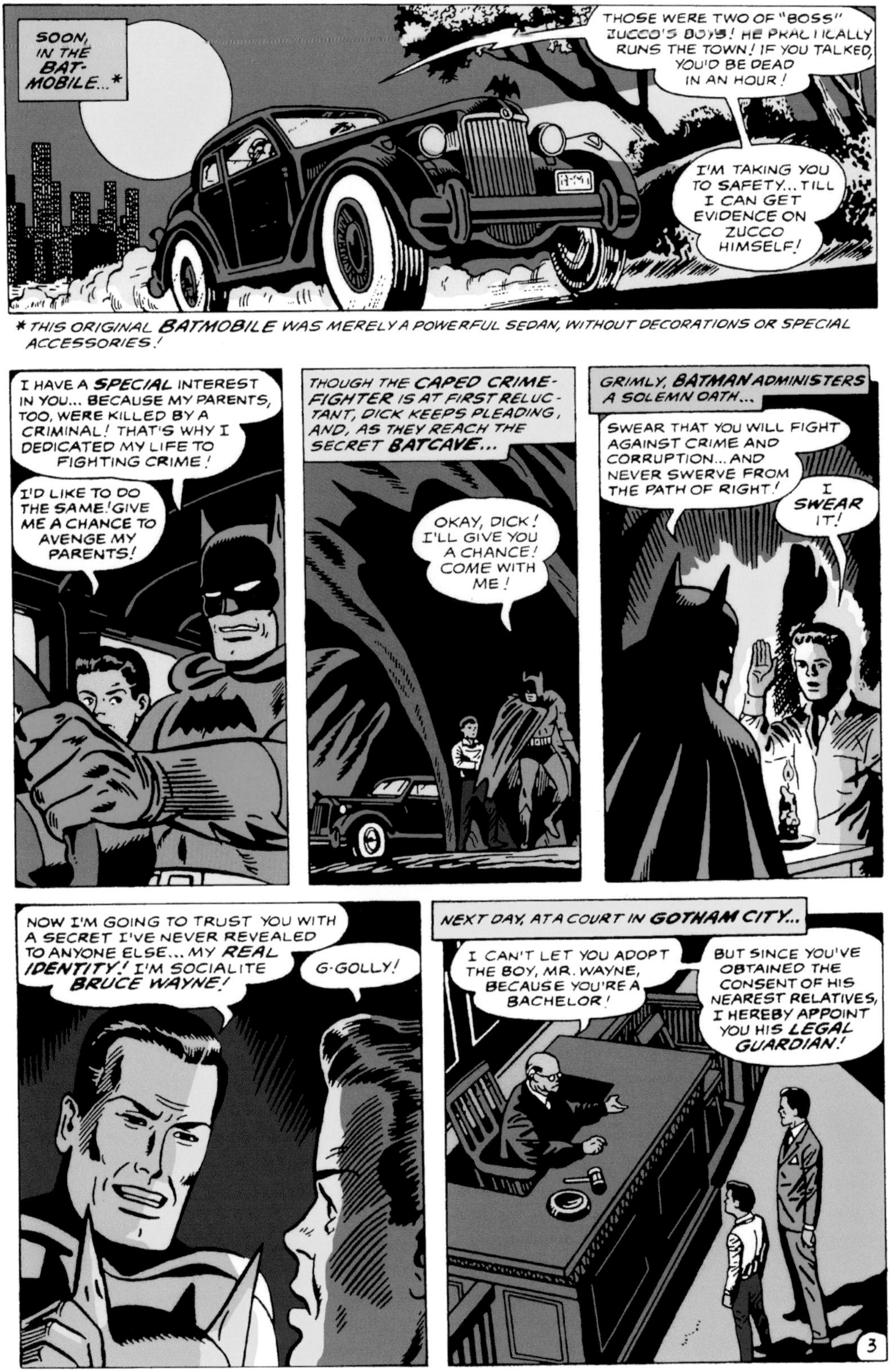

SOON, IN THE BAT-MOBILE...*
THOSE WERE TWO OF "BOSS" ZUCCO'S BOYS! HE PRACTICALLY RUNS THE TOWN! IF YOU TALKED, YOU'D BE DEAD IN AN HOUR!
I'M TAKING YOU TO SAFETY... TILL I CAN GET EVIDENCE ON ZUCCO HIMSELF!
* THIS ORIGINAL BATMOBILE WAS MERELY A POWERFUL SEDAN, WITHOUT DECORATIONS OR SPECIAL ACCESSORIES!
I HAVE A SPECIAL INTEREST IN YOU... BECAUSE MY PARENTS, TOO, WERE KILLED BY A CRIMINAL! THAT'S WHY I DEDICATED MY LIFE TO FIGHTING CRIME!
I'D LIKE TO DO THE SAME! GIVE ME A CHANCE TO AVENGE MY PARENTS!
THOUGH THE CAPED CRIME-FIGHTER IS AT FIRST RELUCTANT, DICK KEEPS PLEADING, AND, AS THEY REACH THE SECRET BATCAVE...
OKAY, DICK! I'LL GIVE YOU A CHANCE! COME WITH ME!
GRIMLY, BATMAN ADMINISTERS A SOLEMN OATH...
SWEAR THAT YOU WILL FIGHT AGAINST CRIME AND CORRUPTION... AND NEVER SWERVE FROM THE PATH OF RIGHT!
I SWEAR IT!
NOW I'M GOING TO TRUST YOU WITH A SECRET I'VE NEVER REVEALED TO ANYONE ELSE... MY REAL IDENTITY! I'M SOCIALITE BRUCE WAYNE!
G-GOLLY!
NEXT DAY, AT A COURT IN GOTHAM CITY...
I CAN'T LET YOU ADOPT THE BOY, MR. WAYNE, BECAUSE YOU'RE A BACHELOR!
BUT SINCE YOU'VE OBTAINED THE CONSENT OF HIS NEAREST RELATIVES, I HEREBY APPOINT YOU HIS LEGAL GUARDIAN!
3

◀ ▶
Batman
Vol. 1, #213
E. Nelson Bridwell,
Ross Andru,
Mike Esposito
Aug. 1969
pp. 2–3

WANDERINGS OF SANMAO

Zhang Leping, 1935-86

Sanmao was created in 1935 by the famous Chinese cartoonist, Zhang Leping. Sanmao's trademark hairstyle reveals a sombre reality: he is unable to grow more hair because he does not have enough to eat. Charismatic and enterprising, Sanmao wanders through a landscape marked by war, poverty and starvation, always maintaining a naïve and curious outlook. In the 1950s, the character evolved into a visual proponent of the Chinese Communist Party. Zhang Leping continued drawing Sanmao until the 1980s.

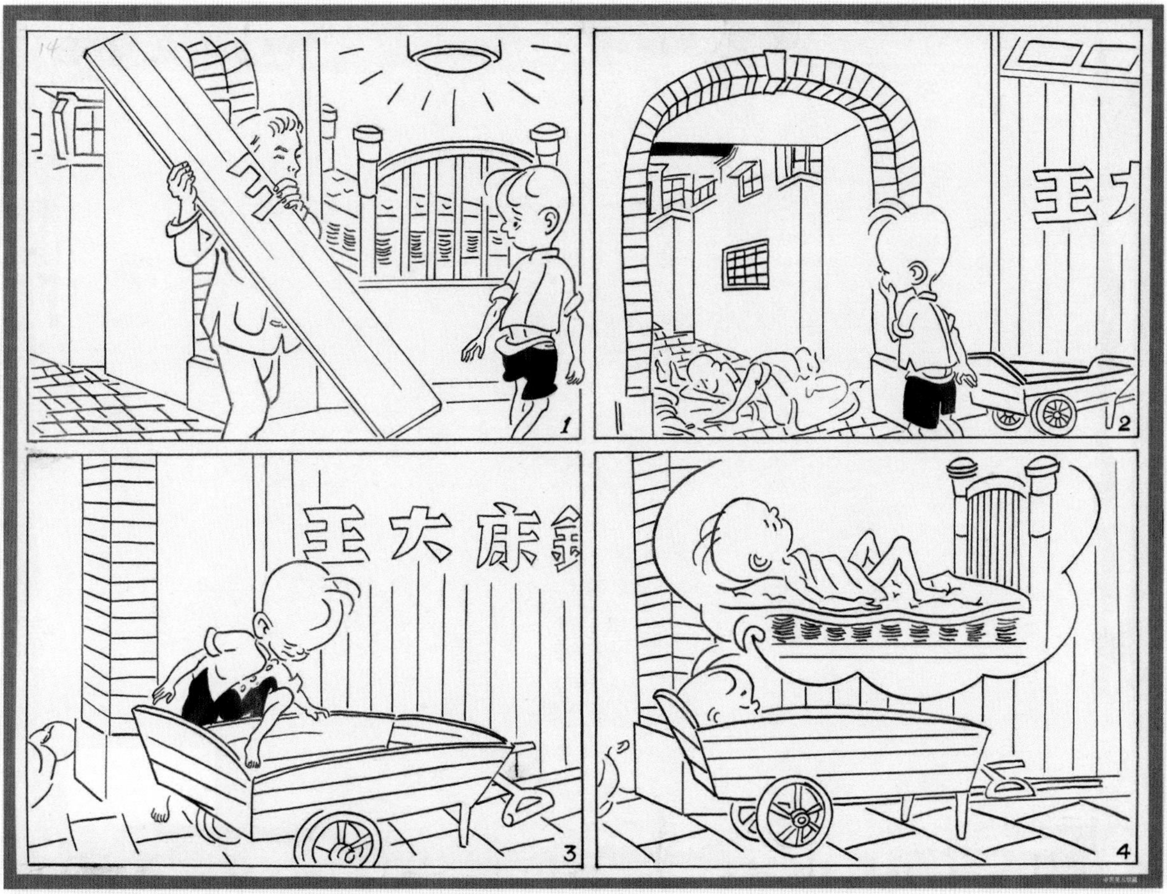
王大庆

▲

Sanmao #17
('A Comfortable Bed')
Zhang Leping
1947–49

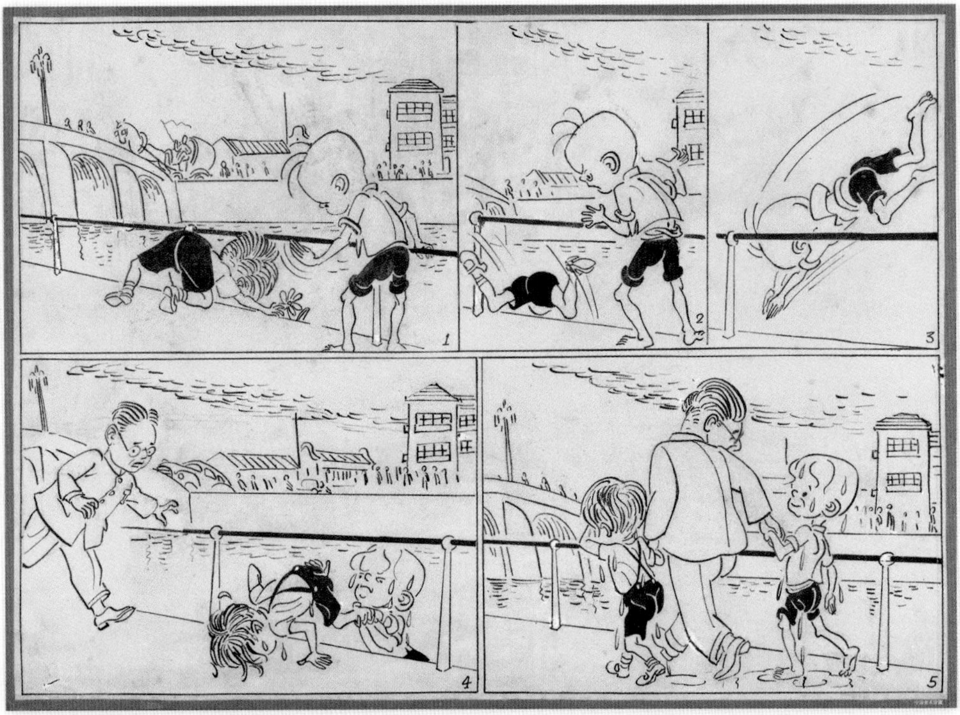

◀
Sanmao #33
('A Brave Deed')
Zhang Leping
1947–49

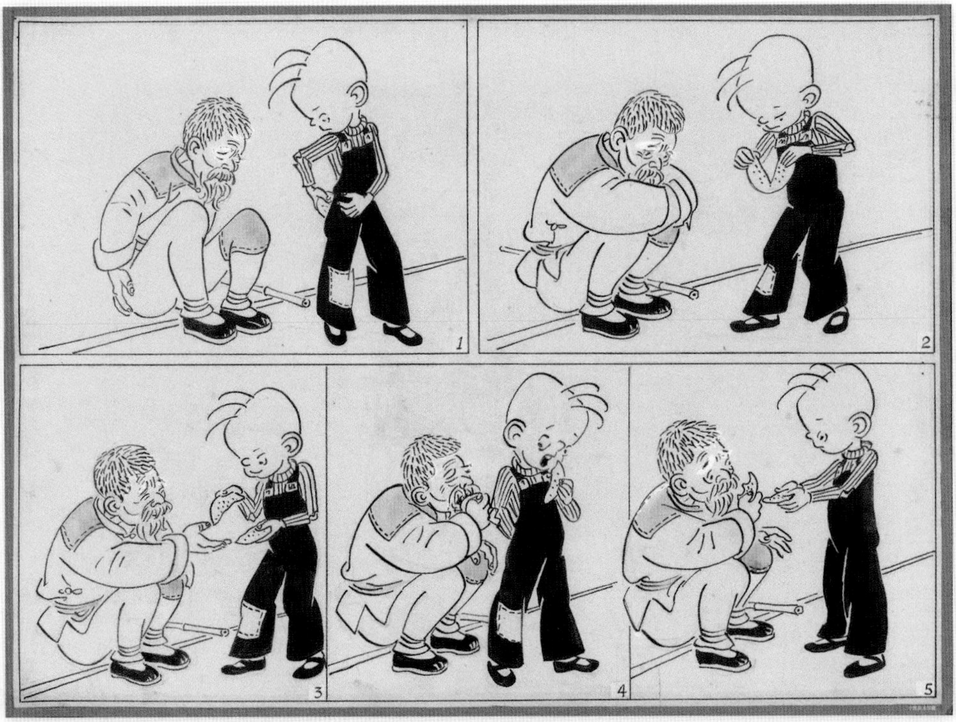

◀
Sanmao #139
('Have It All!')
Zhang Leping
1947–49

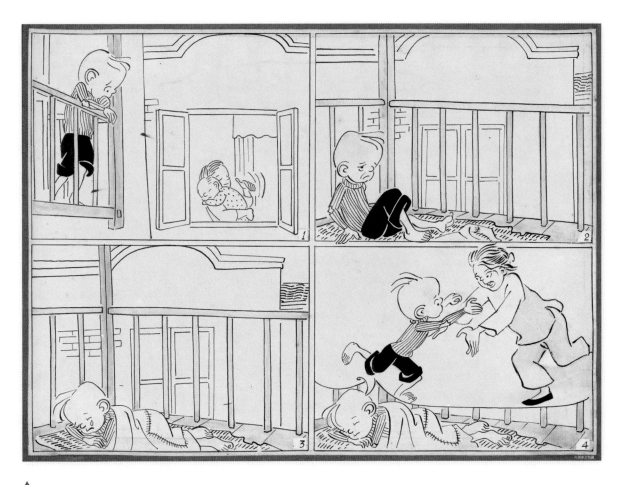

▲
Sanmao #162
('Dreaming of Mum')
Zhang Leping
1947–49

BAREFOOT GEN

Keiji Nakazawa, 1973–87

Barefoot Gen tells the story of Gen Nakaoka, a six-year-old boy who survives the atomic bombing of Hiroshima by American military forces on 6 August 1945. Spread over ten volumes, *Barefoot Gen* documents Gen's escape from the city and his journey to adulthood. The manga is based on Keiji Nakazawa's own experiences, and the nightmarish scenes are intensely immediate and deeply affecting. Nakazawa hoped that Gen's story would show 'the preciousness of peace and the courage we need to live strongly, yet peacefully'.

►
Barefoot Gen
Vol. 2
Keiji Nakazawa
1979, p. 7

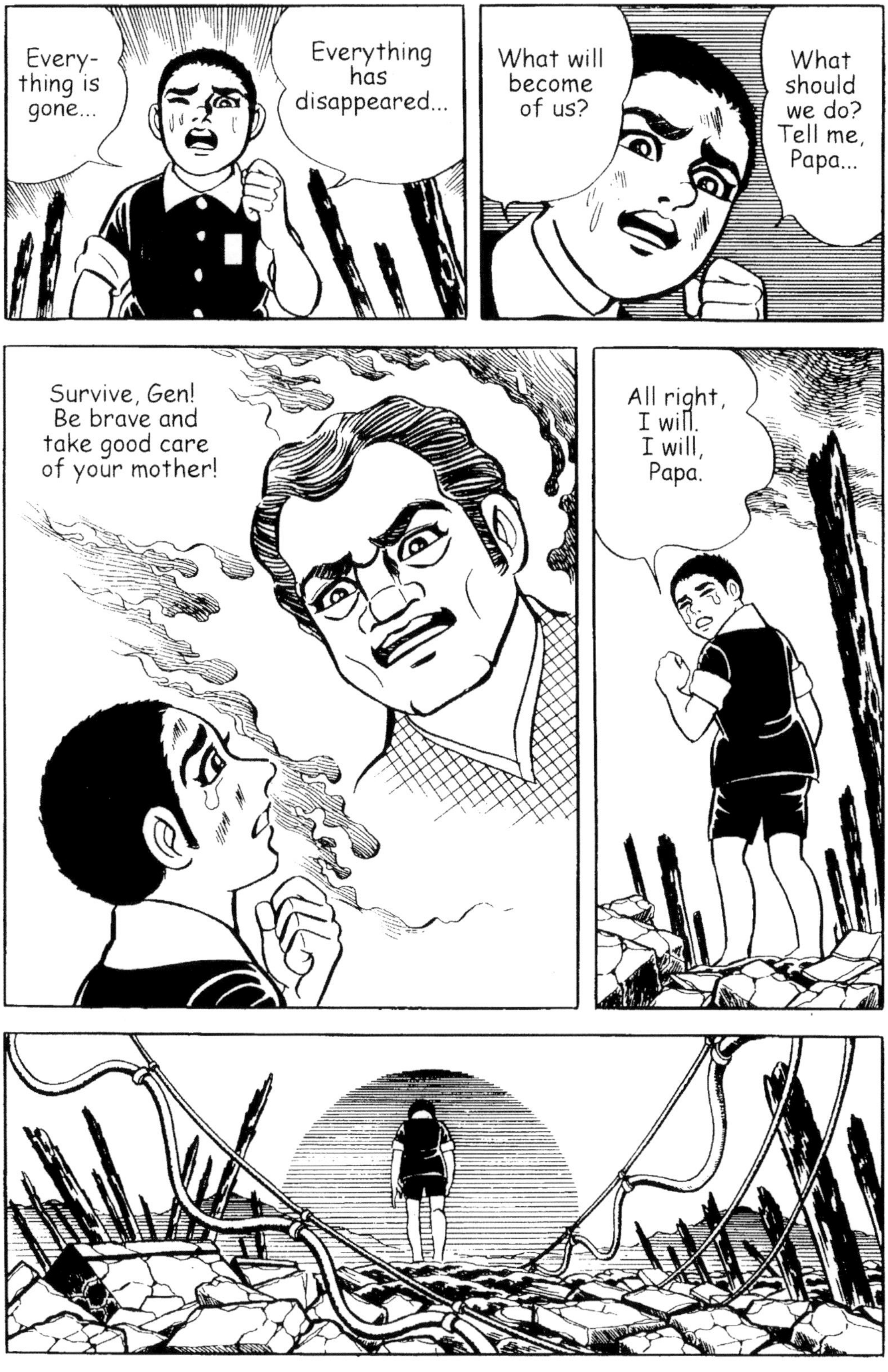
Every-thing is gone...
Everything has disappeared...
What will become of us?
What should we do? Tell me, Papa...
Survive, Gen! Be brave and take good care of your mother!
All right, I will. I will, Papa.

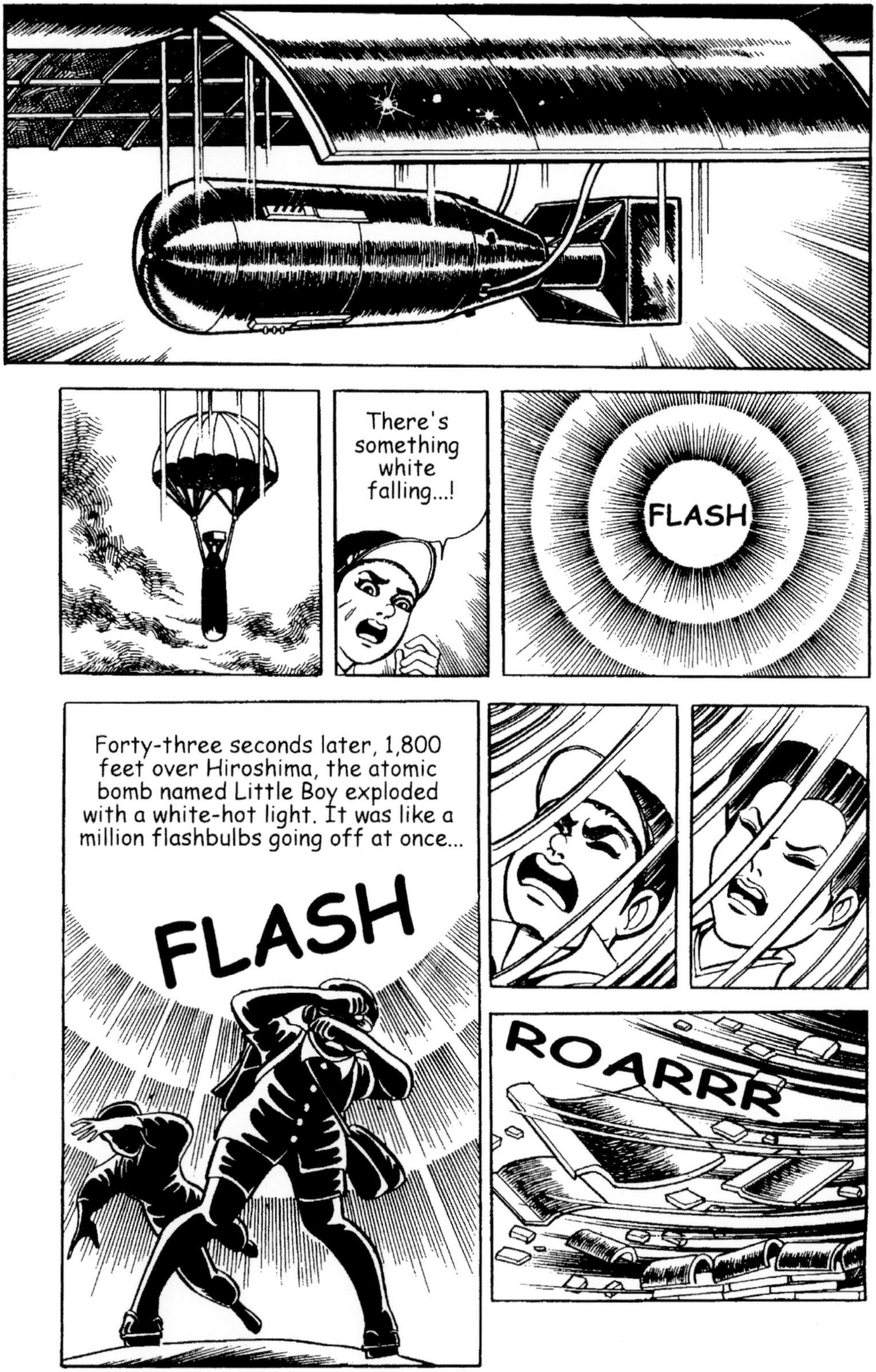
There's something white falling...!
FLASH
Forty-three seconds later, 1,800 feet over Hiroshima, the atomic bomb named Little Boy exploded with a white-hot light. It was like a million flashbulbs going off at once...
FLASH
ROARRR

◀ ▶
Barefoot Gen
Vol. 1
Keiji Nakazawa
1978, pp. 250–1

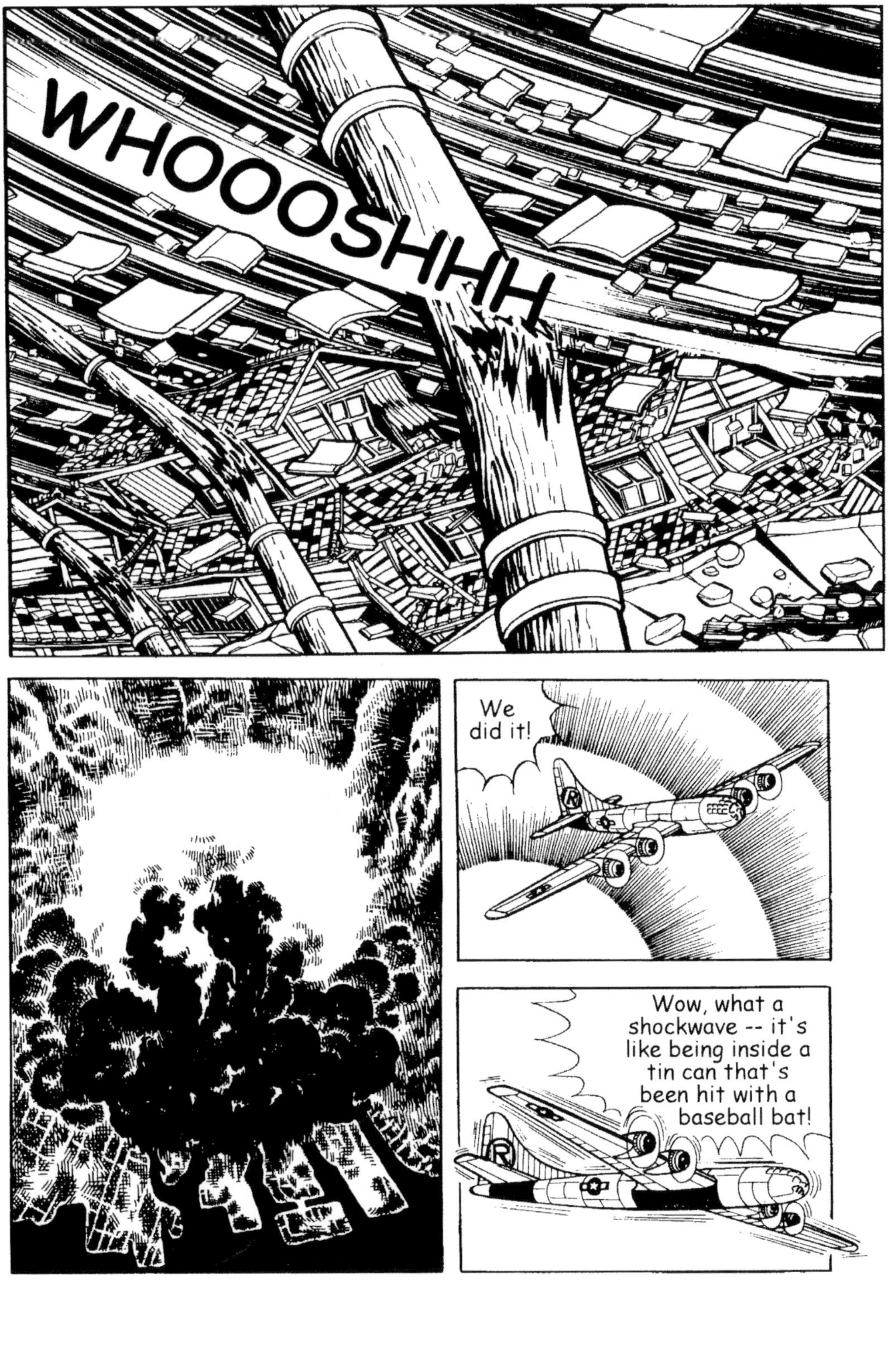
WHOOOSHHH
We did it!
Wow, what a shockwave -- it's like being inside a tin can that's been hit with a baseball bat!

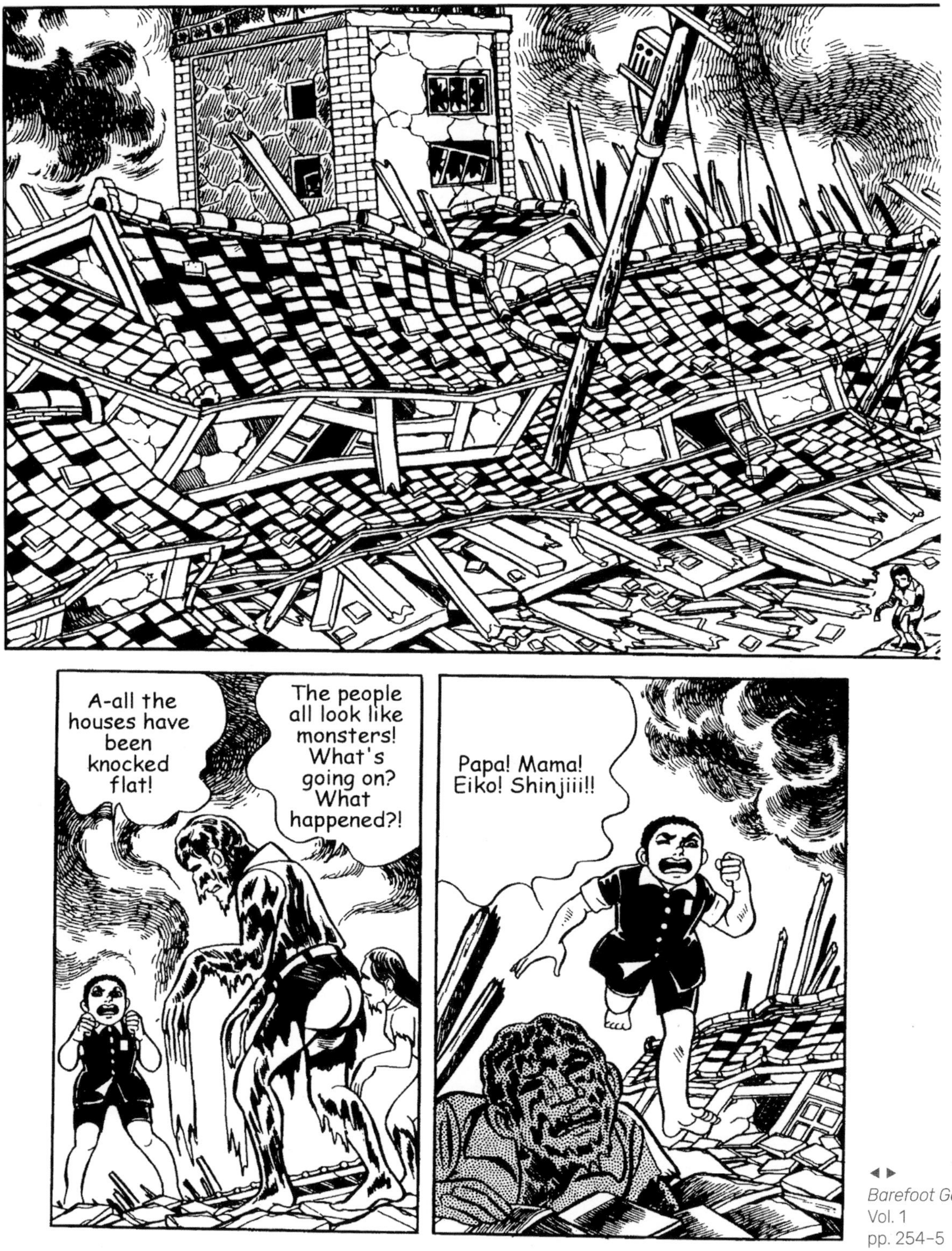
A-all the houses have been knocked flat!
The people all look like monsters! What's going on? What happened?!
Papa! Mama! Eiko! Shinjiii!!

◀ ▶
Barefoot Gen
Vol. 1
pp. 254–5

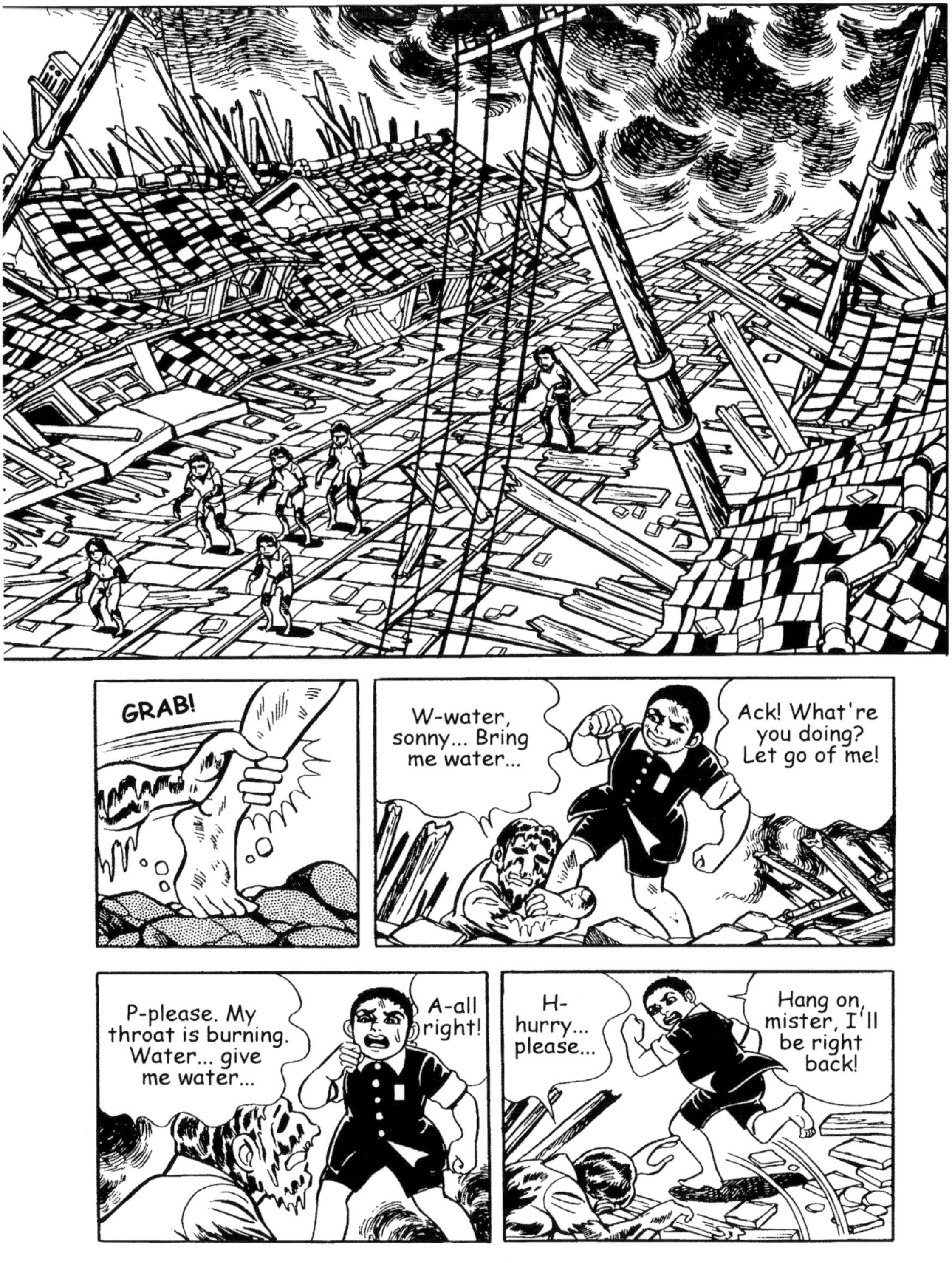
GRAB!
W-water, sonny... Bring me water...
Ack! What're you doing? Let go of me!
P-please. My throat is burning. Water... give me water...
A-all right!
H-hurry... please...
Hang on, mister, I'll be right back!

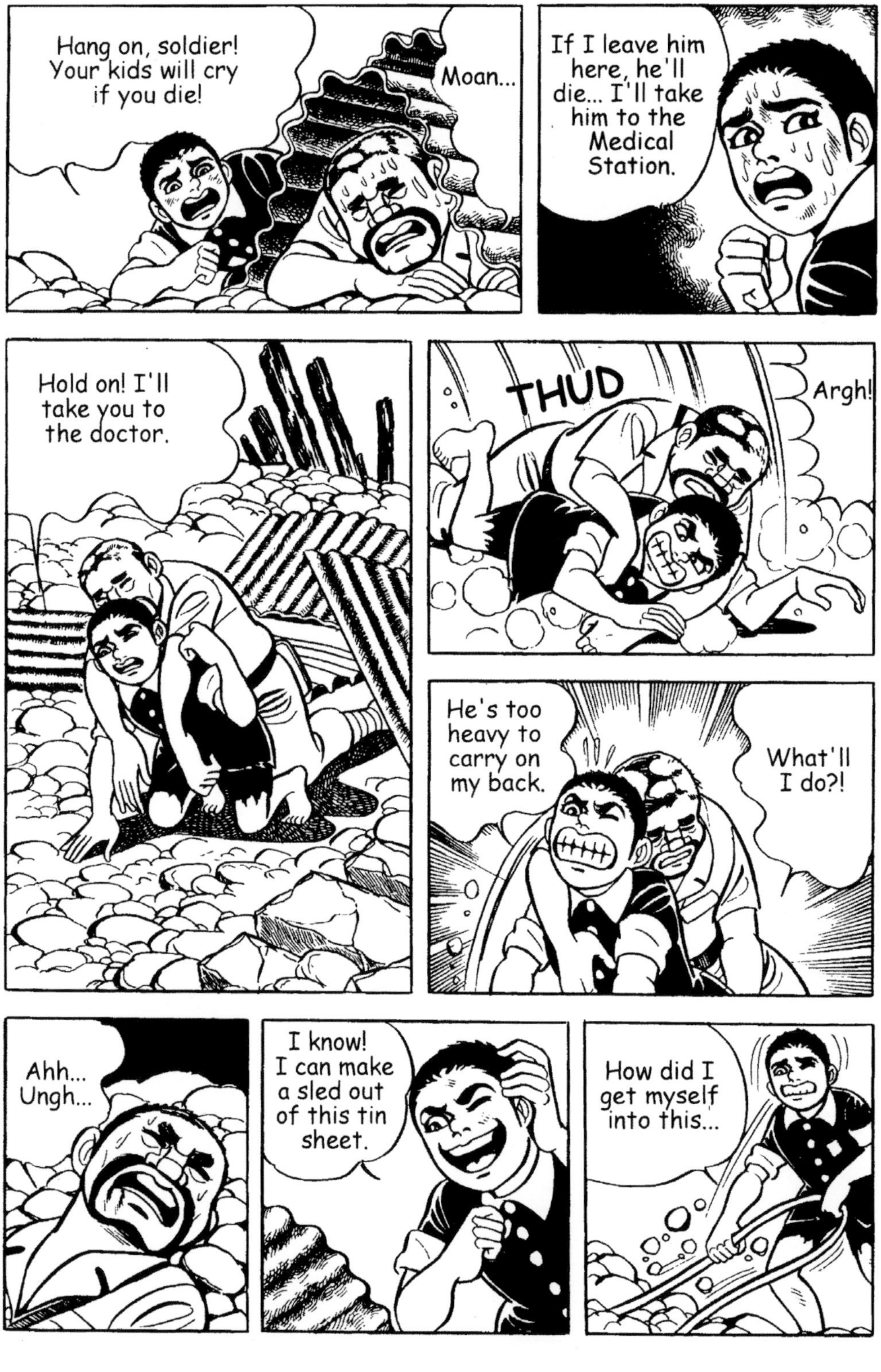

Hang on, soldier! Your kids will cry if you die!
Moan...
If I leave him here, he'll die... I'll take him to the Medical Station.
Hold on! I'll take you to the doctor.
THUD
Argh!
He's too heavy to carry on my back.
What'll I do?!
Ahh... Ungh...
I know! I can make a sled out of this tin sheet.
How did I get myself into this...

◀ ▶
Barefoot Gen
Vol. 2
pp. 38–39

BAM
BAM

Now it's ready.

Hey, am I smart or what!

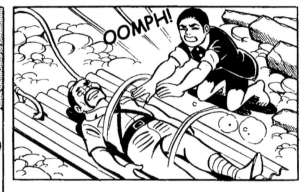

OOMPH!

You've gotta hang on, OK?

Ah... Ah...

Heave-ho. Heave-ho.

This isn't fair! I was the one who was supposed to be taken to the doctor.

RATTLE RATTLE

RATTLE RATTLE RATTLE

Heave-ho. Heave-ho.

PARACUELLOS

Carlos Giménez, 1976

Paracuellos depicts children living in the Social Aid Homes that were established by Francisco Franco following the Spanish Civil War. Carlos Giménez entered the Social Aid system when he was six years old and lived in care until he was fourteen. His drawings reveal an environment in which children are regularly terrorised by violence and cruelty. He published the first strip six months after the death of Franco, and its searing honesty and criticism of the regime sent shockwaves through Spain.

▶
Paracuellos 1
Carlos Giménez
1976
p. 6

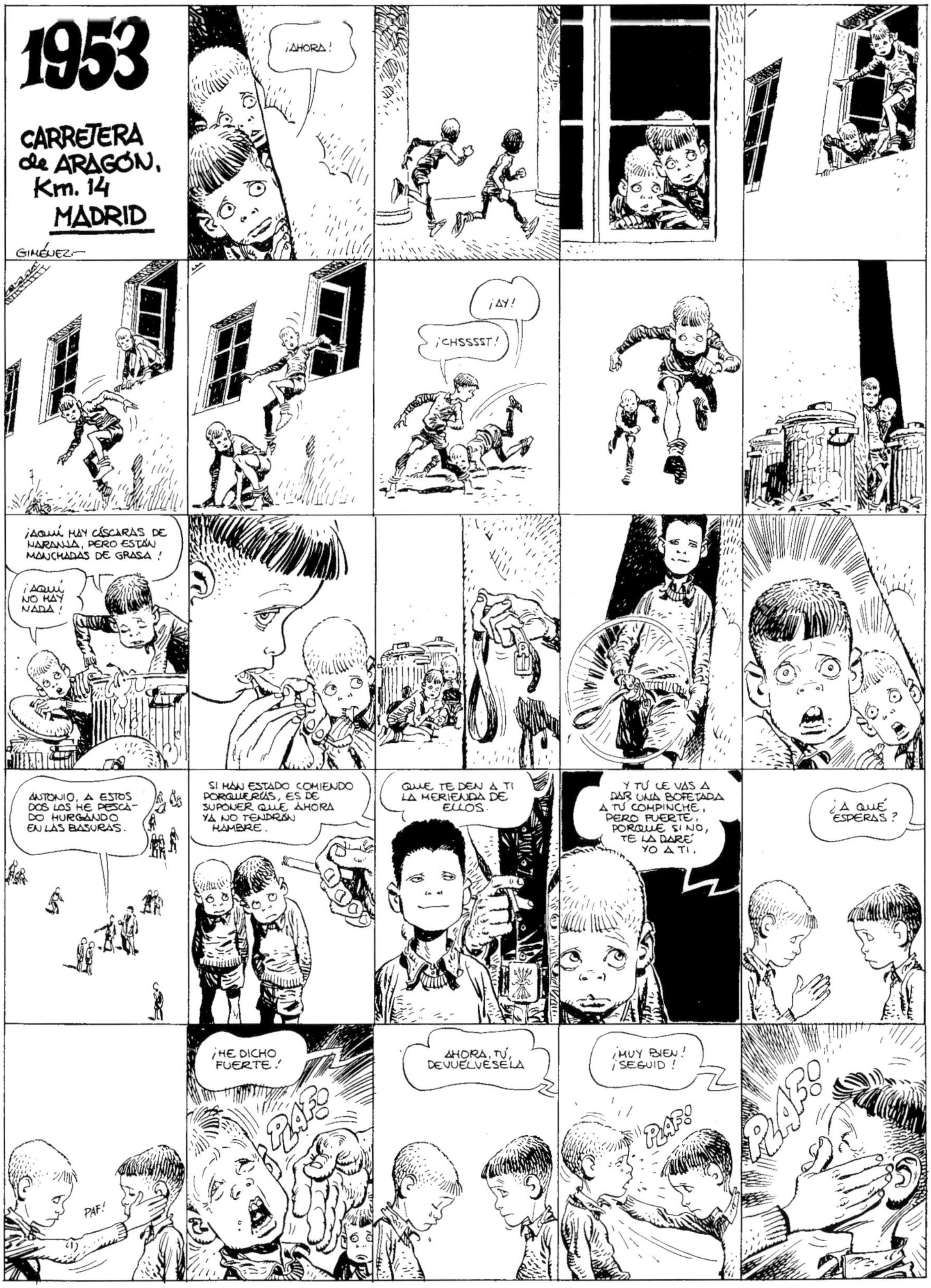

1953
CARRETERA de ARAGÓN, Km. 14 MADRID
GIMÉNEZ
¡AHORA!
¡CHSSSST!
¡AY!
¡AQUÍ HAY CÁSCARAS DE NARANJA, PERO ESTÁN MANCHADAS DE GRASA!
¡AQUÍ NO HAY NADA!
ANTONIO, A ESTOS DOS LOS HE PESCADO HURGANDO EN LAS BASURAS.
SI HAN ESTADO COMIENDO PORQUERÍAS, ES DE SUPONER QUE AHORA YA NO TENDRÁN HAMBRE.
QUE TE DEN A TI LA MERIENDA DE ELLOS.
Y TÚ LE VAS A DAR UNA BOFETADA A TU COMPINCHE, PERO FUERTE, PORQUE SI NO, TE LA DARÉ YO A TI.
¿A QUÉ ESPERAS?
PAF!
¡HE DICHO FUERTE!
PLAF!
AHORA, TÚ, DEVUÉLVESELA
¡MUY BIEN! ¡SEGUID!
PLAF!
PLAF!

STREET ANGEL

Jim Rugg, Brian Maruca, 2004–19

Jessie Sanchez is twelve years old and lives in the most dangerous ghetto in Angel City. Known as the 'Princess of Poverty', Sanchez uses her expert ninja and skateboarding skills to defeat mad scientists and time-travelling pirates in a darkly funny and occasionally surreal comic. While Sanchez is feisty and fearless, she also reveals a vulnerable side, especially when facing the everyday struggles of homelessness.

▶
Street Angel
Jim Rugg and
Brian Maruca,
2004
Draft artwork
for p. 8

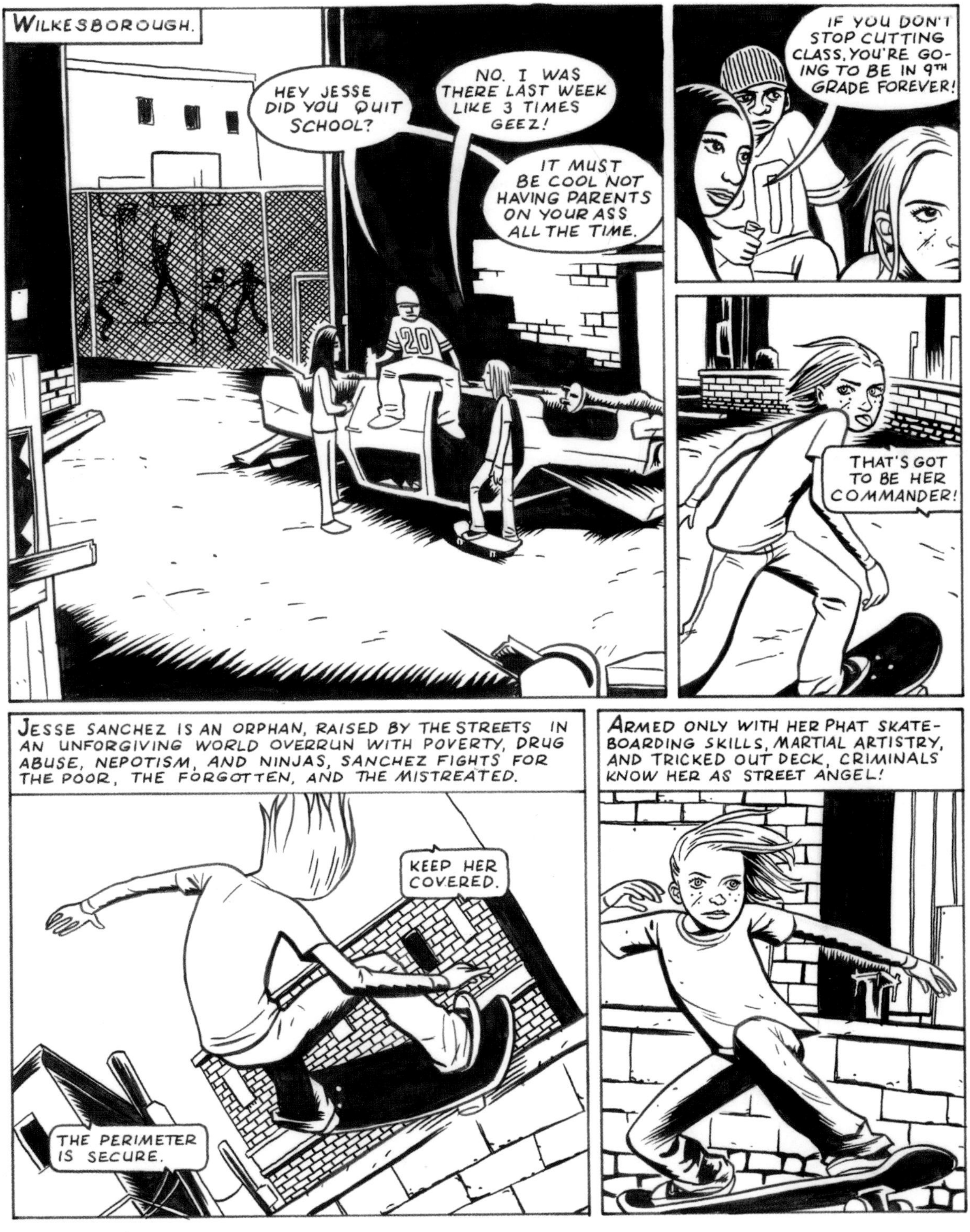

WILKESBOROUGH.
HEY JESSE DID YOU QUIT SCHOOL?
NO. I WAS THERE LAST WEEK LIKE 3 TIMES GEEZ!
IT MUST BE COOL NOT HAVING PARENTS ON YOUR ASS ALL THE TIME.
IF YOU DON'T STOP CUTTING CLASS, YOU'RE GOING TO BE IN 9TH GRADE FOREVER!
THAT'S GOT TO BE HER COMMANDER!
JESSE SANCHEZ IS AN ORPHAN, RAISED BY THE STREETS IN AN UNFORGIVING WORLD OVERRUN WITH POVERTY, DRUG ABUSE, NEPOTISM, AND NINJAS, SANCHEZ FIGHTS FOR THE POOR, THE FORGOTTEN, AND THE MISTREATED.
KEEP HER COVERED.
THE PERIMETER IS SECURE.
ARMED ONLY WITH HER PHAT SKATEBOARDING SKILLS, MARTIAL ARTISTRY, AND TRICKED OUT DECK, CRIMINALS KNOW HER AS STREET ANGEL!

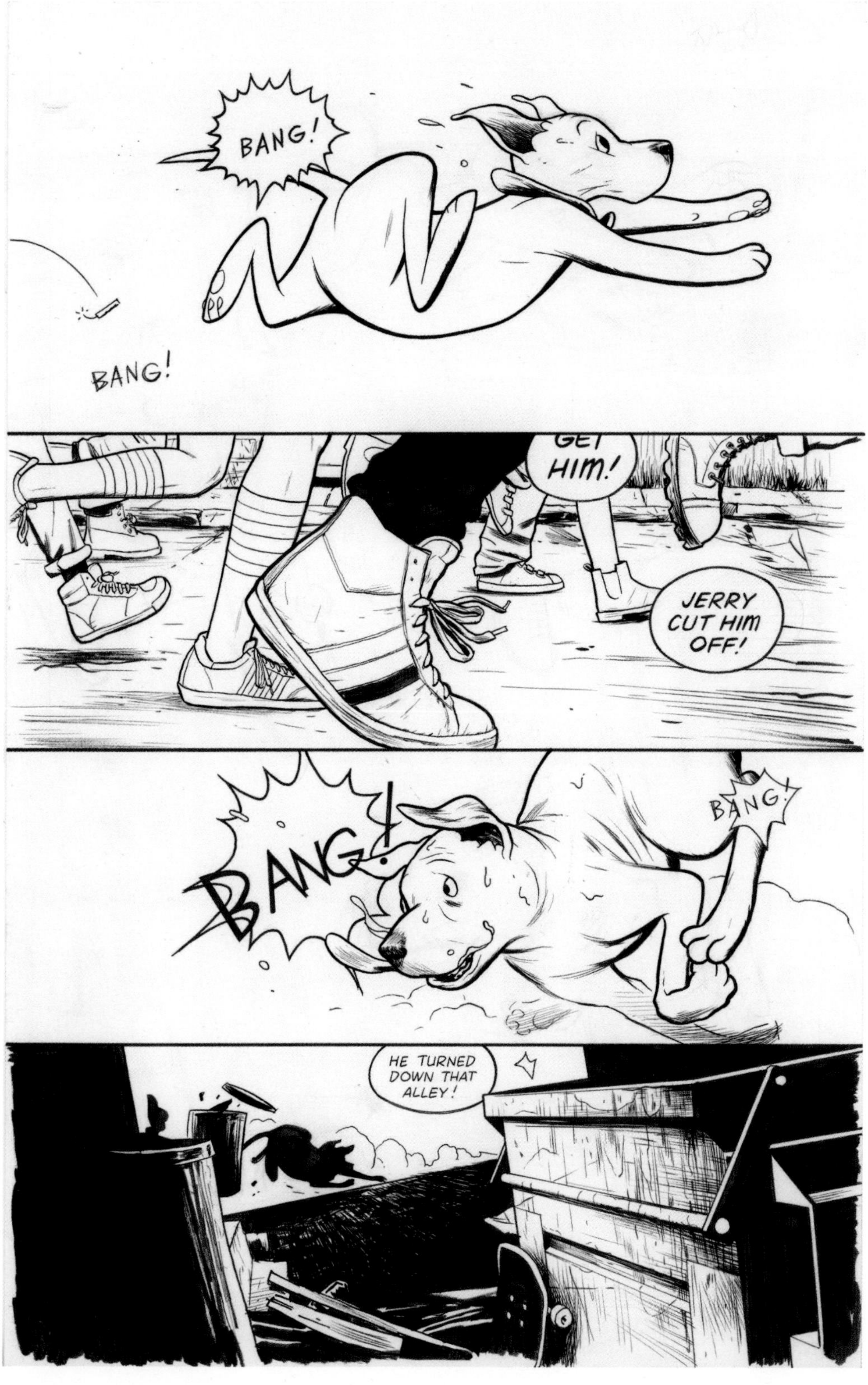
BANG!
BANG!
GET HIM!
JERRY CUT HIM OFF!
BANG!
BANG!
HE TURNED DOWN THAT ALLEY!

Street Angel: Deadliest Girl Alive
Jim Rugg and Brian Maruca, 2019
Draft artwork for pp. 5-6

ORPHANED BY THE WORLD...

SNIFF
SNIFF

RAISED BY THE STREETS...

JESSE SANCHEZ IS A DEADLY KUNG FU FIGHTER...

AND THE WORLD'S GREATEST HOMELESS SKATEBOARDER...

IN WILKESBOROUGH, ANGEL CITY'S WORST GHETTO, SHE FIGHTS NINJAS, DRUGS, NEPOTISM, AND PRE-ALGEBRA AS--

THUD!

WHIMPER

PANT

BANG!

BANG!

YIP!

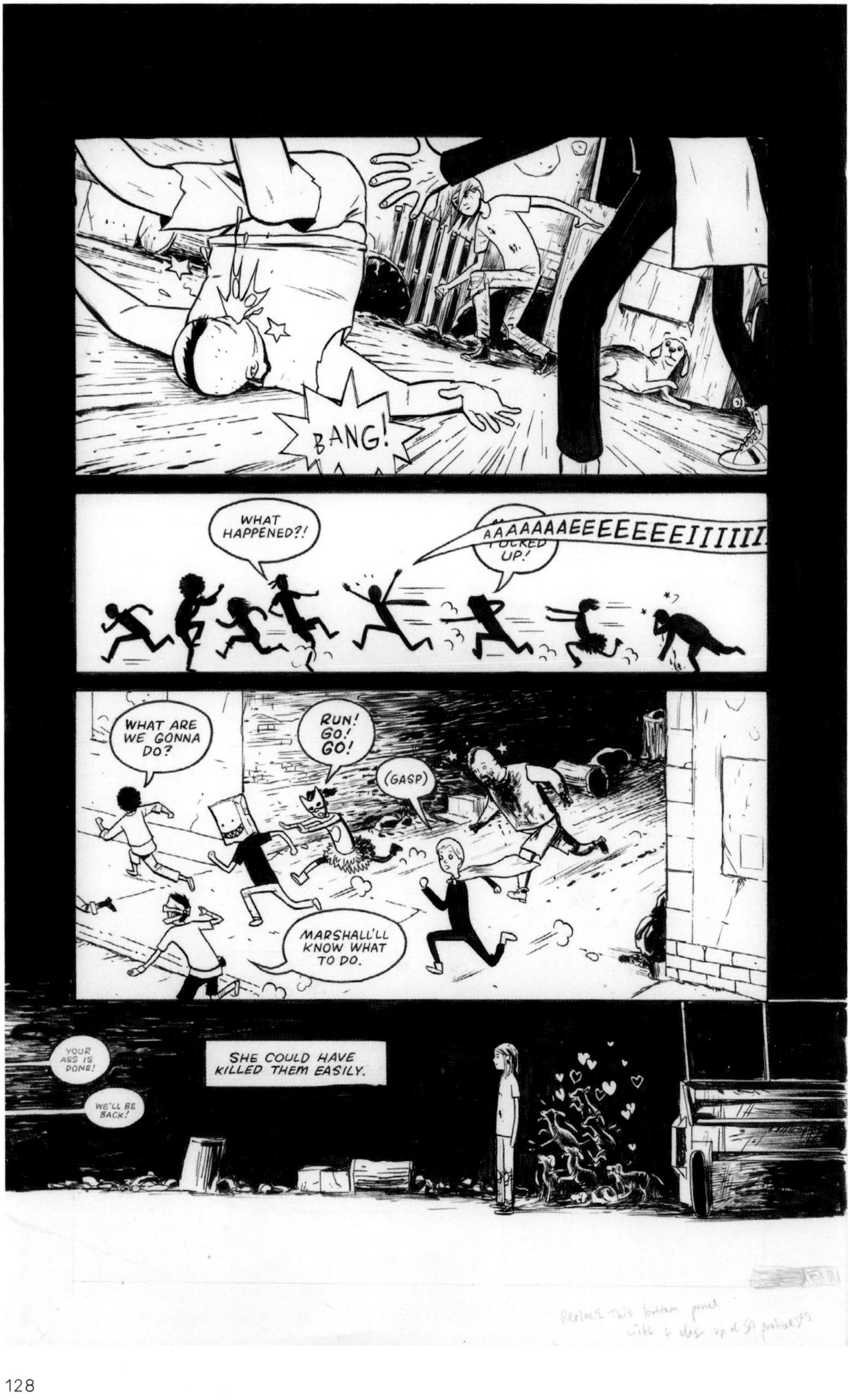

BANG!
WHAT HAPPENED?!
AAAAAAAEEEEEEEIIIIII
UP!
WHAT ARE WE GONNA DO?
RUN! GO! GO!
(GASP)
MARSHALL'LL KNOW WHAT TO DO.
YOUR ASS IS DONE!
WE'LL BE BACK!
SHE COULD HAVE KILLED THEM EASILY.
Replace this bottom panel
with a close up of SA

Street Angel: Deadliest Girl Alive
Draft artwork for pp. 7–8

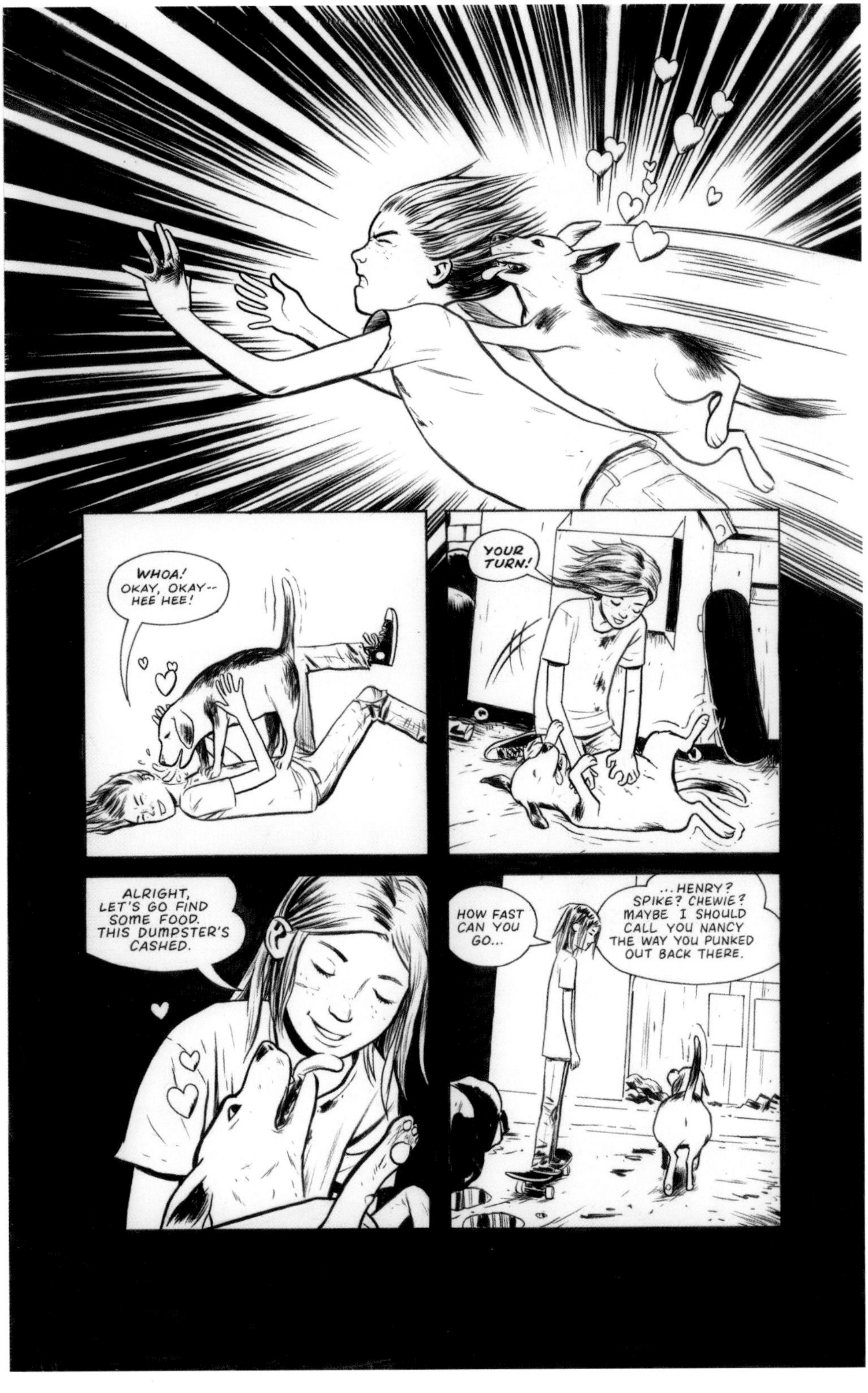

WHOA! OKAY, OKAY-- HEE HEE!
YOUR TURN!
ALRIGHT, LET'S GO FIND SOME FOOD. THIS DUMPSTER'S CASHED.
HOW FAST CAN YOU GO...
...HENRY? SPIKE? CHEWIE? MAYBE I SHOULD CALL YOU NANCY THE WAY YOU PUNKED OUT BACK THERE.

SUNNY

Taiyō Matsumoto, 2010–15

Sunny describes the young residents of the Star Kids children's home (a combination of an orphanage and a group home). Artist Taiyō Matsumoto spent six years as a child in a similar group home in Kansai while his parents lived in Tokyo. The title *Sunny* refers to a broken-down Nissan Sunny parked behind the home that the children use as a place of refuge where their imaginations can run wild. For these children, the Sunny functions as a space for hope.

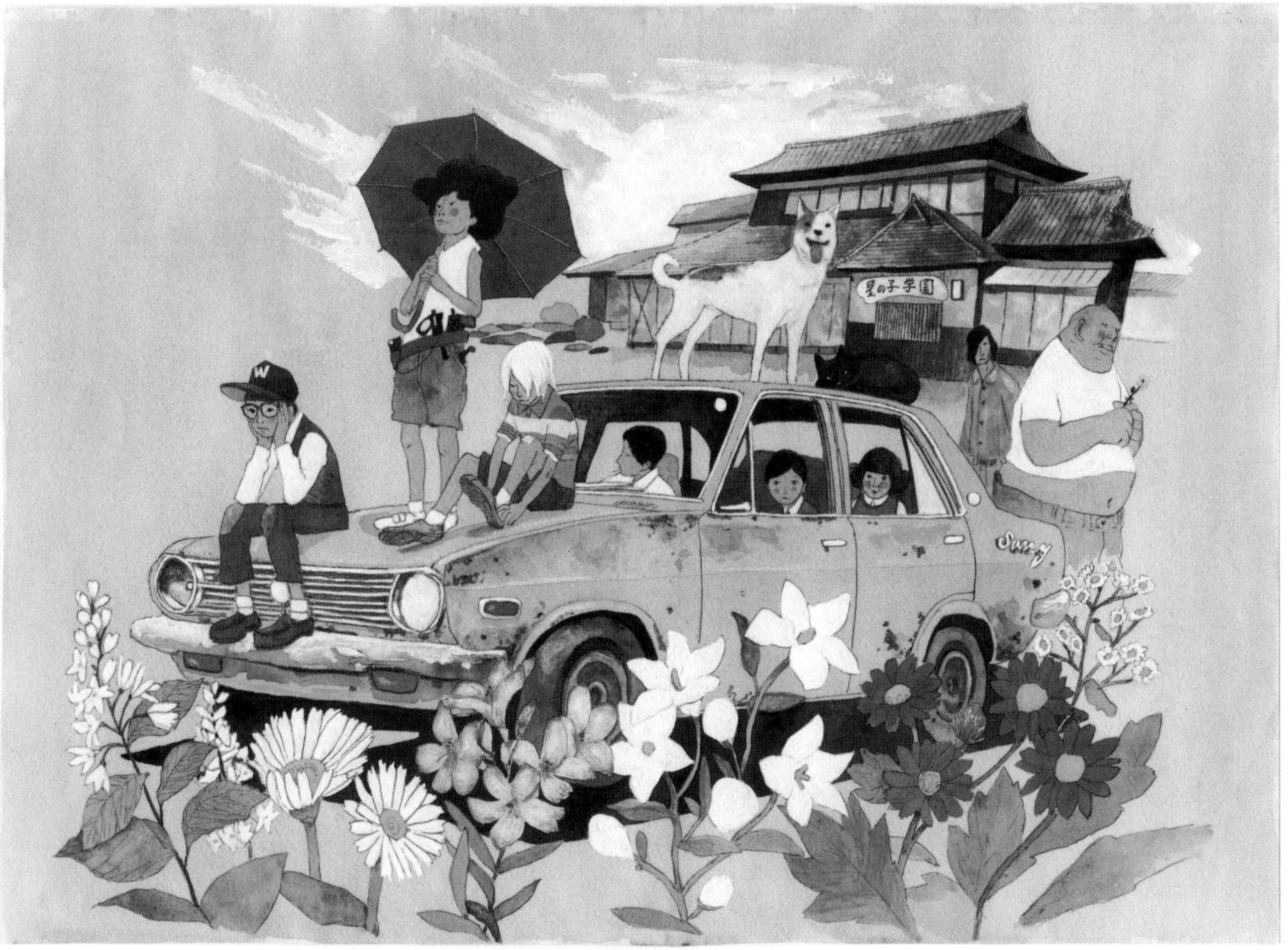
星の子学園
Sunny

▲ *Sunny* Vol. 1
Taiyō Matsumoto, 2011
pp. 10–11

◀ *Sunny* Vol. 5
Taiyō Matsumoto, 2014
pp. 145–146

ZENOBIA

Morten Dürr, Lars Horneman, 2016

◄
Zenobia
Morten Dürr and
Lars Horneman
2016, p. 4

▶
Zenobia
p. 6

Amina is an orphan fleeing a war-torn country on an overcrowded refugee boat. Alone
and afraid, Amina recalls the inspiring adventures her mother used to tell her about the
Syrian warrior queen Zenobia, a woman whose fearless determination transformed her
into the ruler of an empire. Amina strives to be like Zenobia, but this is only possible in her
imagination. Amina's story reflects the reality of so many child refugees around the world.

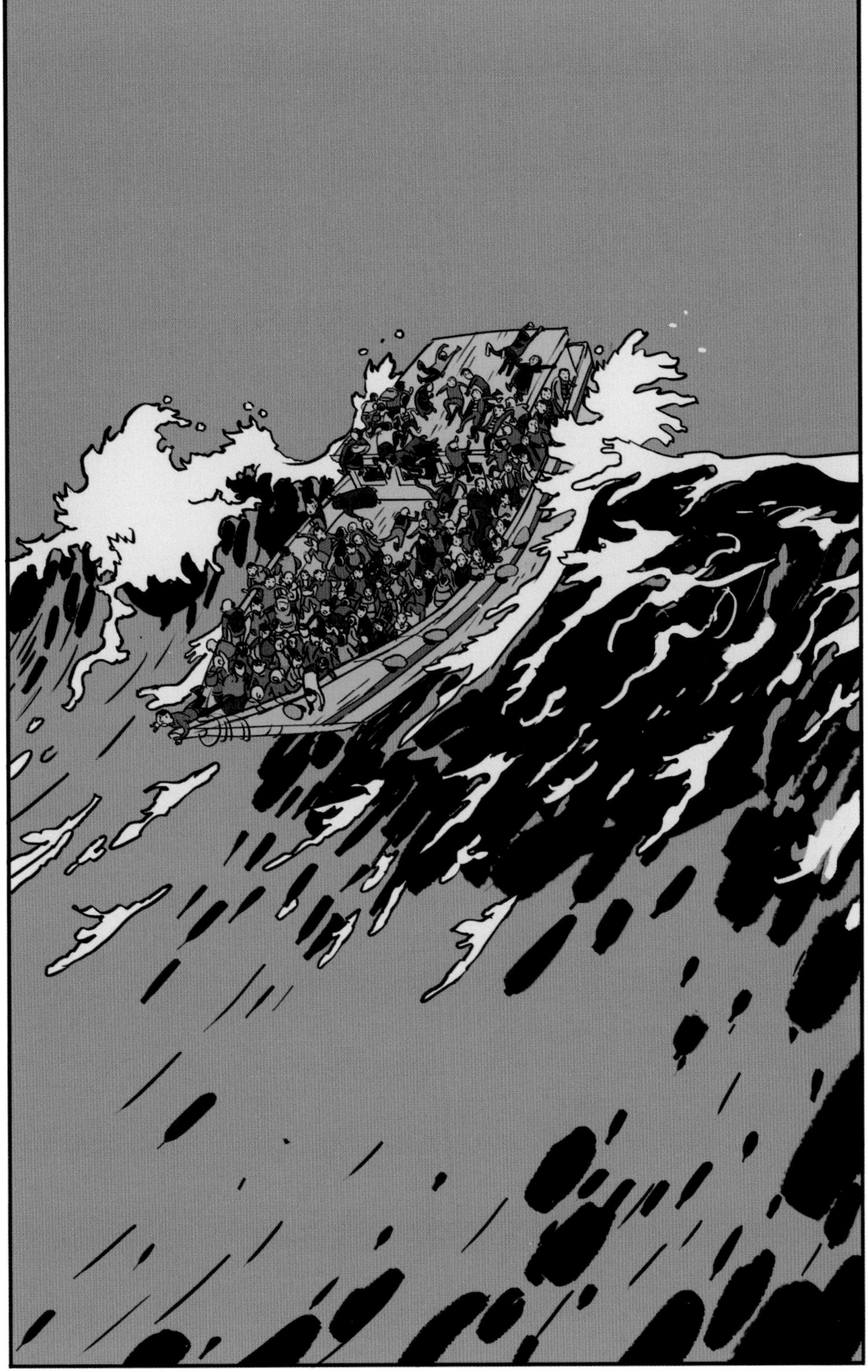

Zenobia
pp. 9–11

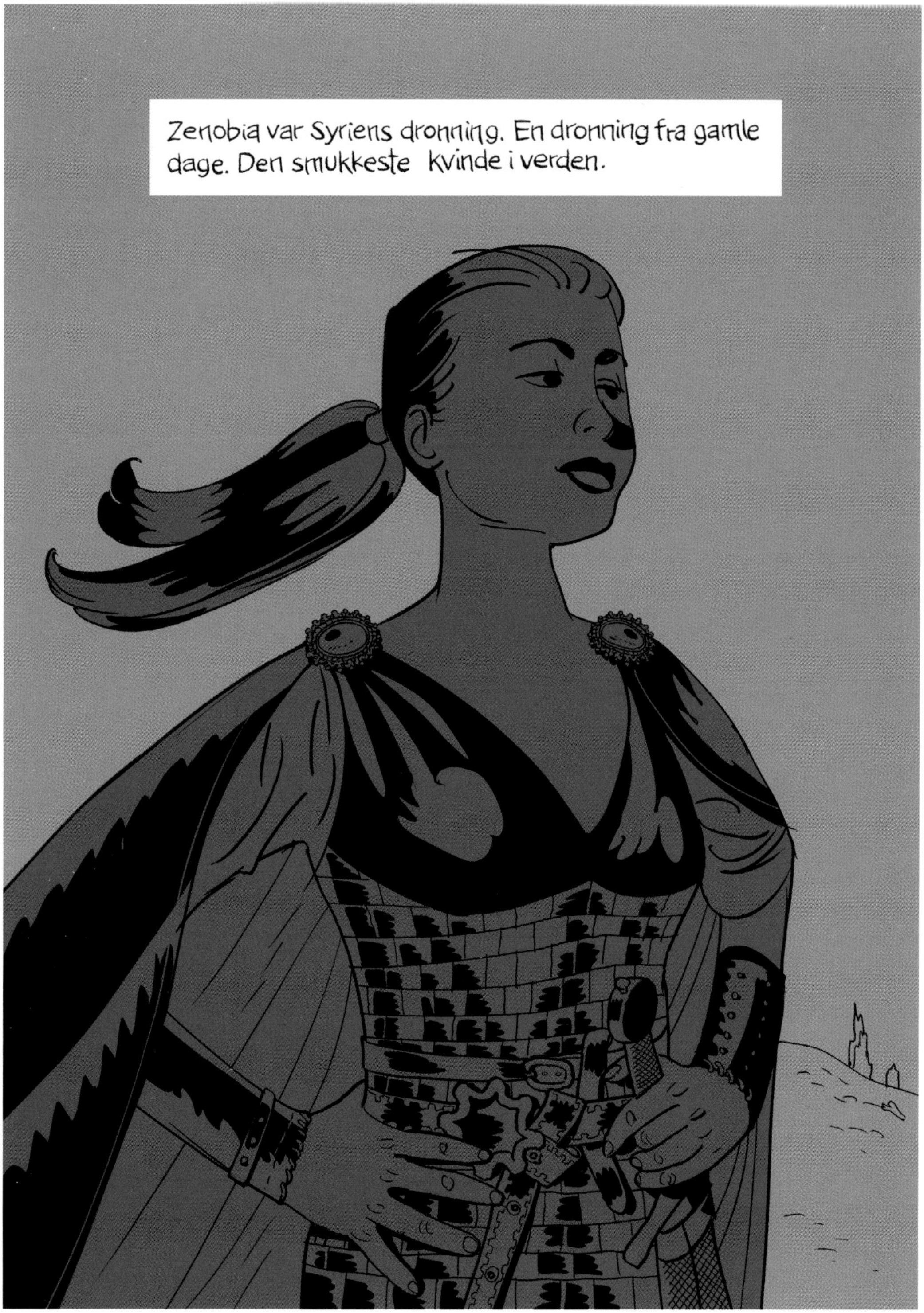
Zenobia var Syriens dronning. En dronning fra gamle dage. Den smukkeste kvinde i verden.

▸ *Zenobia* p. 35

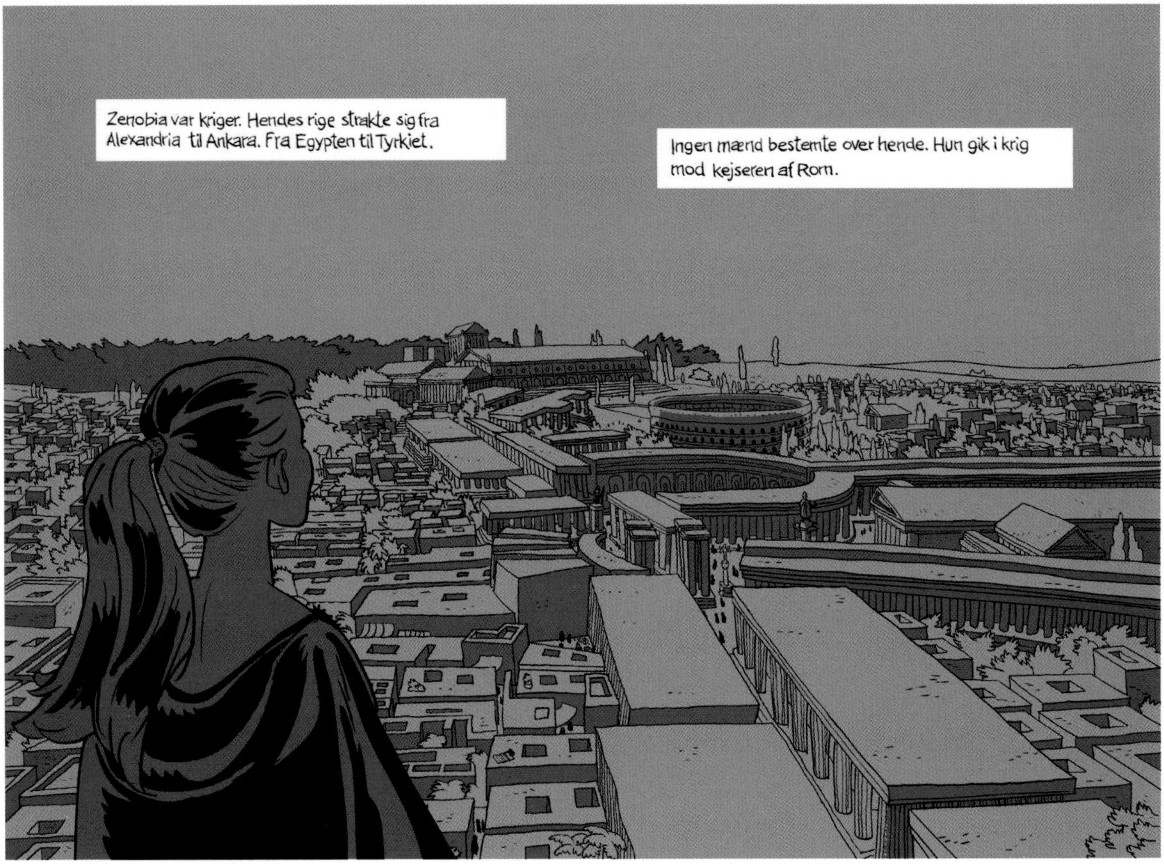
Zenobia var kriger. Hendes rige strakte sig fra Alexandria til Ankara. Fra Egypten til Tyrkiet.
Ingen mænd bestemte over hende. Hun gik i krig mod kejseren af Rom.

▲
Zenobia
pp. 36–37

Zenobia
pp. 44–45

PALIMPSEST

Lisa Wool-Rim Sjöblom, 2019

In *Palimpsest*, Lisa Wool-Rim Sjöblom recounts her experience growing up in Sweden as a Korean adoptee. Determined to find her birth parents, Sjöblom faces many unexpected challenges while trying to uncover the details – and questionable legality – of her adoption. Her quest to learn more about her origins generates profound reflections on her feelings of belonging in both Sweden and Korea, as well as her own experience of motherhood.

▶
Palimpsest
Lisa Wool-Rim
Sjöblom, 2019
p. 143

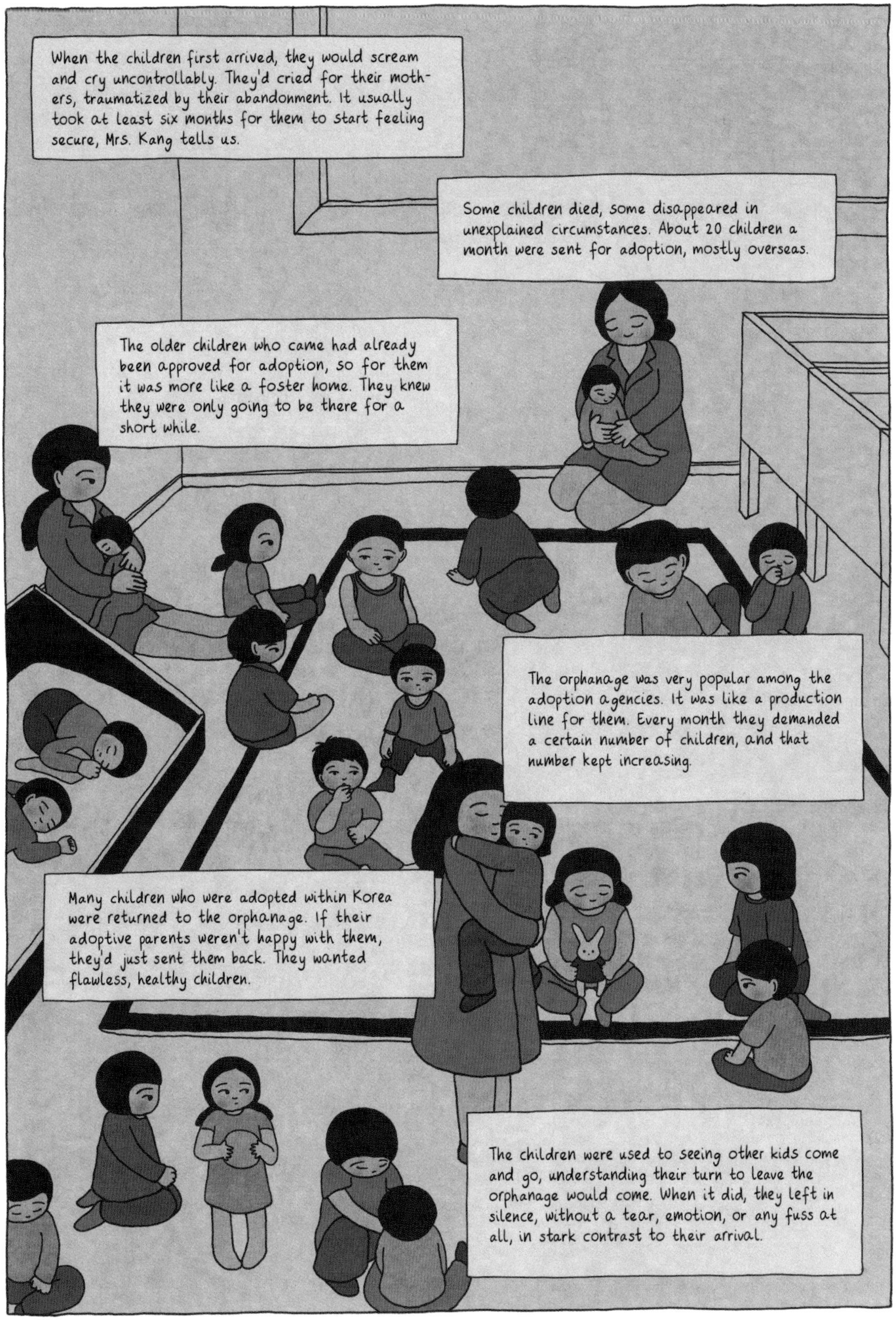
When the children first arrived, they would scream and cry uncontrollably. They'd cried for their mothers, traumatized by their abandonment. It usually took at least six months for them to start feeling secure, Mrs. Kang tells us.
Some children died, some disappeared in unexplained circumstances. About 20 children a month were sent for adoption, mostly overseas.
The older children who came had already been approved for adoption, so for them it was more like a foster home. They knew they were only going to be there for a short while.
The orphanage was very popular among the adoption agencies. It was like a production line for them. Every month they demanded a certain number of children, and that number kept increasing.
Many children who were adopted within Korea were returned to the orphanage. If their adoptive parents weren't happy with them, they'd just sent them back. They wanted flawless, healthy children.
The children were used to seeing other kids come and go, understanding their turn to leave the orphanage would come. When it did, they left in silence, without a tear, emotion, or any fuss at all, in stark contrast to their arrival.

NUBIA: REAL ONE

Robyn Smith, L.L. McKinney, 2021
Published by DC

Nubia is the first Black female superhero to appear in the DC universe. First introduced in *Wonder Woman* #204 (1973) as the titular character's estranged twin sister, she assumed various supporting roles before disappearing from the comic for nearly twenty years. In the graphic novel *Nubia: Real One*, Nubia is reimagined as a high school student who struggles to conceal her superhuman abilities when confronting racism, misogyny and school violence. Nubia must find a way to fulfil her heroic destiny in a society that doesn't see her potential.

▶

Nubia: Real One
Robyn Smith and
L.L. McKinney
2021, p. 139

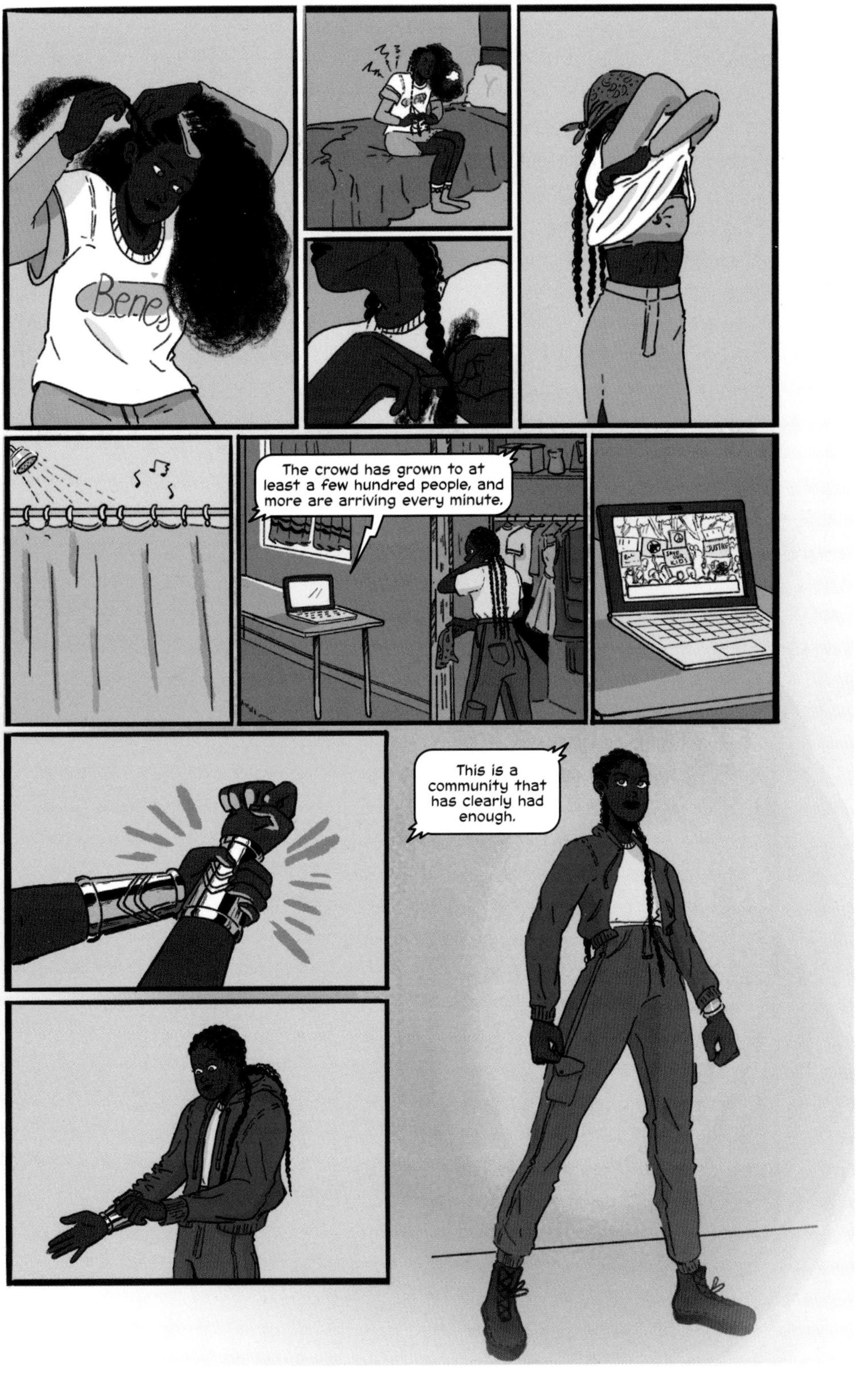

Benes
The crowd has grown to at least a few hundred people, and more are arriving every minute.
JUSTICE
This is a community that has clearly had enough.

PICTURE CREDITS

pp. 2, 6: © The Foundling Museum

pp. 4, 8, 11, 12, 27–29, 37–42, 44, 46–49, 51–55, 57, 95–109, 141 and cover: All DC characters and images are © & ™ DC. All Rights Reserved. Used with permission

pp. 9, 22, 25, 26, 35, 91, 93 and cover: © 2001 Tribune Content Agency

p. 13: © 2021 Hamish Brown

pp. 15-18, 20, 21, 123 and cover: © 1976 Carlos Giménez. Used with permission of the artist

pp. 30, 116–119: © 1978 Keiji Nakazawa. Used with permission of the publisher, Last Gasp

pp. 31, 115, 120, 121: © 1979 Keiji Nakazawa. Used with permission of the publisher, Last Gasp

pp. 32, 33, 60–62, 65–67, 69, 70, 72–75, 139: © 2019 Lisa Wool-Rim Sjöblom. Used with permission of the artist

pp. 77–83: © 2021 Asia Alfasi. Used with permission of the artist

p. 85: © 2021 Bex Glendining. Used with permission of the artist

pp. 86, 87: © 2021 Woodrow Phoenix. Used with permission of the artist

pp. 111–113: © Sanmao Image Group

p. 125 and cover: © 2004 Jim Rugg and Brian Maruca. Used with permission of the artists

pp. 126–129 and cover: © 2019 Jim Rugg and Brian Maruca. Used with permission of the artists

pp. 130, 131: © Taiyou Matsumoto/ Shogakukan

pp. 132–137 and cover: © 2016 Morten Dürr and Lars Horneman. Used with permission of the artists

EXHIBITED ARTWORKS

V&A NATIONAL ART LIBRARY

New York World's Fair Comics, Vol. 1, #20, March 1940. DC.

World's Finest Comics, Vol. 1, #46, July 1950. DC.

Superman, Vol. 1, #209, August 1968. DC.

Action Comics, Vol. 1, #375, April 1969. DC.

Action Comics, Vol. 1, #575, January 1986. DC.

Batman, Vol. 1, #51, February 1949. DC.

Batman, Vol. 1, #213, August 1969. DC.

Detective Comics, Vol. 1, #389, July 1969. DC.

The Amazing Spider-Man, Vol. 1, #12, May 1964. Marvel Comics.

The Amazing Spider-Man, Vol. 1, #87, August 1970. Marvel Comics.

The Amazing Spider-Man, Vol. 1, #100, September 1971. Marvel Comics.

Black Panther, Vol. 1, #1, January 1977. Marvel Comics.

Black Panther, Vol. 1, #7, January 1978. Marvel Comics.

Black Panther, Vol. 1, #8, March 1978. Marvel Comics.

The X-Men, Vol. 1, #12, July 1965. Marvel Comics.

The X-Men, Vol. 1, #24, September 1966. Marvel Comics.

The X-Men, Vol. 1, #96, December 1975. Marvel Comics.

The X-Men, Vol. 1, #101, October 1976. Marvel Comics.

The X-Men, Vol. 1, #113, September 1976. Marvel Comics.

Special Edition X-Men, Vol. 1, #1, February 1983. Marvel Comics.

The Last Marvel Team-Up: Spider-Man and The Uncanny X-Men, Vol. 1, #150, February 1985. Marvel Comics.

Kalimán, Vol. 1, #375, February 1973. Promotora K.

BILLY IRELAND CARTOON LIBRARY & MUSEUM

'McFadden's Row of Flats,' *Hogan's Alley*. Richard F. Outcault, 18 October 1896. *New York Journal*.

'A Few Things the Versatile Yellow Kid Might Do For A Living,' *Hogan's Alley*. Richard F. Outcault, 22 November 1896. *New York Journal*.

Little Orphan Annie. Harold Gray, 2 November 1924. *Chicago Tribune*.

Little Orphan Annie. Harold Gray, 7 December 1924. *Chicago Tribune*.

Little Orphan Annie. Harold Gray, 16 May 1948. *Idaho Sunday Statesman*.

Little Orphan Annie. Harold Gray, 23 May 1948. *Idaho Sunday Statesman*.

Gasoline Alley. Frank King, 12 February 1922. *Chicago Sunday Tribune*.

Gasoline Alley. Frank King, 31 December 1922. *Chicago Sunday Tribune*.

Gasoline Alley. Frank King, 21 October 1923. *Chicago Sunday Tribune*.

Gasoline Alley. Frank King, 28 June 1925.
  Chicago Sunday Tribune.
Gasoline Alley. Frank King, 22 May 1927.
  Chicago Sunday Tribune.
Gasoline Alley. Frank King, 22 April 1934.
  Chicago Sunday Tribune.

THE BRITISH LIBRARY

World's Finest Comics, Vol. 1 #1. Mimosa
  Comics. Artwork originally published in
  World's Finest Comics, Vol. 1 #55, Dec.
  1951. DC.
World's Finest Comics, Vol. 1 #6. Mimosa
  Comics. Artwork originally published in
  World's Finest Comics, Vol. 1 #54, Oct.
  1951. DC.
Superman, Vol. 1 #18. Mimosa Comics.
  Story originally published in *Superman*,
  Vol. 1 #57, Aug. 1949. DC.
Superman, Vol. 1 #38. Mimosa Comics.
  Artwork originally published in
  Superman, Vol. 1 #77, Jul. 1952. DC.
Superman, Vol. 1 #39. Mimosa Comics.
  Story originally published in *Superman*,
  Vol. 1 #72, Dec. 1951.
Batman, Vol. 1 #11. Mimosa Comics. Story
  originally published in *Detective Comics*,
  Vol. 1 #235, Sept. 1956.
Batman, Vol. 1 #16. Mimosa Comics.
  Artwork originally published in *Batman*,
  Vol. 1 #148, Jun. 1962.
Barefoot Gen, Volumes 1 and 2. 1978; 1979.
  Project Gen.
Captain Marvel Jr., Vol. 1 #85. 1954.
  Fawcett Comics.

ARTWORK LOANED
BY INDIVIDUAL ARTISTS

Paracuellos 1. Carlos Giménez, 1976.
Palimpsest. Lisa Wool-Rim Sjöblom, 2019.
Nubia: Real One. Robyn Smith and
  L. L. McKinney, 2021. Artwork loaned
  with permission from DC.
Street Angel. Jim Rugg and Brian Maruca,
  2004.
Street Angel: Deadliest Girl Alive. Jim Rugg
  and Brian Maruca, 2019.
Zenobia. Morten Dürr and Lars Horneman,
  2016.
Up In Flames. Woodrow Phoenix, 2021.
Begin Again. Bex Glendining, 2021.
Baseerah. Asia Alfasi, 2021.

SHOGAKUKAN

Tekkonkinkreet, Taiyō Matsumoto, 1993.
  Shogakukan.
Sunny Vol. 1. Taiyō Matsumoto, 2010.
  Shogakukan.
Sunny Vol. 5. Taiyō Matsumoto, 2014.
  Shogakukan.
Sunny Vol. 6. Taiyō Matsumoto, 2015.
  Shogakukan.

THE CARTOON MUSEUM

Pam and Peter. Molly Higgins, 1960.
  Princess Magazine.

SANMAO IMAGE GROUP

Wanderings of Sanmao. Zhang Leping,
  1947-49.